Management of the Business Classroom

National Business Education Association Yearbook, No. 39

2001

Editor
Betty J. Brown
Ball State University
Muncie, Indiana

Published by

NBEA

National Business Education Association
1914 Association Drive
Reston, VA 20191-1596
(703) 860-8300 • Fax: (703) 620-4483
www.nbea.org

Management of the Business Classroom

Copyright © 2001 by the National Business Education Association

National Business Education Association
1914 Association Drive
Reston, VA 20191-1596

ISBN 0-933964-55-2

Any views or recommendations expressed in this book do not necessarily constitute official policy of the National Business Education Association.

The Web addresses listed were accurate when this book was written but may have changed since publication.

TABLE OF CONTENTS

Part I: An Introduction

Management of Business Education: A Perspective

Betty J. Brown
Ball State University
Muncie, Indiana

Part II: Managing the Curriculum

The Basic Business and Economic Education Curriculum

John E. Clow
Professor Emeritus
State University of New York
College at Oneonta
Oneonta, New York

Managing the Technology-Related Curriculum in Business Education

Michael L. McDonald
University of Southern Mississippi
Hattiesburg, Mississippi

Lonnie Echternacht
Professor Emeritus
University of Missouri
Columbia, Missouri

Part III: Managing the Learning Process

PREFACE

In this *Yearbook*, "management of business education" is considered in a very broad sense. All aspects are addressed: curriculum, programs, courses, students, facilities, instructors, media for instruction, delivery systems, and classroom management tools.

Managing the curriculum is the first major topic of this *Yearbook*. The business education curriculum is often described as encompassing two broad areas: education *about* business and education *for* business. As consumers, employees/employers, and citizens in our society, individuals have a tremendous need for economic and basic business education. Business education teachers have a golden opportunity to help students understand the economic system and learn how to manage their personal financial and business affairs—education *about* business. Integration of business education with all other areas of the curriculum involves focusing on the skills and knowledge that students need to manage their own affairs at present and to plan for their futures.

Education *for* business prepares students with the skills and knowledge needed to function successfully in the workplace. Technology is one aspect of that preparation. As technology continues to change rapidly, business educators must focus on technology as a tool, as a means to an end rather than an end in itself. Business education has a major objective of meeting the needs of employers for capable workers and the needs of students to become effective managers of work-related resources.

In this *Yearbook* School-to-Career initiatives are discussed, and business educators are urged to consider how they can integrate and manage such initiatives throughout the curriculum. In all business education programs, students become aware of the opportunities available to them at every level: elementary school, middle school, high school, postsecondary school, and college/university. Everyone is a consumer; business education therefore is essential for all students, regardless of their career goals or plans for further education.

Change is a constant in business education, as in all other areas of education. Strategies for managing programs and handling curriculum change are addressed in the discussion of curriculum.

The second part of this *Yearbook* addresses the learning process. How do classroom teachers handle today's classroom settings and diverse student populations? What tools are effective for working with students of various backgrounds who have different ability levels, interests, learning styles, and goals? The authors discuss the learning process in business education programs at all levels and address teachers' concerns about incorporating more technology and new facilities and delivery systems into their curricula and programs.

The final chapter of the *Yearbook* is a compilation of research ideas that business educators can address. For each of the topics of the first two sections of the *Yearbook*, the authors have identified research questions that require answers. This chapter, I hope, will provide some real "food for thought" and inspire business educators to begin the search for those answers.

I express my sincere thanks and appreciation to all who contributed to this *Yearbook*. The chapter authors, the NBEA Publications Committee members and staff, and reviewers have made it possible to prepare this *Yearbook* as a learning tool for business educators—those already in the classroom and those who will soon join us as new professionals in the field.

Betty J. Brown, Editor
Ball State University
Muncie, Indiana

ACKNOWLEDGMENTS

The following business educators devoted their time, effort, and expertise to reviewing the 2001 *NBEA Yearbook, Management of the Business Classroom*:

R. Jon Ackley
Virginia Commonwealth University
Richmond, Virginia

Judith Lambrecht
University of Minnesota
St. Paul, Minnesota

Clora Mae Baker
Southern Illinois University
Carbondale, Illinois

Ken Martin
University of Cincinnati
Cincinnati, Ohio

Shirley Barton
Kent State University
Kent, Ohio

J. William Murphy
Winona State University
Winona, Minnesota

Linda Bean
Arkansas Tech University
Russellville, Arkansas

James Calvert Scott
Utah State University
Logan, Utah

Alice Citano
Kent State University, Ashtabula
Campus
Ashtabula, Ohio

Donna Stewart
University of Southern Mississippi
Hattiesburg, Mississippi

Vickie J. Stout
University of Tennessee
Knoxville, Tennessee

Margaret Erthal
Southern Illinois University
Edwardsville, Illinois

Linda F. Szul
Indiana University of Pennsylvania
Indiana, Pennsylvania

Marcia James
University of Wisconsin-Whitewater
Whitewater, Wisconsin

Colleen Vawdrey
Utah Valley State College
Orem, Utah

Myrena Jennings
Eastern Kentucky University
Richmond, Kentucky

Glenda Kunar
Youngstown State University
Youngstown, Ohio

Management of Business Education: A Perspective

Betty J. Brown
Ball State University
Muncie, Indiana

The phrase "management of business education" encompasses a wide range of concepts. At one end of the spectrum, it involves overseeing a classroom, working with groups of students, and making decisions about learning materials. At the other end of the spectrum, it entails devising curricula, selecting instructional resources, and creating virtual classrooms. This *Yearbook* addresses the management of curriculum development, facilities, technology, integration activities, and the classroom to ensure that students with various talents, needs, backgrounds, and experiences are accommodated skillfully. In today's world, management often involves coping with change. Few disciplines experience the degree and pace of change that is inherent in business education. Changes in curriculum and in the expectations of parents, businesses, the community, and society, as well as a movement toward a standards-based framework, present daunting challenges to business educators.

Business Education: A Perspective

A framework for building and maintaining effective business education programs at all levels was identified in the early 1930s when business education programs were added to many secondary schools. Early business educators defined effective business education programs as those that educated for and about business. Education for business involved the preparation of students to enter the workplace upon completion of their studies. Education about business included all courses designed to provide the skills and knowledge necessary for students to efficiently manage their personal business responsibilities and be effective citizens. To serve the needs of all students, regardless of their background, socioeconomic level, and career aspirations, business education must still fulfill the dual mission of educating for and about business.

To prepare for the workplace, business education students learn accounting skills, as well as advanced computer applications involving multimedia presentations, desktop publishing, database management, and complex document production. To equip students with the skills and knowledge they need to manage their personal business responsibilities, the business education curriculum includes courses such as computer applications, personal finance, business foundations, business law, and economics. The plethora of hardware and software, now available at reasonable prices, has made it possible for business education programs at all levels to add technology to their classrooms.

Managing Curriculum and Programs

The management of curriculum and programs is critical to the entire teaching-learning process. In response to the modern standards movement, the Northwest Regional Educational Laboratory (1995) outlined a process for developing a high-quality curriculum. The first step is to develop a curriculum framework that outlines all structured learning experiences, student outcomes, teacher roles, the context in which teaching and learning take place, and everything that affects what happens in the classroom and, consequently, student learning. Considered in this broad context, the curriculum becomes a set of building blocks, or a road map, for everything that is done by teachers for learners.

Planning, the second step in the process, involves defining the program's mission, goals, and objectives. The programs for all levels of business education have evolved over time. Collegiate and university business education has two facets: education for business and business teacher education. Postsecondary business education became a significant component of community and junior colleges as they grew in number, especially during the 1960s. Business education has been a part of most secondary schools since the 1930s. Middle school business education emerged as keyboarding courses in the earliest stages, followed by courses such as introduction to business and computer applications. Elementary business education is a relatively new component of the business education curriculum. As computers become tools for everyone, rather than primarily equipment for the business world, and as a continuing need for personal financial literacy is reemphasized, courses that formerly were offered in the high school may be offered in the middle school. Many business educators predict that some skills and knowledge now gained in the middle school will then move to the elementary school. How business educators respond to such shifts is crucial to a coherent curriculum.

Such shifts have been noted, and a framework has evolved for business education, resulting in business education programs in virtually every secondary school in the United States. This framework is the basis for the *National Standards for Business Education: What America's Students Should Know and Be Able to Do in Business* (1995), published by the National Business Education Association.

Program planning, based on the curriculum framework, contributes to viable, up-to-date business education offerings at all levels. Professional development and preparation of competent teachers to design and offer courses that meet the needs of students as consumers, workers, and citizens is critical to keeping programs relevant and up-to-date. Business education curricula at all educational levels—from elementary to postsecondary/collegiate—experience change at a more rapid pace than many other disciplines do. In order to manage curricula and programs in a manner that fulfills goals and objectives, business educators must cope with constant change. They must use change as a guide for updating, refining, and revising their programs and courses, and as a mandate for professional renewal.

As curricula, programs, and courses are implemented in the classroom, they must be monitored, reflected upon, and evaluated. As a result of this process, they should be refined to meet the needs of all business education students. To ensure that this is the case, business educators must incorporate strategies that reflect a sensitivity to diversity of gender, age, race, socioeconomic level, ethnicity, parental status, geographic location, physical ability, marital status, and work background.

A substantial body of research conducted over the past several decades has identified the relationships between academic achievement and individual learning styles. Dunn and Dunn (1978), for example, used a Learning Style Inventory, which they developed for use with students of all ages and in various educational settings to determine the relationship between learning style and achievement. Their research has consistently supported the contention that students learn in different ways and that when students are taught using approaches and resources that complement their learning styles, their achievement levels increase significantly. Research about learning styles is just one resource that can help business educators raise student achievement levels.

The Impact of Education Standards

Emphasis on performance-based educational programs and evolving standards boards has had an impact on all educational programs. The federal government's identification of goals for American education led to higher standards. A national assessment movement in the 1990s focused attention on performance-based assessment and resulted in standards that require demonstration of competence, with learners and teachers alike having to show what they know and are able to do. National, state, and local standards for business education at all levels and for business teacher education at the college/university level have been one of the most influential forces for change in the past decade or more. Important questions at all levels—from elementary school through collegiate/university business education programs—involve what the learner should be able to do and how the learner can demonstrate satisfactory performance. The key words in those questions are "do" and "demonstrate." Performance-based standards emphasize "doing" so observers can evaluate whether standards are met.

These standards have broadened the scope of curriculum to include everything that affects what happens in the classroom and consequently affects student learning. A "traditional" plan of instruction identified structured learning experiences and outcomes for students. It specified the details of student learning, instructional strategies, the teacher's role, and the context in which teaching and learning take place. The standards-based curriculum includes not only goals, objectives, and standards, but also everything that is done to enable those outcomes and to foster reflection and revision of the curriculum to ensure continued student growth. Standards drive not only instruction and curriculum, but also assessment, professional development, parent and community involvement, instructional leadership, and the use of technology and other resources.

The objective of standards-based education reform is higher student achievement, based on explicit definitions of what students must do to demonstrate proficiency at each level. To ensure that students meet higher expectations, other participants in the educational system must explore various ways to enhance the ability of the system and its teachers to improve student learning. For business educators, the standards movement means they will be involved in determining what they want students to know and to be able to do. A curriculum framework aligns goals and standards from all levels—national, state, and local. That framework guides each school's curriculum. In business education, an ongoing process of developing and refining standards provides a framework for designing a curriculum that educates for and about business.

Increasingly, all educators must be aware of national, regional, and state organizations that encourage or mandate the use of standards. National certification is one option for teachers to demonstrate their competence at meeting national standards. School-to-Work legislation has emphasized high standards for students being prepared for the workplace. Additionally, standards developed by the Interstate New Teacher Assessment and Support Consortium (INTASC) and corresponding national and state standards have had a dramatic impact on business teacher education.

Since the early 1980s various reports from commissions have called attention to the need for changes in education. As a result, educators have been charged with the responsibility of devising curricula, programs, and courses that prepare students with the skills needed for a fast-changing world.

Performance-based programs require some restructuring of programs and classroom activities. Business educators have an advantage over many other educators because for years much of business education has been performance-based, requiring educators to observe students' activities and ascertain the degree to which standards have been met.

Managing Facilities

As more powerful, less expensive, and more adaptable computers have been developed, business educators have expanded curricular offerings to include computer-based learning at all educational levels. Secondary, postsecondary, and collegiate/university programs use computers and computer-based equipment both as learning tools and as teaching tools. With the rapid spread of technology, elementary and middle school business education programs are now also using technology in ways similar to those being instituted in high school and postsecondary programs.

Management of facilities involves more than management of computer classrooms and labs. It must address how technology can be incorporated into the general-purpose classroom so that it can be used as a teaching tool. The educational design of all classroom facilities is complicated by the fact that it is impossible to predict what technological changes the future will bring.

Distance education has rapidly altered the way business education classes are offered to students. The use of television, videotape, videoconferencing, satellite, and Web technology has revolutionized many aspects of business education, as well as all other disciplines. Being able to manage the technology required to provide well-designed, pedagogically sound business education courses to off-site students is critical. If the technology is not well managed, students may receive an offering that is inferior to an on-campus course. Often, it is assumed that all Web-based and distance education courses are postsecondary/collegiate/university courses. However, a growing number of secondary schools are using the technology to enable their students to enroll in courses that may not be available within the district.

Technology requires considerably more attention in business education than it does in most other disciplines. Changes in technology, both hardware and software, occur quickly and require adaptations to physical facilities. Management of technology has become a major responsibility of business educators. It is a responsibility that is compounded by technology's constant changes. Bill Gates (1995) described the information highway as a road that "is going to give us all access to seemingly unlimited information, anytime and anyplace we care to use it. It's an exhilarating prospect, because putting this technology to use to improve education will lead to downstream benefits in every area of society" (p. 184). He described the present as an "exciting time in the Information Age." Information technology will change our lives. But the question in many people's minds is, for better or for worse? Gates was optimistic about the impact of new technologies. He envisioned them as tools to "humanize" the educational environment—to make learning practical and enjoyable—and to "enhance leisure time and enrich culture by expanding the distribution of information." He went on to say that technological advances "will relieve pressures on urban areas by enabling individuals to work from home or remote-site offices" (p. 250).

Technological changes are a boon to business education in many ways, but in other ways they can be a source of frustration. Business educators must struggle to stay abreast of rapid technological change and to incorporate new technology into their programs. Business education facilities require vision and planning to ensure that technology is financed and used to the best advantage.

Technology is only one aspect of the business education setting. This chapter also describes some of the other management issues that are addressed in more detail in the ensuing chapters of this *Yearbook*.

Managing the Classroom Setting

For decades the study of education has included classroom management, and instructors have been challenged to be cognizant of and manage all aspects of facilities, students, interactions, and the myriad dynamics of the classroom to ensure that teaching and learning were facilitated. The typical business education classroom has a heterogeneous population of students with various needs, backgrounds, experiences, talents, skills, and attitudes toward learning. The challenge for an instructor is to consider diversity, including diversity of gender, ethnic and socioeconomic background, learning style, learning and physical ability, behavior mode, and motivation level. Managing the learning process requires the instructor, at all levels—from elementary to collegiate/university—to challenge, interest, motivate, and entice students to learn and develop. Students learn and respond to various stimuli in different ways. Research about teaching and learning has made business educators aware of the diversity of students' responses to classroom activities.

Research into effective instructional practices has identified some that can be used as benchmarks for the business education curriculum, classroom management and instruction, and positive teacher-student interactions. Although these practices are not unique to business education, they can be used as guides for business educators. The following are examples of effective practices:

- A preplanned curriculum guides instruction. Teachers develop learning goals, sequence them to facilitate student learning, and ensure that resources are available and instructional time is used wisely.
- Instruction integrates traditional school subjects, as appropriate. Teachers use a variety of resources and performance assessments that allow students to demonstrate their acquisition of knowledge and skills.

- Instructional groups fit students' academic and affective needs. Teachers use whole-group instruction; form smaller groups as needed for student learning; and ensure that groups exhibit gender, cultural, ability-disability, and socioeconomic balance.
- Learning time is used efficiently. Teachers give assignments that are suited to the age and ability level of students.
- Teachers establish smooth, efficient classroom routines and apply standards for classroom conduct fairly and consistently.
- Teachers carefully orient students to learning and provide clear and focused instruction.
- Students receive feedback and reinforcement of their learning progress.
- Teachers use validated strategies to help students build their critical- and creative-thinking skills.
- Teachers hold high expectations for student learning and provide incentives and recognition to promote excellence.
- Teachers provide equitable learning opportunities to all students, regardless of their background, race, gender, culture, or socioeconomic level (Northwest Regional Educational Laboratory, 1995).

Challenges for Business Educators

The proliferation of URLs (Web sites) in the chapters of this *Yearbook* is a reminder of what an important tool the Internet has become for business educators. As a source of information and resources, the Internet has broadened the scope of content in the classroom to an extent that teachers could not have foreseen 10 years ago. Teachers are able to share ideas, resources, and concerns to a degree that would be impossible without instant access to each other. Not only is the Internet a tool for the teacher, it also provides students access to vast stores of information. Throughout this *Yearbook*, the authors suggest ways for students to use the Internet as their tool for learning—a tool that generates interest as well as content.

Business educators are continually affected by rapid changes in technology. Technological innovations make possible alternative delivery systems for curriculum. With technology, distance education has become a reality, and business educators have become facilitators of a vast array of resources and tools for learning, rather than being directors of classrooms.

The National Commission on Teaching and America's Future (1996) concluded after two years of study that elementary and secondary education must focus on redesigning schools to support high-quality teaching and learning. New courses and curricula are important starting points, but the Commission pointed out that they are meaningless unless teachers use them well. Educators must focus on teaching well, helping diverse learners master challenging content, and encouraging students to think and experience their subject matter so they can learn.

Business educators should be clear about what students need to learn to succeed in the world that awaits them. Teachers must also determine what they need to know and be able to do to help students master critical skills and knowledge. Developing the kind of high-quality educational experiences that prepare students for their future endeavors is fundamental to all curricula.

In the Future

As technology becomes more sophisticated and user-friendly, hardware and software will be regarded as tools for learning to a greater extent than they were in the past. Computer applications courses, for example, will focus more on the critical-thinking and problem-solving skills required to use hardware and software as tools, or means to an end, rather than an end in themselves. This shift in the role of technology is essential to a business education curriculum that provides students with the skills and knowledge for and about business. Rapid advances in technology will lead to new tools that will enable students to use computers and computer-based devices for their personal lives and in the workplace.

All students are consumers; all must manage their personal business responsibilities. The business education curriculum must be managed so as to prepare students for their roles as consumers and citizens and provide the financial literacy/economic knowledge and skills needed for those roles. The curriculum components that encompass knowledge about business must not be neglected. Technology will provide students with tools for managing their personal business responsibilities, but it cannot guarantee that their financial management decisions will be based on sound reasoning. A good foundation in financial literacy and economic education can enhance the decision-making skills that will enable students to manage well.

Summary

Management of business education entails building a curriculum framework, designing and implementing courses to achieve curriculum objectives, providing facilities to meet the needs of learners and teachers, identifying alternative delivery systems such as distance learning and Web-based instruction, designing and implementing effective instructional materials, and creating a classroom setting for effective teaching and learning. This broad interpretation of "management" encompasses all the activities in which business educators engage. The ensuing chapters of this *Yearbook* discuss in depth some of the responsibilities, concerns, and activities of business educators at all levels—elementary through collegiate/ university. Stakeholders mandate high-quality educational programs, and business educators must meet the challenges brought about by change, technological innovation, the standards movement, and diverse learners.

References

Dunn, R., & Dunn, K. (1978). *Teaching students through their individual learning styles: A practical approach.* Reston, VA: Reston Publishing Company.

Gates, W. H. (1995). *The road ahead.* New York: The Penguin Group.

National Business Education Association. (1995). *National standards for business education: What America's students should know and be able to do in business.* Reston, VA: Author.

National Commission on Teaching and America's Future. (1996). *What matters most: Teaching for America's future.* New York: Author.

Northwest Regional Educational Laboratory. (1995). *Effective schooling practices: A research synthesis.* Retrieved from the World Wide Web: www.nwrel.org.scpd/esp/

The Basic Business and Economic Education Curriculum

John E. Clow
Professor Emeritus
State University of New York
College at Oneonta
Oneonta, New York

The basic business and economic education segment of business education is an area of great promise. As the secondary schools have increased their academic requirements in the last 10 years, enrollment in secondary occupational technical education courses has declined considerably. Postsecondary two-year institutions have assumed responsibility for much of the occupational and technical education previously completed at the high school level, and business education at the middle and secondary levels has begun to focus on education that is for all students. Previously, business education at the secondary level was oriented toward the occupational and career preparatory aspects of business education. The embracing of the economics and basic business area by business educators in the years ahead could bring a new "golden age" for business education at the elementary, middle, and secondary levels.

This chapter focuses on the nature of basic business and economic education, the reasons it should be included in the school curriculum, and ways to make it a dynamic part of the business education curriculum. The many materials and other resources that are available to educators are also described.

What Is Basic Business and Economic Education?

The basic business and economic education segment of the curriculum has two components. One of them is basic economics, which includes concepts such as scarcity, opportunity cost, incentives, economic systems, supply and demand, competition, market structure, the nature of money, fiscal policy, and monetary policy. Thinking in economic terms, which involves weighing the costs and benefits of various alternatives, is also an integral part of economics. A fuller explanation of these concepts and generalizations can be found in the economics portion of the *National Standards for Business Education* (National Business Education Association, 1995) and in the *Voluntary National Content Standards in Economics* (National Council on Economic Education, 1995).

In the basic business component, students apply economic concepts and thinking processes to their roles as consumer and investor (personal finance), wage earner (career education), and entrepreneur and business leader (entrepreneurship and business administration). Each of these areas includes content that is separate from economics, but various economic concepts are addressed. For example, in personal finance, an important area of study is credit, which is not generally considered an "economics" concept. Yet being able to apply cost/ benefit analysis (an economic process) is important when choosing a credit source. When studying the stock market, a student should understand the difference between secondary and primary stocks as well as the various stock exchanges—all pursuits that are not necessarily considered part of "economics" studies. Students, though, cannot have a complete understanding of why the price fluctuates for a stock unless they have grasped how supply and demand work in a market. When planning a business, the entrepreneur must know how to recognize opportunities, which is technically not an economic concept. Yet, the entrepreneur must understand the types and effects of competition when analyzing the viability of specific opportunities. A fuller explanation of the content of personal finance, career education, and entrepreneurship education is delineated in the *National Standards for Business Education*.

Why Are Economics and Basic Business Education Important for All Students?

Our country has a market-oriented economic system with many individual freedoms, including the important freedom of choice. We can choose the goods and services we want—even how we want to buy them. We can choose the careers that we want to pursue; the government does not tell us we must follow a certain career path. We can start businesses to produce goods or services that we think others want; the government does not keep us from business failure. We also have the freedom to vote in the polling booth; the candidates we choose and issues we approve affect us economically.

Freedom of choice is indeed a wonderful privilege. Informed choice making or decision making, though, does not occur by happenstance. Individuals need good content background in a field plus the ability to use the information to make sound judgments. To prepare students to make more informed decisions as citizens, consumers, wage earners, entrepreneurs, and business leaders, basic business and economic courses or units of study are essential.

Typical courses in the business education curriculum that focus on basic business and economics topics include business foundations or introduction to business, economics, consumer education or personal finance, business law, business management, entrepreneurship, and international business.

What Is the Track Record of Schools in Developing Economic and Basic Business Understandings?

Current research shows that students are not very well prepared in the areas of basic business and economics. Kourilsky (1995) reported that a Gallup poll completed in the mid-nineties showed that "high school students do not know much about entrepreneurship. Ninety percent of the students rated their personal knowledge of entrepreneurship as very poor to fair. The self-assessment was accurate: high school students polled responded correctly to only 44 percent of basic knowledge questions concerning entrepreneurship" (p. 11).

Mandell (1998) and the Jump$tart Coalition (2000) reported that personal financial literacy declined among 12th graders throughout the nation between 1997 and 2000. In the survey Mandell completed in 2000 for the Jump$tart Coalition for Personal Financial Literacy, only 51.9 percent of the questions on the normed instrument were answered correctly, down from 57.3 percent of the questions answered correctly in 1997. The same concepts and generalizations were tested both years. The questions focused on the guidelines for personal financial literacy developed in four areas—money management, saving and investing, income decisions, and credit and spending.

Louis Harris and Associates, Inc., (1999) completed a poll in 1999 of American adults and high school students to determine their knowledge of basic economic concepts. The concepts were taken from the *Voluntary National Content Standards in Economics* published by the National Council on Economic Education (NCEE). Fifty-seven percent of the items were answered correctly by the more than 1,000 students and adults who were surveyed. For students in grades nine through twelve, the average grade was 48 percent. Students and adults surveyed lacked a basic understanding of scarcity, money, and inflation. The study results suggested that nearly two-thirds of American students and adults did not know that money does not hold its value in times of inflation.

Indeed, research shows that the content in the basic business and economic areas is not being learned. Increasing numbers of businesses and individuals who declare bankruptcy are some of the casualties associated with such illiteracy. Additionally, family counselors have indicated that money management problems are one of the primary causes of marital breakups.

Is Basic Business and Economic Education Instruction in Demand?

Several studies indicate that basic business and economic education is in great demand. In the previously mentioned Gallup poll, high school students, small business owners, and the general public showed a real interest in having schools offer more instruction about entrepreneurship and how to start a business.

Eighty-four percent of the students surveyed and 80 percent of the general public and small business owners and managers surveyed indicated that it was "important to very important" that schools provide entrepreneurship instruction (Kourilsky, 1995).

Many people feel that entrepreneurship instruction should be required of all students (Clow, 1997). Although relatively little discussion has taken place about instituting this course of action, support for it is growing. One reason is the belief that everyone should understand the role and importance of the entrepreneur in the U.S. economy. Indeed, the primary source of the sustained economic growth that occurred during the 1990s was the development of small businesses, many of them newly formed businesses. Futurists (Morrison, 1996) tell us that this trend is likely to continue. Entrepreneurship education would help students understand essential business concepts and would prepare them to work for employers who now want individuals with more than technical skills (Mann, 1992).

The demand for economic education is evident in school curriculum requirements. Clow (1999) found that 39 states included economics in their adopted education standards, guidelines, or proficiencies. Twenty-eight of those states required that the standards for economics be implemented in the schools, with 25 administering tests to determine whether students have met the standards. If economic standards are being implemented on a K–12 basis, the standards are generally fulfilled in social studies courses. If fulfilled at the middle and high school levels, the concepts are found in a variety of subject areas, including business education.

Personal finance and entrepreneurship are not so thoroughly woven into curriculum requirements. Clow (1999) found that fewer than half of the states (21 states) included "developing personal financial literacy" in the educational standards for their schools. Only one state required that all students take a course in personal finance. But this may change in response to growing demand for the inclusion of more personal finance instruction for all students.

How Can Economic and Basic Business Education Be Promoted?

If the economic and basic business area is to gain prominence in business education, several changes must be made; they are delineated here.

First, basic business and economic instruction must be perceived as a very important objective. Through the years, the basic business and economic area has been the "stepchild" in the business education family in many ways. Most business education instruction at the K–12 level has focused on vocational and occupational education.

This emphasis on occupational skills has been maintained because of the primary interests of many of the leaders and teachers in the field. Over the years

13

at national, regional, and state meetings they have indicated that the objective of business education is to train students for the business world. Certainly, the vocational and occupational education objective is an important one for business education. However, for decades business education has had two objectives: education *for* and education *about* business. As pointed out by early leaders in business education, such as Herman Enterline and Paul Lomax, teaching about business is one of the two major objectives of business education; it is not a secondary objective of business education.

Second, business educators must become comfortable with teaching basic business courses. Until the 1990s many graduates of business teacher education programs chose office education/technology concentrations. Many of them took courses in economics, marketing, management, accounting, and finance; but their primary focus was in office education and technology. In the secondary schools, they found that teaching business foundations or introduction to business (a basic business course) was less to their liking than teaching keyboarding. Why? Greater familiarity with the content of keyboarding than with the content of business foundations may be one reason. Business foundations draws from a very broad content base: consumer education, economics education, career education, entrepreneurship, and business administration. Keyboarding is much more focused. Furthermore, many of the teacher education candidates had more background in the keyboarding area than in the various basic business areas.

The discomfort that many graduates of business teacher education programs experienced may also relate to methods for teaching the course. Teaching a course that is skills-related, such as keyboarding, is different from teaching a course that focuses primarily on cognition. The methods can and should be considerably different. In keyboarding, especially at the early stages, considerable teacher-centered instruction occurs. A primary purpose of the introductory keyboarding course is to develop motor skills; lengthy discussion about how to develop keyboarding skills is no substitute for the actual development of skills through goal-directed practice. In business foundations, a considerable amount of student-centered instruction, such as group discussion, role-playing, panel discussion, and cooperative learning, takes place. Many teachers are more comfortable with psychomotor-oriented methodology than cognition-oriented methodology.

An abundance of innovative, creative materials has been tested in the schools that can be used by new or experienced teachers. These materials can fill the gaps that otherwise can make teachers uncomfortable with teaching basic business and economics. These materials also provide tested teaching strategies or tools with which teachers may be unfamiliar.

Changes in teacher education indicate that future business teachers may well be more comfortable teaching economics and basic business courses. Current business teacher education programs based on the National Association for Business Teacher Education's *Business Teacher Education Curriculum Guide & Program Standards* provide an excellent background for the basic business area. A solid core of business administration and economics courses is recommended for every business education major. Such a core is not always found in business education programs, especially if they are deemed "vocational" business education programs.

Another development in teacher education is the adoption of a five-year program for teacher education. In some universities each teacher education student must have an undergraduate major in his or her content area, taking the professional education component at the graduate level or during the fifth year. The candidates in these programs generally have a good background in business administration and economics, as many of them have undergraduate majors in marketing, management, accounting, management information systems, finance, or economics. These candidates are comfortable and enthusiastic about teaching the basic business and economics courses because of their familiarity with the content. This characteristic was not common among business teachers of earlier decades.

Third, courses in basic business and economics can be experientially based. Mandell's (Jump$tart Coalition, 2000) study of the achievements of high school seniors on a test of personal finance showed that students who took traditional courses in personal finance and economics did not do any better on the test than those who did not take such courses. A survey of 16- to 22-year olds completed by the American Savings Education Council in 1999 yielded similar results. Students who took a personal finance course seemed to feel more knowledgeable about money management, but they were no more likely than noncourse takers to think it is important to save money on a regular basis or to save money from a job and/or allowance. Similarly, course takers were not more likely to budget their income and expenditures or to compare prices before making a purchase than those who had no course work.

In the case of the economics study conducted by Louis Harris and Associates, Inc., (1999) students who had an economics course did better on the test than those who did not take an economics course. But there is no convincing evidence that traditional course work is actually developing the knowledge base necessary for students to use personal finance concepts in their lives.

Mandell (Jump$tart Coalition, 2000) found that interactive learning seemed to play a part in helping students comprehend and use personal finance concepts. Students who used the stock market game, an interactive simulation, did better on the investment questions and on the entire test than those who did not use the simulation. With the stock market game, students are "doing;" but the game generally involves some classroom instruction that requires the students to reflect on what they are doing. Certainly, Mandell's finding is congruent with the currently popular constructivist theory that students learn from experiencing by such means as doing, reflecting, and sharing with others. Just "doing" does not seem to be enough, as is evidenced by Mandell's findings that students who simply owned stocks in their own name or received a regular allowance did no better on the test than those who did not have their own stocks or an allowance.

Fourth, business educators can work together to encourage each school district to require a course in basic business and economics and to allow business educators to teach economics. In New York the State Board of Regents granted approval in 1999 for secondary business education teachers to teach the required economics course (a semester in length). Prior to 1999 only social studies teachers could teach the required course. Through letters to the Regents and face-to-face contact with some of the Regents, the Business Teacher Association of New York State (BTANYS) was able to secure passage of this ruling. The Association demonstrated that most business education teachers prepared in the State of New York have a similar or better collegiate course background in economics than their counterparts in social studies. After 1999 either business education or social studies teachers could teach the course. Another change in the course occurred in 2001; the content of the course in New York included a combination of economics, personal finance, and entrepreneurship.

A 1999 study (Clow) showed that 16 states had a mandated course in economics, with 13 of the 16 requiring it of all students. The study also showed that high school social studies and business education teachers taught the course. Indeed, there is precedent for business educators teaching the required economics course.

In some instances, it is not possible to secure approval of a full semester course in a crowded curriculum. In those cases, some nontraditional approaches to offering economics and basic business units of study or courses at the middle and senior high school levels may be effective. In schools that allot time for a course every day, five days a week, a required economics and personal finance course could be offered three days a week instead of five—allowing another course to be offered the other two days. Some individuals may be concerned that such action could result in the economics and personal finance course being perceived as "second-class," or less rigorous than other courses. But in the "academic"-oriented curriculum of the early 2000s, some presence is better than no presence. If the course is found to be valuable for students, it could eventually be moved to meeting five days a week.

Another approach is to develop an economics and basic business course on the Internet. This writer's experience with a one-hour college credit course on investing showed that students with initiative and drive enjoyed and thrived in the online course. Students could take it after school or at home. This arrangement would especially appeal to the gifted, highly motivated student whose course schedule is full. He or she still needs an understanding of the economic world and how to get the most from his or her resources with an online course. An array of online secondary-level courses is now available and includes the National Foundation for Teaching Entrepreneurship's course entitled Biztech. Indeed, this and other innovative approaches to getting more and better basic business experiences into the curriculum may be necessary.

Finally, educators can take advantage of a wealth of instructional resources that are very accessible. These materials and teacher education activities will not only provide teachers the background needed to make this subject "come alive," but they will enable teachers to stay current on methodology and content. In the area of economics and basic business education, the problem is not a lack of materials; the problem is choosing the ones that best meet the classroom teacher's needs.

What Are Some Materials and Programs That Can Be Useful in Teaching Basic Business and Economics?

A complete listing of the opportunities and materials available to teachers would not be possible here. Most of the providers of the sources listed below are from the nonprofit sector, and each one has earned an enviable reputation of producing quality materials and programs.

Workshops for teachers. Many different sources of workshops and courses exist. Colleges and universities offer graduate-level courses or noncredit courses related to teaching economic and basic business topics in their business education, economics, family and consumer science, economic education, and social science departments. It is a good idea to consult your local college or university to determine what is available.

Many college and university workshops in the economic and basic business area are implemented by the Centers and Councils for Economic Education of the NCEE network. NCEE was established in 1949 to help all students think in economic terms and develop problem-solving skills to use in their roles as consumers, savers, investors, members of the workforce, responsible citizens, and effective participants in a global economy. Currently, the NCEE has established 49 affiliated state and regional Councils on Economic Education, as well as more than 260 affiliated university/college-based centers for economic education. The state councils and centers implement a number of programs for teachers, focusing on various economic topics as they apply to personal finance, career choice making, entrepreneurship and citizenship education. In fact, they generally serve about 120,000 teachers a year. A listing of the councils and centers can be found on the National Council's Web page (www.nationalcouncil.org). Business educators can benefit by becoming involved in local center and state council activities and in the networking such involvement promotes. Additionally, the centers and councils are a good source of teacher education courses and quality materials for the classroom.

The Center for Entrepreneurial Leadership of the Ewing Marion Kauffman Foundation provides monies for entrepreneurship education workshops and materials for youth. A number of the NCEE centers and councils on economic education provide these workshops for teachers. With funding from the Foundation, The National Business Education Association (NBEA) has for several years implemented workshops at its national conventions and hosted regional programs on entrepreneurship education.

An underlying theme of the programs and materials supported by the Foundation is that students should "actually do" entrepreneurship—experiencing the "thrills and heartaches" of the entrepreneur. For example, in the middle school program, The New Youth Entrepreneur, students use the opportunity recognition process to determine a business venture that they want to pursue in their own community; they then set up and operate the business. In the Mini-Society program for the elementary level, students establish a society that includes functioning businesses. The programs are experiential—again focusing on the theme of doing and reflecting. More information about the programs of this Foundation is available at www.emkf.org/.

There are a number of other sources of workshops. Many Federal Reserve Banks provide workshops for teachers—generally on economic and personal finance topics. The New York Stock Exchange generally provides summer workshops for teachers to acquaint them with the Exchange and financial markets. Trade associations, such as insurance and credit groups, provide periodic workshops for teachers. Additionally, some local chambers of commerce provide workshops that may not be specifically for teachers, but that address economic and business concerns. Teachers can be added to mailing lists of these groups to stay abreast of when workshops and courses are being offered.

Organizations and materials. NCEE has an extensive array of materials on economics, personal finance, entrepreneurship, and career choice making in the following categories:

- Standards and benchmarks in economics, which focus on economic concepts that should be mastered at various grade levels based upon the developmental level of students
- Exemplary lesson plans for economics and advanced placement economics courses and for integrating economics into other K–12 courses
- Exemplary lesson plans for personal finance economics for grades K–12, which feature lesson plans tied to the standards in economics as well as to guidelines for personal financial management issued by the Jump$tart Coalition for Personal Financial Literacy

- Exemplary lesson plans for career choice making, which include instructional materials on decision making, the importance of education (human capital), and characteristics of the labor market
- Exemplary lesson plans for integrating entrepreneurship education into various courses
- Materials for a semester-length entrepreneurship education course, which include a package of reading materials with a teacher's guide and student worksheets for a semester-length course
- Materials on international economics, which feature lessons on various economic concepts that are particularly relevant to the international marketplace and useful in an international business course

NCEE's Web site lists many additional publications, as well as services for instructors who want to use the Internet for teaching. Lesson plans on economics are tied to NCEE's *Voluntary National Content Standards in Economics* and can be used in economics, personal finance, entrepreneurship, and School-to-Career units or courses.

The economic education link, www.econedlink.org, includes lessons and explanations tying economic concepts to various current events. The "cyber teach" section has articles and examples of using the Internet to teach economics. The Web link lists sites that provide materials for student research projects and instructional materials for teachers. For example, the sites of various Federal Reserve Banks are linked. The data links provide up-to-date statistical data, such as the latest consumer price index, federal budget surplus or deficit figures, and the gross domestic product, that can be used by teachers and students for lessons or assignments. The Web site also includes a sequence of lessons, all computer-based, that focus on the process of buying a house. The lessons emphasize the importance of savings and credit, as well as the steps involved in choosing and financing a home.

The NCEE has an extensive research arm that field tests materials to determine whether they will be effective in the classroom. Research has shown that the test scores of students with a teacher trained in NCEE workshops and using NCEE materials are better than those of students who do not have such exposure.

Junior Achievement is another important source for educational materials and resources. Junior Achievement operates in more than 3,300 communities nationwide with 60,000 classroom volunteers and 163 offices or centers throughout the nation, as well as offices in various foreign countries (www.ja.org).

Junior Achievement's sequential and integrated K–12 curriculum is delivered by volunteers, generally employees of local business firms who work with teachers and students in the classroom. The volunteers are trained by Junior

Achievement to implement the lessons with students and to leave with the teacher any needed follow-up activities. For many of their programs, the volunteers visit the classrooms periodically during an 8- to 10-week period. At the elementary level (grades K–6), lessons focus on how various economic concepts are demonstrated in the world of the individual, the family, the community, the city, the region, the nation, and the world. The middle school programs address personal economics, the international marketplace, characteristics of our economic system and the role of business in it, the economic aspects of sports and entertainment, and the economic benefits of staying in school. High school programs include a semester-length course in economics, a program focusing on ensuring success in the work world, a cross-cultural experience emphasizing the fundamentals of international trade, and materials that focus on how to start a business.

The various offices of the Junior Achievement network provide materials for schools. An outside evaluator has shown that the programs have been effective in promoting the comprehension of economic and basic business concepts.

The Security Industry Foundation for Economic Education (SIFEE) is another source of materials. SIFEE's mission is to promote understanding of the securities industry by developing programs in economic education. A primary product of the Foundation is an educational program called The Stock Market Game. The game allows players to trade an imaginary $100,000 in funds to build a portfolio by investing in common stocks. Students form teams to make decisions about the stocks for a period of time (generally 10 weeks). A small fee is required for teams that participate in the game, which can be played on the computer or with paper and pencil. Supporting instructional materials, such as sample lesson plans, can help students reflect upon what they are doing. *Learning from the Market,* published by NCEE with support from SIFEE, includes some innovative lesson plans for a variety of grade levels.

Training workshops on how to use the game are provided by various groups. The State Councils and Centers for Economic Education of the NCEE and/or area newspapers commonly implement such workshops. More information about SIFEE, and how to use the game, is available at www.smgww.org/.

The Wall Street Journal Classroom Edition is another valuable resource for economics and basic business classes. It is a monthly student newspaper with regular features on marketing, economics, entrepreneurship, careers, and personal finance. Its articles are selected from those appearing in *The Wall Street Journal.* A teacher's guide, lesson plans, and full-color posters are provided with the student newspaper. A fee for these materials may be underwritten by sponsoring businesses or individuals. A videotape of current events related to articles within the issue is also available for a nominal cost. The Web site http://

webserve.dowjones.com/classroom/index.html describes available materials and links to materials on economic indicators such as consumer confidence and gross domestic product. The site also includes national and international business news and the best cartoons from the *Wall Street Journal*.

The Jump$tart Coalition for Personal Financial Literacy seeks to enhance the personal financial knowledge of young people by evaluating the financial literacy of students, encouraging schools to implement the guidelines for personal financial literacy for grades K–12, spearheading national efforts to encourage more personal financial literacy in the schools, and maintaining a clearinghouse of educational materials. More information about this organization can be found at http://www.jumpstartcoalition.org. One item of particular interest on the Web site is the database of educational materials. For example, a teacher can key the word "credit" into the database for an annotated listing of materials on that topic. Additionally, the guidelines and benchmarks for personal financial management are available on the Web site. These guidelines and benchmarks describe what Jump$tart Coalition believes students should learn about personal finance at various grade levels.

Another clearinghouse for materials, the National Institute for Consumer Education (NICE), can be found on the Internet at www.nice.emich.edu/. Teachers can use this Web site to find teaching materials and ideas for topics related to consumer education. NICE also implements workshops, which are announced on its Web site.

The National Endowment for Financial Education (NEFE), as its name implies, is interested in financial literacy. The Foundation, in cooperation with the Cooperative Extension System and U.S. credit unions, has an extensive seven-unit course that acquaints students with basic financial planning concepts and illustrates how these concepts apply to everyday life. This High School Financial Planning Program relates well to the guidelines for personal financial management published by the Jump$tart Coalition for Personal Financial Literacy. More about the Foundation and its materials and programs is available at www.nefe.org/.

Materials from other organizations. A myriad of other educational materials for business educators is published by businesses, trade groups, and various foundations. The Internet is a valuable source of information and activities for active learning. However, many items on the Internet are advertisements, including some of the materials labeled "educational." Still, an abundance of up-to-date educational materials can be found on the Web and used in conjunction with various units in basic business and economics courses. Although problems with students viewing inappropriate sites can occur, teachers can add safeguards to ensure that students use the Internet appropriately.

Basic business and economics teachers can use the Internet in many ways. Three are presented here:

1. Instruct students to do research using the Internet and complete a study guide sheet. For example, there are many laws on credit. Ask students to read about them on the Federal Trade Commission Web site at www.ftc.gov and then answer questions on a study guide. The author has found students often are more motivated to read materials from a computer screen than from a book.

2. Give students a problem that has a definite answer. Have students solve the problem by searching the Internet. One such activity involves using the Federal Reserve Bank of New York Web site at www.ny.frb.org to compare the consumer price index for various years and point out how it has changed. Another activity involves having students find the current rates for credit cards issued to students and adults by going to www.cardtrak.com. Students can also determine the price of a house they could afford with a given amount of income, down payment, and savings, by using the financial calculator at www.fincalc.com.

3. Give students a problem that requires information from many different Web sites. As an example, in an economics course, students can develop an economic forecast for the following year using the many statistics available on the Econo*magic*.com Web site at www.economagic.com/, the Resources for Economists Web site at www.rfe.org, and the EconData.Net site at www.econdata.net. Students can also quote economists' predictions from Internet sites or the print media. They also might want to ask people in a chat room what they believe will happen during the next year (not an unbiased sampling, but one that should yield some interesting perceptions).

Appendix A includes other Web sites that are useful in teaching economics and basic business.

Summary

Our society has a tremendous need and demand for economic and basic business education. Teachers have a unique opportunity to help students understand the economic system and learn how to manage their personal financial and business affairs now and in the future. Many business teachers have excellent content backgrounds to teach courses in this area. Additionally, an abundance of creative materials and programs is available that can be used to update teachers' knowledge and to make this area of study come alive for students. Business educators can develop a new "golden age for business education" if they embrace the family of courses that has been a part of their heritage for decades.

References

American Savings Education Council. (1999). *Youth and money*. Washington, DC: Author.

Clow, J. E. (1997). Entrepreneurship education. In C. P. Brantley & B. J. Davis (Eds.), *The changing dimensions of business education* (Yearbook No. 35, pp. 148–159). Reston: VA: National Business Education Association.

Clow, J. E. (1999). *National survey of economic education: Final report*. New York: National Council on Economic Education.

Harris, L. and Associates. (1999). *Survey of economic literacy*. New York: National Council on Economic Education.

Jump$tart Coalition for Personal Financial Literacy. (2000, April 6). *Financial literacy declining among twelfth graders* [Press release]. Washington, DC: Author.

Kourilsky, M. (1995). Entrepreneurship education: Opportunity in search of curriculum. *Business Education Forum, 50*(1), 11–15.

Mandell, L. (1998). *Our vulnerable youth—The financial literacy of American twelfth graders*. Washington, DC: Jump$tart Coalition for Personal Financial Literacy.

Mann, P. H. (1992). Entrepreneurship and the world of small business. *Gifted Child Today, 15*(1), 26–27.

Morrison, I. (1996). *The second curve: Managing the velocity of change*. New York: Ballantine Books.

National Business Education Association. (1995). *National standards for business education: What America's students should know and be able to do in business*. Reston, VA: Author.

National Council on Economic Education. (1995). *Voluntary national content standards in economics*. New York: Author.

Appendix A

BANKING, SAVINGS, AND CREDIT

- www.bankrate.com—current rates for savings instruments and various types of loans
- www.ny.frb.org—Federal Reserve activities and materials, especially those at the Federal Reserve Bank of New York
- www.aba.com—banking services
- www.asec.org—savings plans and activities
- www.cardtrak.com—credit card rates
- www.equifax.com and www.experian.com—credit reports
- www.ftc.gov—credit law information
- www.nfcc.org and www.nccs.org—how to deal with consumer debt problems

CONSUMER INFORMATION ABOUT MANY TOPICS

- www.consumer.gov —information on product safety, money, careers, food, and other areas
- www.pueblo.gsa.gov —government publications from the Consumer Education Center
- www.bbb.org —Better Business Bureau reports on business activities and complaints

FRAUD

- www.fraud.org —National Consumer League reports of fraud against consumers

AUTOMOBILES

- www.edmunds.com and www.kbb.com—new- and used-car prices
- www.leasesource.com—leasing information about cars

HOUSING

- www.fincalc.com—financial calculators

INVESTMENTS

- www.quote.com and www.wsrn.com and www.quote.yahoo.com—stock quotes
- www.amex.com and www.nyse.com and www.nasdaq.com—stock market information

ECONOMIC STATISTICS

- www.economagic.com/ and www.rfe.org and www.econdata.net

Managing the Technology-Related Curriculum in Business Education

Michael L. McDonald
University of Southern Mississippi
Hattiesburg, Mississippi

Lonnie Echternacht
Professor Emeritus
University of Missouri
Columbia, Missouri

Due to the rapid advancements occurring in technology, the business curriculum is undergoing considerable change. Describing today's typical business program is a difficult task. The difficulty of this task is reflected in the differences in programs from state to state, district to district, school to school, and campus to campus. In addition to technology, business programs are impacted by a variety of educational initiatives and reforms. For example, some local K–12 programs are influenced by School-to-Career initiatives, statewide standards, and technology infrastructures, whereas others are adhering to quite different, yet related, current movements, such as Tech Prep, project-based learning, and basic skills initiatives. Generally, business programs reflect the values of local boards, administrators, and teachers, who typically focus on the immediate as well as future needs of program graduates and the business community. At the postsecondary and collegiate levels, changes in hardware, software, and workplace procedures, such as telecommuting, wireless communication, and remote work sites, are influencing the curriculum.

No matter what influences create differences in business programs, all programs should reflect common goals of meeting the needs of business employers by supplying a capable workforce, educating students to be effective consumers, and developing leadership skills applicable to today's society. To achieve these goals effectively, educators must use available instructional resources in the most efficient manner. They must manage their time, materials, information, systems, technology, and space to achieve high performance. Both articulation and coordination within the business curriculum are necessary to ensure instructional effectiveness and efficiency.

Planning for an Articulated and Coordinated Business Curriculum

Technology-related courses have become popular at all levels of education, from middle school through postsecondary/collegiate levels as well as adult education and training programs. During the last decade computer literacy and software courses have contributed to rising enrollments in business education programs at the middle and high school levels. The marketability of various types and levels of computer-related courses has attracted students and maintained or even increased enrollments in many business education programs. However, often there is a lack of articulation and coordination in these software applications courses.

An effective technology-based curriculum should ensure that computer-related instruction is properly sequenced throughout the business program. Basic computer instruction offered in secondary programs should build on skills and knowledge introduced in the elementary and middle school grades. Advanced instruction that not only builds higher levels of skills and conceptual understandings but also focuses on a "real-world" business applications, processes, and procedures should be implemented as students progress through the curriculum.

Students' technical skills and problem-solving abilities can be further enhanced by incorporating the use of technology-related skills in the nontechnology-based business courses. Students should use technology to solve problems in a variety of situations and at different levels of learning. By systematically aligning and articulating the teaching and learning of computer applications skills, business programs can more effectively enhance student skills; reduce curriculum redundancies; utilize instructional resources, including time and talent; and prepare students for today's workplace.

Postsecondary business programs have historically enjoyed high student enrollment levels. Currently, postsecondary business programs offer instruction that focuses on computer software applications, including word processing, database, spreadsheet, desktop publishing, multimedia, and Internet skills. Instruction on these same software applications is also typically taught at the secondary level, often using the same software and sometimes the same prepared instructional materials. The potential for a significant amount of redundancy in students' programs is considerable in computer-related courses at all levels.

Students typically are introduced to computer software application programs at the junior high/middle school level and again at the high school level. Introductory level computer software applications courses also are offered at postsecondary and collegiate/university institutions. Although an argument may be made that students cannot practice these important technical skills too often, this curriculum redundancy may waste valuable instructional time and reduce the chance of moving students to problem solving and integration of all their skills. They may not reach the level of true "application"—using technology as a tool for problem solving, a means to an end, not an end in itself.

Business education programs, as well as businesses, will benefit from an articulated computer software applications curriculum, extending from the K–12 level through the university level. In a well-articulated curriculum, students who can demonstrate mastery of a particular subject or skill will not repeat that instruction. According to VanHuss (1997), "To maximize learning, instruction must be tailored to avoid duplicating those skills that have been mastered and to provide additional time to build skills in areas of deficiencies" (p. 32). A highly structured, competency-driven, performance-based curriculum is needed to achieve this goal. The technology-related curriculum must not involve just instruction on computer applications but must be designed to advance students from their various skill levels to a highly productive, workplace-ready level.

Approaches for Delivering Technology-Related Instruction

Two major approaches for delivering technology-related instruction are generally used in educational institutions today. The first is the separate course approach. Courses are designed specifically to provide computer software applications instruction. Individual courses focus on delivering beginning, intermediate, and/or advanced levels of instruction on one or more types of application software, an integrated package, or a suite of related programs.

Computer technology instructors must convey to students the principle that the computer is a business tool used to solve problems. In 1984, the Policies Commission for Business and Economic Education issued Statement 34, which noted, "Business students should demonstrate the ability to use the computer as a tool in performing such information processing applications as accounting, word processing, data processing, and records management" (1997, p. 72). When the separate course approach is used, efforts should be made to ensure that instruction reflects applications in the business world. While offering a direct method for teaching computer technology, the separate course approach often requires additional instructional materials and may add courses to an already crowded business program.

The second approach for delivering technology-related instruction is the infusion approach. The idea behind this approach is to "infuse" or incorporate technology instruction into content-based business courses. For example, spreadsheet instruction and practice can be incorporated into accounting courses, word processing and database instruction into management courses, and computerized presentations into marketing or communication courses.

A major advantage of the infusion approach is that it links computer technology instruction with business applications, processes, and procedures. For instance, using a spreadsheet to solve accounting problems is an important business application of computer technology. However, the infusion method also has some major disadvantages. Often, in content-based business courses there is not sufficient time for in-depth technology instruction and skill development.

The computer skill level developed in content-based courses may not be as advanced as when the separate course approach is used. Instructors who specialize in teaching content areas such as accounting, economics, communication, management, and marketing may not devote the time or resources needed to keep abreast of ever-changing computer software and technology. Instead, they may choose to devote their professional development and in-service activities to keeping up with changes and advancements in their particular areas of expertise.

Using Technology to Enhance Instruction

The multimedia capabilities of computers make them obvious tools for delivering virtually all types of instruction, both in classrooms and at workstations. By using up-to-date technologies in classrooms, teachers increase their credibility, raise their level of professionalism, and maintain a higher level of attention from students.

Computer-assisted instruction (CAI) offers opportunities to simulate real-world scenarios and promotes problem solving and decision making among students. High-quality CAI software programs provide students with opportunities to experience realistic accounting problems, business law cases, economic principles, and communication scenarios. CAI programs are available for many different areas of business, and additional instructional programs are being continually developed.

Teachers need to be selective when implementing CAI and adopting software products. Using an instructional software evaluation form can help eliminate personal bias, promote objectivity, and facilitate group or team decisions about selection. An evaluation form for instructional software should address, but not be limited to, the following questions:

- Is appropriate documentation available for the software?
- Does the documentation include specific directions for handling information storage, e.g., on floppy disk, hard drive, or zip disk?
- Does the documentation provide sample lesson plans and a listing of up-to-date resources?
- Are the instructions in a user-friendly and logical sequence?
- Does the reading level of the instructions match that of the intended audience?
- Are the instructions to proceed consistent, e.g., always press the space bar or Enter key to continue?
- Can the user return to the instructions while the program is running?
- Does the program give examples of the input it requires and accept only correctly formatted input?
- Are the screens attractively and logically formatted (not cluttered with excessive graphics, text, etc.)?

- Does the program make appropriate use of sound and animation?
- Does the material match the course and lesson objectives?
- Does the program provide immediate feedback, and does it personalize the feedback, e.g., use the respondent's name?
- Does the program provide random problems or situations and responses to the user?
- Is the material accurate and up-to-date?
- Does the program allow users to enter at different levels, exit at different points, and return to the correct point later?
- Does the company provide a hot line to answer questions?
- Does the company provide a sample of the program for review?
- Does the company provide a backup disk or allow the program disk to be copied?

Supplementing and Enhancing the Business Curriculum With the Internet

The Internet is the largest source of information available today. The Internet and World Wide Web have made it easy for teachers and students to access business information, conduct research, and bring today's work world into the classroom. Students can visit many business Web sites that offer considerable in-depth information on various aspects of companies, as well as stock quotes, business news, sales trends, and product and financial reports. In addition to providing valuable business information, the Internet also offers unprecedented opportunities for long-distance collaboration and communication. Through e-mail and listservs, students can communicate with business, industry, and government leaders and with peers in other cities, states, regions, and countries.

However, potential hazards in bringing the Internet into the classroom must be considered. First, the amount of material on the Internet that is inappropriate for educational purposes continues to increase. Creators of such sites go to great lengths to make sure that individuals inadvertently visit their locations. Students will probably happen onto these inappropriate sites. Precautions should be taken by teachers, especially those who teach minors. An acceptable-use policy (AUP)—developed and signed by the teacher, the student, and most importantly, a parent or legal guardian—should include the following standard provisions:

- The use of computer network resources must support educational objectives and be consistent with the school's mission.
- Users must abide by copyright law; software contracts; and other local, state, and federal laws; as well as institutional policies and regulations.
- The use of network resources for commercial business or profit is prohibited.
- Extensive personal use of network resources is prohibited.
- Internet accounts should be accessed only by the authorized owners of the accounts.

- Confidentiality of passwords and user accounts must be protected. Individuals can be held accountable when their accounts are used by others.
- Intentional use of Internet resources to access or process obscene material, inappropriate text or graphic files, or files that are dangerous to the integrity of the network is prohibited.
- Teachers who sponsor student use of telecommuting shall review with students the AUP and maintain supervision of students using the network.
- Students' phone numbers, addresses, or other personal information shall not be transmitted or posted.

The specific steps that educators and institutions are expected to take to maintain proper use of the Internet should be listed in the school's AUP. The most important step is careful monitoring. Software designed to monitor the appropriateness of Internet sites is at best helpful, but certainly does not guarantee proper use. School personnel must be present and diligent in monitoring computers that provide Internet access. The AUP should also include a statement that acknowledges that inappropriate materials may be accidentally viewed by students, and all parties—students, teachers, administrators, and parents—should work together to reduce these occurrences.

It is possible that students will use the Internet to hack into or gain access to private or sensitive information, not only viewing the information but also using or altering it unethically. Students' may try to use the Internet to deliver threats and other inappropriate messages or to make private and personal information public. These kinds of problems, as well as others that may result from the misuse of the Internet, should be dealt with in the AUP and through careful monitoring.

The Emerging Role of E-Business

A fast-growing segment of the Internet that has special relevance for the business curriculum is electronic commerce (e-commerce) and/or the more inclusive term, electronic business (e-business). E-business may be defined as any business activity that takes place using the Internet. A definition of e-business offered by Balachandran and Smith (2000) is, "... all business activity conducted electronically to take advantage of speed and access" (p. 37).

The use of e-business is changing rapidly. According to Ascentrix Technologies, "predictions indicate that by 2001 e-commerce will increase from the current level of $450 million to over $6.5 billion" (Balachandran & Smith, 2000, p. 37). If business educators are to provide instruction on the most relevant trends in business, e-business concepts, processes, and procedures should certainly be included in the business curriculum. Students may find themselves employed in businesses that rely greatly on e-business, or they may choose to start their own e-businesses and offer products or services via the Internet. In addition, students are current and future consumers who will use the Internet for purchases and for securing product information.

The greatest challenge for business programs and teachers who offer e-business courses will be determining the content to be delivered. Technology skills and knowledge of business concepts, processes, and procedures are essential competencies for success in e-business. Obviously, the technological skills related to using the Internet and creating and maintaining Web sites are critical. However, special-purpose software programs that provide templates or shells for designing and creating Web pages have become more sophisticated and user-friendly, and current applications programs can convert documents into HTML format for use as Web pages. Using these software programs to create Web sites is remarkably easy and allows users to concentrate on business and marketing strategies and effective Web page design.

E-business involves several critical issues that should be addressed. The first is security. Balachandran and Smith (2000) have reported:

> "Security issues have been mostly resolved through encryption, authentication, and authorization technologies" ("E-Commerce: E-nevitable," 1998, p. 76). Electronic transfer of funds can eliminate the use of credit cards, but there is still an element of fear for some consumers. (p. 39)

Currently, this issue does not appear to be resolved, when the number of news reports concerning the seemingly high number of breaches of security and the vulnerability of high-level Internet servers is considered. Consumers continue to be hesitant to reveal private information to unseen entities over the Internet.

What is done with this personal information after it has been divulged over the Internet by a user? Sometimes this information is sold to telemarketers who use it to launch a barrage of sales attempts via e-mail, telephone, fax, or even traditional mail. Students should be expected to apply ethical standards when dealing with personal information that has been entrusted to them by consumers and has resulted from business transactions.

Integration of Basic Workplace Skills Into Technology-Related Courses

In today's highly technical workplace, nontechnical skills, such as writing, are extremely important. According to Carnevale, Gainer, and Meltzer (1990), "Certainly, top business administrators consistently rank writing competency among their highest priorities for job applicants and employees" (p. 21).

The 1992 SCANS report (U.S. Department of Labor) defined the foundational skills and workplace competencies required for effective job performance. The skills listed in the report included both technical and nontechnical skills and reflected the need for balance in business education programs. Nontechnical skills included, but were not limited to, the ability to

- Manage time
- Manage money
- Manage material and facility resources
- Manage human resources
- Participate as a member of a team
- Teach others
- Serve clients/customers
- Exercise leadership
- Negotiate to arrive at a decision
- Work with cultural diversity (p. 81)

Coomer (1998) has also identified a set of basic skills that should become the focus of learning in today's business classrooms. They include the following:

- The ability to read for understanding
- Communication skills
- High-level math skills
- Computer skills
- The ability to locate information
- Problem-solving skills
- Teaming, networking, and leading skills
- The ability to manage career development
- Mentoring skills (p. 42)

According to each of these sources, basic workplace skills must be addressed in all courses, including technology-related courses. Business educators must continue to emphasize basic workplace skills—interpersonal skills, self-management skills, and workplace enhancement skills—because they impact the ability of organizations to succeed. Attention should be given to "spiraling" these basic skills, as well as business applications, processes, and systems, into software application courses through the use of case studies, modeling, projects, portfolios, simulations, and work-based experiences.

An integrated approach to developing curriculum and delivering instruction provides students with experiences that move them from an introduction to technology to workplace-based experiences. The integrated approach enables students to apply their skills and knowledge to situations or simulations that require problem solving and to increase their expertise in this area. An integrated approach to teaching both technical skills and basic workplace skills enables students to use all types of technology as tools for problem solving and increasing productivity. Typically, the problem provides the environment and need for a project. The project serves as a motivational experience and provides an authentic context for students to learn how to use technology tools and develop higher-level skills.

Addressing Future Needs

Higher student enrollments have encouraged many business educators to add computer literacy and software applications courses to their programs. However, business programs have a much broader mission than just delivering computer instruction. According to the National Business Education Association (1995),

> The primary mission of business education is to provide instruction for and about business. The discipline of business education prepares students to become contributing citizens who are capable of making astute personal economic decisions. In business education classrooms, students learn the basics of personal finance, develop techniques for making wise consumer decisions, master economic principles, and learn how businesses operate. (p. 1)

Fundamental nontechnical business concepts and skills are needed by employees, required by employers, and valued by consumers. Knowledge of business concepts remains important as computer technologies advance. Business education must continue to focus on the need for a balanced "for and about" curriculum. The content taught in courses such as business law, communication, management, economics, and accounting provides students with invaluable information (knowledge about business) to help them be competent, highly productive workers and knowledgeable, effective consumers.

However, technical business skills and computer-related skills (knowledge for business) should still be emphasized. New technologies have altered business and office environments and have made new skills necessary for employees in administrative and management positions. Davis (1997) has studied the computer skills employers expect of recent college graduates and has reported the following comments from employers:

> Many employers agreed that "computer literacy is important to all," and that "if a student graduates without any [skills], he/she will have a distinct disadvantage in the workforce." Lacking these skills would not exclude most college graduates from the job market; however "the more skills they exhibit, the more attractive they would be" to potential employers. (p. 7)

The ability to acquire and use information effectively has become an important technical skill for today's workplace. More information than ever is being stored systematically in databases and disseminated electronically. The ability to search extensively and retrieve information efficiently from comprehensive and specialized databases is a necessary skill for today's business workers.

Using Multiple Instructional Strategies

To ensure a high-quality technology-related business curriculum, careful attention must be given to facilitating and managing the instructional/learning process. Business educators must structure their time and activities to communicate high expectations. They must accept multiple levels of technology skills in their classes as a challenge, arrange classrooms thoughtfully and creatively to facilitate student learning, address everyday computer and technology problems and concerns calmly, provide access to the latest technology possible, and focus on each student's total development. The professional development of educators is a key to improving the educational system. Professional development needs to be focused, planned, and ongoing—a part of the day-to-day, week-to-week life of an educator. Every educator needs to be a lifelong learner.

The following instructional strategies can be used to enhance the technology-related business curriculum. They can help ensure that students will be highly productive, employable, and well prepared with information for and about business.

- Demonstrate computer and software procedures in large group, small group, and individualized settings. Include skill-building principles and accommodate individual student learning styles.
- Introduce changes in routines, activities, instructional materials, and computer software enthusiastically.
- Develop instructional/learning activities that allow students to be creative and to demonstrate their problem-solving skills.
- Use actual business examples in class to which students can relate (for example, use annual reports from companies such as Nike, Tommy Hilfiger, Dell, Compaq, Microsoft, and Wal-Mart).
- Observe student performance systematically to determine areas where teaching and learning emphases need to be placed.
- Adjust instruction for both individual and group differences, varying timing of activities, incorporating supplementary materials, and encouraging repetition of exercises and problems.
- During skill-building activities, provide feedback that is positive, constructive, immediate, and specific so students can correct their responses immediately.
- Motivate students to develop the right attitude, evaluate their own work, participate in competitive team efforts, and strive to achieve at high performance levels.
- Create assignments that incorporate increasing levels of difficulty (progressing from simple to complex) so all learners perceive that they are achieving higher-level skills and being challenged.
- Organize the classroom as a learning laboratory that encourages problem solving, trial and error, experimentation, concept refinement, and skill enhancement.

- Use an electronic journal for dialog or a listserv where students can freely communicate questions, needs, and observations about their learning experiences.
- Incorporate cooperative-learning activities in technology-related learning experiences so students can contribute to and learn from their peers. Assign problems or tasks that require groups to work together as they gather data, think critically, solve problems, and synthesize ideas.
- Display checklists, rubrics, and finished projects for self-evaluation of completed work; establish recognizable, achievable goals.
- Depict the many different types of businesses, organizations, and industries that use computers extensively through "topical collages," for which each student is required to contribute at least one item.
- Discuss legal and ethical aspects of software copyright and piracy issues.
- Examine different types of viruses and evaluate antivirus software programs.
- Describe the potential for invasion of privacy that may result from the use of computers, networks, intranets, the Internet, and the World Wide Web.
- Identify ways that computer systems can be protected from unauthorized access.
- Explain the legal ramifications of "hacking" into another computer or computer system.
- Create a classroom resource center consisting of recent computer, software, and technology magazines; company brochures; and product descriptions and ask students to review, contrast, and/or summarize articles about the computer industry and about current issues, emerging trends, and high-profile concerns.
- Have students research possible environmental issues related to computers and peripherals, e.g., landfills and recycling.
- Describe the need for and ways of backing up programs, files, and data, and how systematic procedures can prevent costly losses of information.
- Identify health risks and discuss the need for ergonomic awareness related to prolonged and inappropriate computer use.
- Discuss issues surrounding the upgrading of hardware and software, e.g., compatibility, efficiency, capabilities, cost, and the pursuit of a cutting-edge image.
- Develop a course-related Web site for posting pertinent information, updates, assignments, assessments, grades, and "helpful hints."
- Examine popular search engines to determine the search strategies they utilize and the different types of information they provide.
- Explain the security and financial issues related to the buying and selling of products and services over the Internet.
- Discuss the advantages and risks of downloading files from the Internet.
- Have students analyze and contrast two or more business or organization Web sites and identify their major characteristics, unique features, and overall structures.

- Identify new computer careers opening up because of technological advancements (e.g., network administration, Web site development/ maintenance, electronic publishing, and e-business), and their education/ training requirements.
- Using spreadsheet or presentation software, have students generate tables or graphics from actual data taken from companies' annual reports or newspaper articles.
- Have students access the help screen to review and perform efficiently functions deemed critical for a computer end user.

Summary

Technology-related courses have become an increasingly important part of the business curriculum at all levels, from middle school through the postsecond-ary/collegiate level. The two missions of business education, teaching for and about business, remain equally important, though. If the technology-related curriculum is to contribute to the objectives of preparing students to manage their own business affairs successfully and join the workforce with the skills and knowledge that employers need, both areas must be emphasized. The technology-related curriculum should assist students in integrating their skills and knowledge in ways that enable them to meet both goals effectively.

Technology has two roles: it is a tool for technology-based courses and a tool integrated into courses that focus primarily on business content, processes, and procedures. As a tool integrated into the curriculum, technology enables students to develop their problem-solving skills and carry out complex tasks, using hardware and software as means to an end, not as ends in themselves.

In delivering the technology-related portion of the business curriculum, attention must be given to coordinating and articulating instruction at all levels; incorporating technology to improve instruction; exploring the emerg-ing role of e-business; continuing to stress the importance of basic workplace skills; and maintaining a future-oriented, balanced approach. This chapter includes multiple strategies that should enable business educators to develop both technical and nontechnical skills in the technology-related business curriculum.

References

Balachandran, M. E., & Smith, M. O. (2000, April). E-commerce: The new frontier in marketing. *Business Education Forum, 54*(4), 37–39.

Carnevale, A. P., Gainer, L. J., & Meltzer, A. S. (1990). *Workplace basics: The essential skills employers want.* San Francisco, CA: Jossey-Bass Publishers.

Coomer, C. (1998, December). Teaching the new basic skills. *Business Education Forum, 53*(2), 42–43.

Davis, P. (1997, September). What computer skills do employers expect from recent college graduates? *T.H.E. Journal.* Retrieved from the World Wide Web:

http://www.thejournal.com/magazine/ vault/A1921.cfm

National Business Education Association. (1995). *National standards for business education: What America's students should know and be able to do in business.* Reston, VA: Author.

Policies Commission for Business and Economic Education. (1997). This we believe about computer literacy, Statement 34, 1984. *Policy Statements 1959–1996.* Cincinnati, OH: South-Western Educational Publishing.

U.S. Department of Labor. (1992). *Learning a living: A blueprint for high performance: A SCANS Report for America 2000.* Washington, DC: U.S. Government Printing Office.

VanHuss, S. H. (1997, December). Integrated applications keep keyboarding alive and well. *Business Education Forum, 52*(2), 30–32.

Integrating Business Education Programs With Other Disciplines

Sandra R. Williams
University of Montana
Missoula, Montana

Billie J. Herrin
Professor Emeritus
University of Montana
Missoula, Montana

Robyn J. Taylor
Petersburg High School
Petersburg, Alaska

What is curriculum integration? Beane (1995) has defined it as "a way of thinking about what schools are for, about the sources of curriculum, and about the uses of knowledge" (p. 616). Curriculum integration goes beyond the mastery of fragmented information within the boundaries of subject areas to focus on the skills and knowledge students need for effective transition from school to work and further education.

When integration occurs between business education programs and other programs, teachers from disciplines such as math, science, English, and history can work with business teachers to help students apply what they learn to real-world situations and develop problem-solving and critical-thinking skills. The integrated setting can become an exciting arena for students as they respond to new methods of teaching and learning. Teachers can profit by collaborating, observing, and participating in new teaching experiences.

Many of the more contemporary approaches to integration currently in use include integrated curricula, cognitive and work-based apprenticeships, career academies, magnet schools, and Tech Prep and School-to-Career programs. These varied approaches require teachers to develop new methods suitable to their evolving roles as lifelong learners, collaborators, and facilitators of learning. These approaches also require teachers to become as familiar with the workplace as they are with their school settings and to make school settings reflect professional standards (Naylor, 1997).

For several years educators have been discussing such topics as curriculum integration and nonprogrammatic delivery of education. Theorists have developed ideas related to these different systems of delivering education; however, there is little documentation available on schools that have adopted new approaches to facilitating integration and other curriculum reform. Stasz, Kaganoff, and Eden (1994) have stated that "programs that integrate academic and business education can take several years to design and implement and several more [years] before they graduate students" (p. 87).

Elementary schools, high schools, postsecondary institutions, colleges, and universities are all facing increasing external pressures to design curricula that will help students integrate and apply concepts learned in all subjects. Often, the reforms advocated by policy makers, educators, employers, scholars, and social critics, lack a clear focus of exactly what integration should address. This may be due in part to the fact that each reform constituency has its own perspective on what educational or social problems integration might help solve. Additionally, questions remain about whether integration reform should be curricular, pedagogical, organizational, or all three (Stasz, Kaganoff, & Eden, 1994).

Meeting societal needs in the 21st century is another factor affecting the reform challenges that must be faced by schools. Evolving student and classroom demographics, teaching expectations, administrative requirements, and general school philosophies result in a need for change. Is integration of curriculum *one* solution or *the* solution for meeting today's challenges, dealing with change, and enacting effective reform?

Historical Perspectives

The transition from the 18th century Latin schools, which primarily prepared boys for college, to the tuition academies of the 19th century, which offered both academic and practical studies for boys and girls, brought about increasingly varied curricula and the inclusion of a wider portion of the population. At the dawn of the 19th century, Americans became committed to what was known as the "common school." The advocates of the common school were dedicated to providing an education for all people (Wraga, 1998).

In the latter half of the 19th century and even in the 20th century, secondary education remained the realm of a select few, with only one out of ten adolescents enrolled. The foundation of education at this time was traditional, academic-focused studies that catered to people from the higher socioeconomic strata. It was not until the Industrial Revolution that new economic realities caused educators and other groups to call for an education that would prepare young people for employment. Thus, the vocational education movement began with widespread agreement among educators and businesspeople that vocational education should be a component of secondary education. Controversy soon arose, however, as to whether vocational education and academics should be under separate or dual control. Proponents of a dual system argued that under separate control vocational schools would further segregate people according to vocational lines (Wraga, 1998).

The Smith-Hughes Act of 1918, the federal act that brought vocational education into the schools by providing funding for vocational programs and regulating the expenditures of the monies provided, settled the issue in favor of the comprehensive high school. As business education (first introduced as "commercial education") became a part of the accepted curriculum in the comprehensive high school, it had two missions: to teach students *about* business so that they could understand the economic world in which they functioned as producers and consumers, and to teach them *for* business so that they would have the skills and knowledge needed to be productive employees, to manage their own businesses, and to meet employers' expectations. This dual mission of business education was vital to its role in the comprehensive high school. Teaching students about business is the foundation for integration of business education with other curriculum areas.

Integrated Curriculum Reform
Integration, as discussed by a host of different groups, is analyzed in the following sections.

Stasz, Kaganoff, and Eden (1994) have stated that integration is viewed as a curricular reform that responds to changing and uncertain future skill demands. Federal legislators look at integration as a way to make the United States and its educational system more competitive in the world economy. They believe that developing more fully all academic skills offered in the curriculum will help prepare students to work and compete in a technologically advanced society (Stasz, Kaganoff, & Eden, 1994). The enhancement of basic skills has been the focus of business educators for many years.

Many employers believe that new job entrants lack many of the basic, problem-solving, teamwork, and communication skills needed to survive in the workplace of the 21st century. In their eyes, integration is key to modifying curricula and enhancing basic and workplace skills (Stasz, Kaganoff, & Eden, 1994). Many business programs are currently intertwining School-to-Career and Tech Prep programs, integrated curricula, cognitive and work-based apprentice-ships, and career academies. Business educators, however, sometimes find themselves as the only teachers willing to participate in and provide the new programs.

School reformers echo employers' concerns about students' lack of the basic and critical-thinking skills they need to make learning more meaningful and to prepare adequately for the world of work. These reformers want integration to focus on improving student learning and facilitating the transition from school to work (Stasz, Kaganoff, & Eden, 1994).

Educators look at integration as a way for all teachers to collaborate and share teaching methods. For educators, integration is viewed as a pedagogical reform that aims to improve both teaching and learning (Stasz, Kaganoff, & Eden, 1994).

For other critics, such as those of traditional education, integration means giving all students access to all educational opportunities. In the past, high school students have been tracked into "college preparatory" classes, or "vocational" classes. Integration could help alleviate the problem of tracking students.

Rationale for Integration

The 1990 amendments to the Carl D. Perkins Vocational Act of 1984 required that funds be made available for education programs that integrate business education with other subject areas. Although the amendments provided little guidance on what integration meant, they stipulated that students achieve both occupational and academic competencies. The amendments also gave leeway for implementation and did not mandate that integration be in the same courses or course sequences (Stasz, Kaganoff, & Eden, 1994).

Brewer (1999) has stated that "integration of academic and occupational education reinforces the shifting [of the] paradigm from teaching to learning and requires that students become active participants in the construction of their own knowledge" (p.1). Educators are continually facing external pressures to design curricula and instruction in ways that show students how to apply learned concepts. Integration has the potential of broadening occupational education and strengthening its connections to civic goals. Integration can also broaden the focus of occupational education and offer opportunities to a more diverse group of individuals (Brewer, 1999).

Integration can help move the aspects of business education that focus on preparing students for business from traditional skill training to preparation for today's global, high-tech, and diverse workplace. The September 1997 issue of *Keying In* reported that in the 10 years since the emergence of the idea of curriculum integration there had been an expansive growth in the design of interdisciplinary teaching units by instructors from all disciplines.

Teachers can now find many integrated units and resources available for perusal on the Internet. Integration has been especially significant for business education because of integration's efficacy as a method of raising student achievement levels. Business educators can reinforce the importance of business education by demonstrating how they teach critical-thinking skills to students

41

through integration and the use of interdisciplinary teaching units. Integration and interdisciplinary units and lesson plans also help forge strong relationships with other teachers ("Curriculum Integration," 1997).

Models of Integration

Educators, employers, legislators, critics, civic groups, policy makers, parents, and others are advocating integrated curricula. They all have different reasons for embracing it; however, the major advantage of integration is that it gives all students access to both academic and occupational education benefits.

Research indicates that approaches to integration vary considerably, ranging from models of marginal change in existing courses to major reforms that reshape entire schools. Unlike projects that propose to simply remedy business programs or enrich them academically, the more involved changes that include major curriculum revisions require the efforts and support of administrators, boards, teachers, and parents. While many schools have opted for the more radical and ambitious models of reform, the majority set their sights on only limited change.

One of the most pervasive ways of adopting new models of integration in secondary schools involves investing in "off-the-shelf" curriculum packages (e.g., applied math, science, communication, and English, or principles of technology). Another option is to design and develop programs locally using a collaborative approach to implementing interdisciplinary or thematic units (Stasz, Kaganoff, & Eden, 1994).

As cited in McDonnell and Zellman (1992), a 1991 National Center for Research in Vocational Education (NCRVE) study indicated that 34 of the 45 states responding to a question about integrated curricula said they had invested in applied academic materials. The use of these materials can be quite costly and can require major involvement by teachers to revise the materials for individual, team, and school needs (McDonnell & Zellman, 1992).

Schools choosing to develop interdisciplinary or thematic units may also require major involvement and commitment by teachers and administrators. Years of planning may be needed to develop guidelines and materials and to test the feasibility of implementing integrated units.

Middle school level integration. Beane (1992) has described the middle school curriculum with three critical concepts:

The first is that the middle school ought to be a general education school in which the curriculum focuses on widely shared concerns of early adolescents and the larger world, rather than increasing specialization and different subjects. The second is that while the middle school curriculum is subject to many demands, its primary purpose should be to serve the early adolescents who attend school. The third concept involves the revision of the increasingly popular view of early adolescents as victims of their developmental stage . . . (p. 1)

The emerging vision of these three concepts involves the creation of a middle school curriculum organized around meaningful themes instead of artificial subjects. Beane (1992) has stated, "The question in reform remains: are educators willing to make a leap of faith on behalf of the young people schools are intended to serve" (p. 4).

Secondary level integration models. A comprehensive review of education literature indicates that a variety of different forms of integration exist. The following examples encompass modest to complicated forms of modification and summarize eight models:

- Incorporating more content from courses such as English, math, science, and social studies into business education courses
- Requiring teachers to collaborate on curriculum development
- Making courses in areas such as English, math, science, and social studies more workplace relevant
- Developing curricular alignment that modifies or coordinates all courses
- Designing senior projects to be done in lieu of elective courses and then requiring each student to complete a project that integrates the knowledge and skills learned in all courses
- Implementing the academy model, or the school-within-a-school model (generally targeted to selected students within a high school), in which courses align with each other and with an occupational focus
- Aligning occupational high school and magnet school courses with each other so that there is an occupational focus for all students and programs in the entire school
- Creating occupational clusters, career paths, and occupational majors that feature a coherent sequence and alignment of courses within a cluster, often with teachers organized by cluster instead of department (Stasz, Kaganoff, & Eden, 1994)

No matter which model a school decides to implement, extensive planning, coordination, and commitment are required (Hoachlander, 1999).

Postsecondary level integration. Research indicates that much less is known about integration at the postsecondary level than is known about it at the lower levels. Lack of information may be due in part to the fact that reform has been much less urgent at the postsecondary level. With increased external pressures in all areas, however, community and technical colleges are probably experiencing more pressure to design curricula and instruction in ways that help students apply concepts learned in both occupational and academic courses (Brewer, 1999).

Brewer (1999) has contended that the rationale for integration of education at the postsecondary level is like the rationale for integration at the middle school and secondary levels. Postsecondary integration reinforces the shifting of the paradigm from teaching to learning and requires that students become active participants in the construction of their own knowledge. It also has the potential to broaden the educational focus and offer opportunities to a more diverse group of individuals.

But according to Stasz, Kaganoff, and Eden (1994), some aspects of the rationale for and purposes of integration at the postsecondary level are much less clear than those at other levels. Stasz, Kaganoff, and Eden have discussed an NCRVE survey that indicates that postsecondary institutions have implemented a variety of eight different integration models including

- Requiring technical and community college students to enroll in general education courses as well as occupational courses
- Designing and offering courses that link academic subject matter to workplace issues for occupational students
- Instituting cross-curricular programs that incorporate academic content into occupational programs
- Incorporating academic models and modules into occupational courses and curricula
- Designing multidisciplinary courses that combine academic perspectives and occupational concerns focusing on themes such as the role of work for individuals and society, the history of technology and its effects on society, and ethical issues surrounding work and technological change
- Developing tandem and cluster courses to provide a structure for integration in which teachers may reinforce material taught in related courses, analyze similar issues, utilize common examples, design projects for more than one course, and build on concepts taught in other courses
- Developing colleges-within-colleges, also referred to as expanded clusters, which are very rare partly because students seem unwilling or unable to commit to a preset program of this type
- Offering remediation and English as a Second Language (ESL) programs with an occupational focus (Stasz, Kaganoff, & Eden, 1994)

Although these models do not directly coincide with models of integration at the secondary level, some common themes are evident. The chief differences between the models seem to be that fewer of the postsecondary models involve changes within the classroom and fewer postsecondary models require restructuring (Stasz, Kaganoff, & Eden, 1994).

College/university level integration. The reform movement in higher education calls for improvements throughout undergraduate education both in curricular content and in the educational process. Debates about content include arguments for having colleges and universities require students to study a common core of courses, and arguments for adopting curricula that support diversity, economic growth, and global interdependence. In reference to educational processes, most reformers call for pedagogies that promote student involvement and strengthen relationships between faculty and students. Many reformers stress the need for greater coherence and increased efforts to help students connect what they study with their lives (Lattuca & Stark, 1994). The common thread of integration at all levels is the importance of encouraging each student to become an active participant in his or her education.

Many higher education reforms address integrating general course work with specific areas. Research has reported that task forces have been set up in some divisions (e.g., sciences and mathematics, social sciences and humanities) to look at curricular coherence and to establish ways to promote cohesiveness. Some divisions have reported major setbacks when trying to develop curriculum cohesiveness throughout departments, colleges, or schools. Because of the distinctive autonomy of faculty, schools, colleges, departments, programs, and divisions, creating cohesiveness and connecting learning can be challenging.

Teacher education programs. Although colleges and universities have not focused on integrating academic courses with occupational courses, integration of teacher education programs may be an avenue for change. Across the United States, only a limited amount of research on integration in teacher education programs has been published. Proponents of the reform initiatives of the 1980s and early 1990s have argued that improving education requires improving teacher quality and teacher education. To answer calls for reform, teacher education programs have raised admission standards/exit requirements; revised curricula to reflect multiculturalism and new K–12 standards; paid more attention to pedagogy, teaching practices, and relevance; included clinical experiences in public schools and other learning environments; and proposed new model standards/principles for licensing beginning teachers (Lynch, 1997). There has not, however, been an impetus to address curriculum integration.

Teacher education reform includes proposals to restructure teacher preparation programs to incorporate integrated content, integrated academic and work-based learning, partnerships with businesses/industries, and preservice and in-service field experiences, as well as to require courses in applied instructional and curricular technology (Naylor, 1997).

Miller (1996) has asserted that the mission of occupational education should be based on constructivism. "Constructivism is a cognitive approach that emphasizes 'constructing' knowledge through a problem-solving process designed to produce learners who are problem-solvers, lifelong learners, makers of meaning, collaborators, change agents who are also able to change, and practitioners of democratic processes" (p. 69–70).

Lynch (1997) has offered nine principles that may be used as a foundation for business teacher education programs:

- Faculty commitment to students and their professional development as lifelong learners
- Faculty use of curriculum and instructional methods to integrate theory with practice, professional education with subject matter, academic education with workforce education, and learning theory with workforce preparation
- Faculty understanding of the philosophy and effective practice of workforce preparation and development
- Faculty use of dynamic pedagogy based on learning theory and practices
- Faculty partnerships with learning communities through which collaboration and the democratic processes can be modeled
- Dynamic and change-oriented programs for all institutions
- Programs that are grounded in academic education, workplace subject matter, technology, professional education, and clinical field experiences
- Adequate resources to sustain high-quality programs in colleges and universities
- Prioritization of occupational educator preparation

Are these realistic requirements for business teacher education programs? Can we expect all business teacher educators to participate in programs that follow these principles?

Lynch (1997) has described one model for work-based teacher education programs that consists of the following five components: assessment, curriculum framework, standards of knowledge, principles of workplace and technical teacher education, and philosophical foundations. Many teacher education programs currently use a model of this type; however, by incorporating the nine principles cited above as a foundation for this model, business teacher education programs could enhance teaching effectiveness.

Integration and business education. The majority of business teacher education programs are currently housed in colleges/schools of education or colleges/schools of business. The business teacher education program may be the only work-based program housed in a college/school of business or education; however, the opportunity for integrated curriculum still exists.

At one National Association for Business Teacher Education (NABTE) institution, The University of Montana, faculty and undergraduate students in science, math, and business teaching programs have worked together for approximately five years on integrated units in their methods courses. All methods courses are scheduled at the same time in a three- or four-hour block. During the early part of the semester, faculty and students from all areas get together to discuss integration and integrated projects. Students are assigned groups in which there is at least one person from each discipline. They then begin selecting a theme or topic for their integrated unit project. Many frustrations have been encountered and some overcome, and students have prepared many outstanding units, lesson plans, and materials during this effort. (Topics have included space travel; global warming and its effect on glaciers in Glacier National Park; Whirling disease and its effect on Blue Ribbon Trout streams and fly fishing in Montana; gold mining at the 7-Up Pete Ranch Mine in Lincoln, Montana, and the effect of mining on the environment; and many others. A variety of integrated lessons is available at http:// webback.educ.umt.edu/cpgrant). Integration has not followed particular models, principles, or guidelines at The University of Montana; however, many barriers to success could be overcome by adopting the measures used there.

Another example of successful integration took place in a high school setting. At Petersburg High School in Petersburg, Alaska, freshmen and teachers in physical science, English, and business technology courses integrated their classes for an entire semester. During the physical science class period, students developed and created a research project that included experiments. They first spent time in the library, where they learned how to do research, and later focused on doing experiments. During the business technology class period, students learned how to format reports, title pages, and bibliographies. Then, after spending three weeks learning the software application Excel, students were able to enter and manipulate experimental data. The English class period was devoted to writing, editing, and proofreading the report.

At the close of the semester, students and teachers were able to evaluate and assess the project in its entirety. As reported by the teachers involved in integration, the most positive aspect of this project was the understanding students gained about how the information they learned in one class transferred to other classes. The negative aspect was the excessive time involvement and preparation required of the teachers. This project was only one of several running concurrently throughout the school.

Barriers to Integration

Barriers to integration are many and varied and pose challenges to all levels of schools wishing to move ahead with integration initiatives. If integration is going to become successful and systematic, strong school leadership is required.

A review of literature and research reveals several common challenges that those working on integration have had to face including the following:

- Costs are high, real, and certain (Schug & Cross, 1998).

- Accountability is difficult to attain (Schug & Cross, 1998).
- Parents are often reluctant to endorse such efforts (Schug & Cross, 1998).
- Integration requires hard work and dedication (Hoachlander, 1999).
- Integration requires faculty to depart from familiar methodologies (Hoachlander, 1999).
- Students resist new forms of instruction (Hoachlander, 1999).
- Institutions lack leadership in support of curriculum reform (Brewer, 1999).
- Institutions lack people with knowledge of how to integrate (Brewer, 1999).
- Institutions lack resources for release time, planning, and professional development (Brewer, 1999).
- Institutions have insufficient administrative and faculty support (Brewer, 1999).
- Institutions lack necessary curricular materials and technology (Brewer, 1999).
- Integrated programs may cause job loss or major role changes for teachers (Stasz, Kaganoff, & Eden, 1994).
- Business teachers may be perceived as lacking the skills required to adequately incorporate related academic subjects into their courses or programs (Stasz, Kaganoff, & Eden, 1994).

Wherever significant change is initiated, problems and barriers will occur. When integration is pursued carefully and thoughtfully, however, it can offer students a deep and lasting understanding of how they will use knowledge and skills in their work and personal lives (Hoachlander, 1999). Integration can also offer teachers the benefits of working in a collaborative setting. Instead of looking at these challenges as barriers, teachers, if willing, can change some of them into positive experiences.

Programs That Work

Hoachlander (1999) has stated that "whatever form integration takes, it should begin by clearly specifying the educational goals" (p.3). One way of meeting the objectives of integration is to use academic, workplace, and industrial skill standards to direct integrated learning. Nationally and in many states, standards exist that describe what students are expected to know (outcomes) in each of the major academic and applied learning settings. The *National Standards for Business Education* (National Business Education Association, 1995), *Business Teacher Education Curriculum Guide & Program Standards* (National Association for Business Teacher Education, 1997), and state standards are available for elementary, secondary, postsecondary, and higher education business programs. Although standards may vary in both content and attention to differences among grade levels, they are a good starting point for identifying and specifying learning objectives.

Stasz, Kaganoff, and Eden (1994) have stated that integration is essentially a curricular and pedagogical reform that requires a bottom-up solution. Because this type of reform requires or encourages changes in entire school organizations, researchers suggest starting out slow and small.

If integration is to be successful, administrative support is essential. Administrators who encourage risk taking help create an environment that is conducive to innovation. Schools that approach integration as something that has to be done because it has been dictated by a higher authority create a hostile environment that may provoke teacher resistance. Schools that use effective planning and focus on their ability to serve students and incorporate change with a long-term plan find a smoother transition to integration. Additionally, schools with a strong financial base, a history of innovation, and a cooperative administration also experience a smoother transition than those that do not have these characteristics (Stasz, Kaganoff, & Eden, 1994).

Integration may require many important changes in teachers' roles; therefore, it requires significant support from faculty. Because most business teacher education programs have not prepared teachers for integration, adequate staff and curriculum development would immensely improve the transition to integration. Few curricular materials are available for integration; therefore, faculty and staff must have time to collaborate on curriculum, materials, units, lessons, and classroom instruction. Adequate financial backing is necessary to support the acquisition of classroom resource materials and technology.

One method being used to help faculty members adjust to integration is team building. This involves having teachers from different subject areas work together in clusters, or teams. Educators teach or help each other develop curriculum and instructional strategies and guidelines for implementing integration.

Other tools that are available for administrators to use to help teachers through the integration transition include scheduling times for planning and for classes, handling teacher concerns, dealing with teacher resentment, involving teachers in decisions, providing time for committee assignments, providing adequate time for teacher preparation in specific subject areas, providing communication links, and providing use of counselors for support and insight. Incentives that administrators could offer teachers to help them move toward integration include tuition reimbursement for teachers seeking to upgrade their credentials, funds for curriculum development, and reduced teaching loads during the adjustment period (Stasz, Kaganoff, & Eden, 1994).

When integration is pursued carefully and thoughtfully, it can offer students a deep and lasting understanding of how they will use knowledge and skills in their work and personal lives. A generally accepted theory—that learning is enhanced by doing—can be turned into sound and effective educational practice through well-planned integration programs.

Future Directions for Integration and Implications for Business Education

Because integration requires drastic changes in curriculum, pedagogy, and school and program organization, integration may take years to implement. But the rewards are many, including greater student participation in the learning process, and the accessibility of broader career paths to young people.

Although for almost two decades education reformers have suggested that integration be considered a positive move in education, few institutions have jumped on the bandwagon and led the charge for change. Because integration has been such a slow process, prescribed assessments, outcomes, and evaluations of programs have not yet been published. Once information about successful programs is shared, however, institutions will be able to begin establishing criteria on which to base their integrated programs.

How will this affect business education and business teacher education programs? Williams (2000) has stated, "If business education programs and teacher education programs are to function as leaders in addressing the challenges of preparing well-qualified individuals for the nation's workforce, comprehensive and systematic transformation is imperative" (p. 36). For success in an ever-changing, diverse, technological, and competitive global market, workers will be required to possess specific skills, knowledge, and values.

Advances in technology, reorganization of the global business world, and changes in classroom demographics require that modifications to the learning environment be increasingly customized to fit the diverse needs and learning styles of students. Business teacher educators must accept the challenges placed before them and change in order to ensure that their students are prepared for the 21st century (Gallo Villee & Curran, 1999).

By the year 2010, every job will require some skill in using information-processing technology. Awareness of the global economy and the basics of international business will be crucial in preparing students to compete in the business world of the future. According to Zenger and Zenger (1999), future curricula must be developed around major universal themes such as change and adaptability, global interdependence, cultural diversity, quality of life, technological developments, self-actualization, lifelong learning, and world economic systems. Curriculum planners in the 21st century will need to have the knowledge of real-world requirements to be able to set guidelines for the skills needed by all students (Zenger & Zenger, 1999).

Curriculum integration can help broaden student focus in these areas. Integration can also enable teachers to become focused on contextual relationships between subject matter and integrated work-based concepts that are meaningful to students at the time of learning (Williams, 2000).

References

Beane, J. (1992). *Integrated curriculum in the middle schools* (ERIC Document Reproduction Service No. EDO-PS-92-2). ERIC Digest. Retrieved from the World Wide Web: http://ericeece.org/pubs/digests/1992/beane92.html

Beane, J. A. (1995). Curriculum integration and the disciplines of knowledge. *Phi Delta Kappan, 76*(8), 616–622.

Brewer, J. A. (1999). *Integration of academic and occupational education in community/technical colleges.* ERIC Digest. Retrieved from the World Wide Web: http://www.gseis.ucla.edu/ERIC/digests/dig9901.html

Curriculum integration: Status report. (1997, September). *Keying In, 8*(1), 1–2.

Gallo Villee, P. A., & Curran, M. G. (1999). Preface. In P. A. Gallo Villee & M. G. Curran (Eds.), *The 21st Century: Meeting the challenges to business education* (Yearbook No. 37, pp. iii–iv). Reston, VA: National Business Education Association.

Hoachlander, G. (1999). *Integrating academic and vocational curriculum—Why is theory so hard to practice?* Berkley, CA: National Center for Research in Vocational Education. Retrieved from the World Wide Web: http://ncrve.berkeley.edu/CenterPoint/CP7/

Lattuca, L. R., & Stark, J. S. (1994). Will disciplinary perspectives impede curricular reform? *Journal of Higher Education, 65*(4), 401–424.

Lynch, R. L. (1997). *Designing vocational and technical teacher education for the 21st century: Implications from the reform literature* (Information Series No. 368). Columbus, OH: ERIC Clearinghouse on Adult, Career, and Vocational Education.

McDonnell, L., & Zellman, G. (1992). *Education and training for work in the fifty states: An overview of major federal and state policies* (Report No. MDS-184). Berkley, CA: National Center for Research in Vocational Education.

Miller, M. D. (1996). Philosophy: The conceptual framework for designing a system of teacher education. In N. K. Hartley & T. L. Wentling (Eds.), *Beyond tradition* (pp. 53–73). Columbia: University Council for Vocational Education, University of Missouri. (ED 400 443).

National Association for Business Teacher Education. (1997). *Business teacher education curriculum guide & program standards.* Reston, VA: Author.

National Business Education Association. (1995). *National standards for business education: What America's students should know and be able to do in business.* Reston, VA: Author.

Naylor, M. (1997). *Impacts of reform movements on vocational teacher education.* Columbus, OH: ERIC Clearinghouse on Adult, Career, and Vocational Education. (ERIC Digest No. 180; ERIC Document Reproduction Service No. ED 407572 97).

Schug, M. C., & Cross, B. (1998). The dark side of curriculum integration in social studies. *The Social Studies, 89*(2), 54–57.

Stasz, C., Kaganoff, T., & Eden, R. A. (1994). Integrating academic and vocational education: A review of the literature, 1987–1992. *Journal of Vocational Education Research, 19,* 25–72.

Williams, S. (2000). *Curriculum revision and implementation: Implications for business teacher education.* Unpublished doctoral dissertation, The University of Montana.

Wraga, W. G. (1998). The comprehensive high school and educational reform in the United States: Retrospect and prospect. *High School Journal, 81,* 121–135.

Zenger, W. F., & Zenger, S. K. (1999). Schools and curricula for the 21st century: Predictions, visions, and anticipations. *NASSP Bulletin, 83*(606), 49–60.

School-to-Career Initiatives: Integrating Business Education With the Core Curriculum

Joan Whittemore Loock
Wisconsin Department of Public Instruction
Madison, Wisconsin

Michael James Tokheim
Wisconsin Technical College System Board
Madison, Wisconsin

In today's continually changing and therefore challenging environment, educators must seek every opportunity to improve student achievement, and in particular, students' readiness for and performance in the workplace. All students—regardless of when they enter the workforce—will need business skills to function well in a technological, information-rich, knowledge-based environment. Workers will be required to identify and solve problems, set and achieve goals, communicate effectively and efficiently, absorb and apply new information, negotiate with others, and work in teams. They will also need highly adaptable technical skills. How well will students be prepared to meet the professional and technological demands of business in the 21st century?

America's Choice: High Skills or Low Wages, issued by the National Center on Education and the Economy in 1990, and *What Work Requires of Schools*, a 1991 report by the Secretary's Commission on Achieving Necessary Skills, were the impetus for the move away from separating "academic" and "vocational" tracks. Instead the reports called for a curriculum focused on workplace skills and a restructuring of schools to develop these skills. As a result, the nation was forced to examine how to improve the quality of secondary and postsecondary education in ways that contributed to students' successful entry into the workforce. Career educators were enthusiastic about this attention to preparing students for the workplace, and in many cases became leaders of the initiatives that were to follow.

To ensure that schools could better prepare graduates for the future workplace, the federal government enacted measures directing schools to integrate career and technical studies with the required core courses. The Carl D. Perkins Vocational Education Act requires that funds be used to provide school programs that integrate career education and the core curriculum through a coherent sequence of courses that allow students to achieve both academic and occupational competencies.

This directive makes it clear that business education is more than just an elective or a "track"—it is, instead, fundamental, and as such is part of the schools' covenant with society to prepare students for full engagement as citizens and as participants in the nation's economy. Further, this directive suggests that business education is an equal partner in the effort to advance school reform goals.

Research shows that an integrated curriculum raises student achievement levels. As states continue to develop skill standards, students will achieve career competencies in business education and other related courses, thus contributing to rising scores on state assessments. There is one caveat, however: when the curriculum changes in accord with the Perkins directive, assessment techniques will also need to change in order to authentically evaluate whether or not learning has occurred.

This chapter makes the case for integrating career education with the core curriculum, reviews the history of Tech Prep and School-to-Work initiatives, discusses career majors as a focus for an integrated business education curriculum, presents examples of integrated School-to-Career initiatives, and suggests methods for authentically assessing student achievement in business education.

The Integrated Curriculum

An integrated curriculum is one that is planned and organized to

- Enable learners to connect interrelated concepts, content, and processes
- Demonstrate relationships between past, present, and future experiences and learning
- Make the students' experience of schooling meaningful and relevant
- Transform what is often a disjointed series of courses into a connected framework based in the real world—i.e., the world outside school walls
- Favor teaching strategies that more closely resemble how people think in real life, where problems are multifaceted and interrelated rather than one-dimensional and isolated

To effectively develop an integrated curriculum, teachers must collaborate as equal partners, as do team members in the business world. Two or more teachers from different disciplines can coordinate course instruction, develop materials, link academic and occupational skills, and develop varied instructional strategies that play to each of their strengths and that are appropriate for the learning styles of the students in their classes. Curriculum integration does not require having two teachers in the room at the same time, although some schools use this model.

Taking an integrated curriculum to the applied learning stage requires students to combine sometimes disparate knowledge and skills to solve real problems (rather than participate in simulations). In this way, students experience subject matter in a context that is useful to them because it relates to the real world. As in real life, problem solving does not occur in a vacuum. Instead, problem solvers consider alternatives, confer with others, and research solutions to the challenges they face. This process, known as contextual learning, maintains rather than sacrifices high academic and technical standards and is designed to accommodate all students' learning styles. Most courses can—and perhaps should—be taught in context. Applied teaching strategies may be featured throughout a course, or they may be reserved for selected units or activities.

Integration and Achievement

Various factors influence achievement. Many of them cannot be controlled. But others, such as motivation, school structure, or curriculum, which at first appear immutable, can actually be influenced by how teachers and administrators choose to achieve academic goals.

For example, a recent article in *Educational Leadership* profiled Baltimore's Patterson High School, which created small schools, or academies, within the larger building. The teachers and administrators discovered that the personalized atmosphere created a climate more conducive to learning and that student achievement levels increased. In addition, the authors noted that when students became members of a smaller learning community focused on a course of study that they selected because it matched their interests and career goals, the students behaved better and treated their teachers and the school building with more respect (Abbott & Ryan, 1999).

Integrated learning appears to be a significant factor in increasing academic achievement. For example, data in the 1997 report *Science Achievement in Minnesota in the Middle School Years—Results from IEA's Third International Mathematics and Science Study (TIMSS)* by Kristin Voelkl and John Mazzeo provides some evidence that students who participate in integrated science programs fare better academically than those in nonintegrated programs. At the seventh- and eighth-grade levels, Minnesota students who participated in integrated science programs scored above the average for all 41 nations studied. Only Singapore scored significantly higher (and Singapore also uses an integrated science approach).

It is likely that integrating business education and the core curriculum will bring similar gains in student competencies, as well as offer these benefits:

- Increased teacher involvement and enthusiasm for teaching
- Increased expectations that all students will achieve at a higher academic level
- Enhanced student interest, participation, and fulfillment
- New professional development opportunities and recognition for faculty
- Reduced competition for student enrollment among departments

History Recap: Career Education

Yesterday. In 1986 a new Tech Prep (technical preparation) leader in any state office of education seeking to develop a program had to first establish key definitions and data elements that would help to define a Tech Prep student. The Tech Prep leader frequently sought to capitalize on the experiences of experts or peers in other states. Establishing definitions was difficult.

The staggering statistics on the number of students who had not completed a postsecondary degree indicated a lengthy "floundering" period in the workplace: the majority of these students were likely to spend years in minimum wage, dead-end, high-turnover jobs that frustrated them, damaged their self-esteem, and placed them in the poverty cycle. This circumstance gave force to the Tech Prep (designated for grades 9 through 16) and later School-to-Work (designated for grades K through life) initiatives.

Tech Prep design. Tech Prep was emphasized in the Carl D. Perkins Vocational and Applied Technology Education Act of 1990 and was amended in the School-to-Work Opportunities Act of 1994. Tech Prep education is a planned sequence of study in a technical field beginning as early as grade nine. The sequence extends through two years of postsecondary occupational education or an apprenticeship program of at least two years following secondary instruction, and culminates in an associate degree or certificate. Tech Prep has become an important School-to-Work transition strategy, helping all students make the connection between school and employment.

Each state receives federal funds to implement Tech Prep programs. There were approximately 1,029 Tech Prep consortia in 1995, but the number has increased yearly. In 1995, 737,635 students in the United States were involved in Tech Prep initiatives (U.S. Department of Education, 2001).

Unintentional "tracking." Many schools have recognized their mission to prepare individuals to participate in the workforce, the political system, and society at large. If students leave high school without being fully prepared to participate in the workforce, then their chances of participating fully in society are also diminished. This is the source of a dilemma. In many states, Tech Prep was designed as a relatively prestigious program for those students who did not intend to complete the "college prep" program, but who intended to go directly to work or to additional technical training. Although Tech Prep was intended to parallel collegiate preparation programs in their rigor and integrity, in reality Tech Prep was separate and isolated. College prep programs continued to neglect workforce preparation, further differentiating the two curricula and creating a deeper wedge between them.

As educators examined the definition of a Tech Prep student, they assumed they needed a way to distinguish that student from a college prep student or any other student. This was a mistake. A Tech Prep student was, and is, every student. When policy makers ask how many students are Tech Prep students, the response should be, "all of them."

Many educators refer to Tech Prep as a program. It was not intended to be a program. It was intended to be an educational strategy to make workforce preparation and technical education accepted parts of the curriculum. When a group of students is labeled as Tech Prep, it implies that all other students are not being prepared for the workplace. It implies that other students are not engaging in the same level of career exploration or technical/occupational education; they are simply being prepared for college admission. Too often, valuable career guidance, real-world exposure, and technical training are withheld from these "college prep" students, allowing them to postpone decisions about career options and preventing them from exploring the work world and their own capabilities in that world. This often results in simply postponing the "floundering" mentioned earlier.

Categorizing or attempting to categorize students and/or courses or programs invites certain students in while keeping others out. In contrast to many states, Wisconsin and California refuse to separate Tech Prep students from students in college prep programs. Wisconsin's Tech Prep initiative focuses instead on improving the educational system so that it meets the needs of all students.

Today. According to the *Digest of Education Statistics* (National Center for Education Statistics, 2000),

- The dropout rate from high school for 1998 was 11.8 percent.
- About 50 percent of students who enrolled in a four-year college had completed their degrees five years later.
- Twenty-four percent were no longer working toward a bachelor's degree.

These figures indicate that a substantial number of students have "floundered" in their educational careers and in many cases have expended time and energy but failed to meet their goals. Should educators be satisfied with such results? Would these students have been better off with real-world work experiences and technical training? Would real-world experience and technical training have helped them to focus and understand their interests and their abilities better?

It is noteworthy that according to the U.S. Bureau of Labor Statistics, in Wisconsin 23 percent of all residents hold a four-year degree and, thus, 77 percent do not. This question is especially compelling, because it is predicted that roughly 80 percent of the new jobs in the next decade will require some technical training but less than a four-year degree. All educators must ask how well schools serve the needs of the young people who will enter the workforce of the future, and stop blaming parents or school boards for schools' obsession with college prep programs.

It is not the obsession with college prep that is the problem, but rather what is included or not included in the college prep track. Students should have courses that allow them access to college, but more importantly, they should have access to the tools and skills that will facilitate success in college and in work. College prep should embrace rather than shun the elements of career preparation.

Current Carl D. Perkins (III) legislation emphasizes the importance of this approach and of linking secondary and postsecondary programs. The Tech Prep premise—a curriculum centered on applied academics (contextual learning)—is part of this emphasis. Unifying the curriculum is one way to ensure that all students are prepared to succeed in a work world that constantly changes and a society that continues to become more complex.

Tomorrow. Funding for the federal School-to-Work Opportunities Act is diminishing, and therefore, states must reexamine their efforts to restructure education so that, as educational leaders put it, no child is left behind—in school, or in life. In the 21st century it is imperative to integrate career education with the core curriculum and to strengthen the ability of schools to serve all students by teaching them fundamental skills related to entering the workplace.

One sign that this is happening is the increasing use of the umbrella term, "School-to-Career," a concept that combines rigorous school- and work-based learning with greater career exploration and guidance. In this way the educational system strengthens skills and knowledge in all students, regardless of which "track" they follow.

During the past decade, probably the most important component of the unified School-to-Career effort has been the reformed guidance and counseling function. This effort has three stages: career awareness, career exploration, and career preparation.

Career awareness. Ideally, awareness of career choices should be developed in the early grades; otherwise, secondary school career activities will have very little impact. The dearth of counselors in elementary schools makes it necessary for teachers to counsel students and guide them as they explore career options and then evaluate potential career choices based on these experiences.

Parents and young people alike would do well to understand the career choices available to them, the education or training required, and the importance of being able to "move with the market." In addition, students must connect academic learning to the workplace, especially since the ability to be lifelong learners will affect whether or not workers advance as society and the workplace become more complex.

School is the ideal environment for exposing students to a broad range of occupations. At the elementary level, tours of businesses and industries, entrepreneurial simulations, visits from community members, and career fairs are excellent ways to develop career awareness. These activities help students connect what they learn inside the school building with life outside and expose students to career models other than those they see at home, on TV, or in the lives of relatives and friends.

Career exploration. In the middle school, learning should build on the career awareness developed in early childhood and then transition into career exploration. Career exploration includes mastering identified work skills, such as how to be a part of a team or take the lead on a project. Students can also participate in job shadowing, career fairs, and other related activities.

Most career educators agree on the importance of the middle school years for preparing students to master upper-level core curriculum, career, and technical courses in high school. For example, the Vocational Education Standards Committee of the National Board for Professional Teaching Standards (1997) recommended that the standards for (and thereby the assessment of) highly effective teachers include the knowledge and skills necessary to work with early adolescents as they explore career development and as they begin to accumulate and assess their own employability skills.

In this century required core courses at all levels of education will continue to be emphasized. Therefore, it is important for teachers and administrators to integrate career studies with the core curriculum in authentic ways, and for teachers in various disciplines to trust each other's expertise as they plan joint learning experiences, so that students can benefit from a truly interdisciplinary curriculum. Elementary, secondary, and postsecondary teachers who are open to teaching/learning partnerships will help students transition easily from one level to the next.

Career preparation. Work-based learning will be just as important in this century as it has been in the recent past and will include opportunities such as youth apprenticeships, cooperative education, internships, and job shadowing.

Youth apprenticeship and cooperative-education programs generally involve high school juniors and seniors in rigorous learning experiences that combine school- and work-based experiences in an approved business or industry setting. Students earn pay and a regular high school diploma, an industry-approved skill certificate, and academic credits that may be applied toward a technical/community college degree. In some cases, credits may be applied toward university admission requirements. Internships and job shadowing provide additional opportunities for students to learn about careers, the workplace, and the skills and knowledge needed to be successful.

Although a cooperative-education program is defined by its required competencies, the teacher-coordinator determines the method of learning. Competencies in a business cooperative experience, for example, may be achieved in the co-op class, an accounting class, a language arts class, or a math class. They also may be acquired through activities with career and technical student organizations.

Although students may participate in business cooperative activities, their career goals may be in entirely different disciplines. Suppose, for example, a student wants to be a veterinarian; he or she may enroll in a business cooperative-education course and be placed with a veterinarian for work experience. Job duties may include computer record entry, performance of accounting functions, and office management; however, the student may also observe surgeries and other medical practices. What better way for the student to discover if this career "fits"? Yet, even if it does not, the student meanwhile develops transferable skills that can be used in most other careers.

Lifelong learning/continuing education. Parents, and the public in general, understand the need for children, as an integral part of their K–12 education, to learn about careers and to acquire skills that will make them employable. Yet, it is also important to emphasize the need for continuing education beyond the secondary level. Eight of the ten fastest-growing jobs in the next decade will require (some) college education or moderate to long-term training; increased education and training are linked to higher employee wages and productivity, with college graduates earning an average of 77 percent more than individuals who have only a high school degree (Gore, 1999). It is likely, therefore, that the 13th and 14th years of education will be the minimal benchmark for the next generation of American students. Additionally, the majority of workers will need to pursue additional training and professional development to change careers and keep up with technological advances.

Career Majors as a Learning Focus

The integration of career education and the core curriculum with an identified course of study in career majors could appreciably strengthen our educational system. With career majors as a focus, business educators could advocate for opportunities to provide a truly interdisciplinary education and to help students as they decide which careers to explore. It is important for educators, parents, and students to understand, however, that career selection, at least at this point, is not a commitment for life. Students need to be encouraged to be both focused and flexible, especially given that the days of working in one career or for one employer are long gone—students need only look at their parents' generation to realize the truth of this statement.

Indeed, "tracking" might be better replaced with program options based on a system of (perhaps interrelated) career majors. Each student could be invited to think about identifying a career major in his or her junior year of high school and dedicating specific experiences to the career major prior to graduation. This type of program could be designed to enable students to take courses and develop skills that will help them get admitted into college and be successful there. At the same time, students could be learning in a context that encourages them to think about the world around them, the skills that are valued in contemporary society, and their transition into the work world after graduation.

As states and local school district policy makers consider implementing career major programs in secondary schools, they also need to consider which majors offer long-term employment and lifelong learning opportunities, as well as the potential for high wages and advancement opportunities in high-growth fields. Career major programs should be composed of rigorous sequences of courses that include high-level academics, employability skills, work-based learning with identified competencies and instruction in various aspects of the designated industry. Of course, predicting the future—and predicting with 100 percent certainty which occupations and skills will remain viable—is difficult. However, making these predictions in cooperation with business, industry, and postsecondary education representatives and with information from the U.S. Department of Labor's *Occupational Outlook Handbook* increases the likelihood that projections of future work opportunities will be on target.

The U.S. Department of Education has funded the development of curriculum frameworks in relatively new and high-tech industries and career clusters. The three clusters whose frameworks are currently under development are

- Manufacturing
- Health technology
- Business and management

The Department plans to contract for the development of frameworks for three additional high-tech career clusters. Two of these are essential to the business education curriculum:

- Audiovisual/communication technology involves development and operation of communication systems hardware and software for the recording,

storage, processing, and distribution of voice and video data.
• Information technology involves the design, development, and support of hardware, software, and systems integration services.

Leading-edge business educators will initiate and embrace the development of frameworks for these clusters, integrate them into their curricula, and establish articulation agreements with postsecondary institutions.

Managing Integrated School-to-Career Programs

ESL in School-to-Career initiatives. Students learning English as a second language (ESL) are increasingly involved in School-to-Career activities throughout the country. Internships, community service learning, project-based learning, and job-shadowing programs offer opportunities to integrate language study with acquisition of workplace skills. The publication *A Guide to Involving English Language Learners in School-to-Career Initiatives* presents case studies and offers solutions to some of the challenges that arise when dealing with nonnative English speakers participating in these programs (Allen, DiBona, and Reilly, 1998).

Thematic curriculum projects. Teachers at Arroyo Grande High School in Arroyo Grande, California, have organized an integrated business education curriculum by creating "academies" that encompass social studies, English, and business education (K. Orrell, personal communication, February 2001). The curriculum is thematic (e.g., topics include economic expansion, change, teamwork, etc.) and students complete projects that are due and evaluated at the end of each grading period.

In the teamwork curriculum, for example, 11th- and 12th-grade students may

• Follow the stock market, create displays with graphed data, and orally present results as a culmination of acquiring and evaluating information, writing to persuade, and reading *Farewell to Manzanar* (English) as well as studying U.S. history between 1930 and 1945 (the stock market crash, the Great Depression, WWII, etc.) (social studies)
• Create a trifold stock market brochure and graph stock market results using spreadsheet software after tabulating statistical data (information processing) and integrating graphs and tables that represent the stock market crash and supply and demand concepts (word processing)
• Prepare a proposal and budget to install a LAN at a given site after studying network addressing and design (computer science and information technology)
• Present conclusions after analyzing a merchandising business' corporate report, posting to general ledger accounts, and preparing income statements (accounting)
• Collect and interpret data from a survey after studying buying and distribution practices and pricing (retail merchandising and marketing)

Business-education partnerships. Some school districts have looked to business-education partnerships, which may be funded by Perkins III legislation, as a way of advancing school reform goals and at the same time integrating business education with the core academic courses. BaySCAN, San Francisco's School-to-Career Action Network, is one example of an effective business-industry partnership.

The BaySCAN program serves 1,000,000 students. Unlike traditional business-education partnerships, which have tended to focus on internships, "adopt-a-school" models, and corporate-giving campaigns, BaySCAN works to strategically solve workforce development issues by leveraging time, content, and all available resources. As a result, a coalition rather than a one-to-one, business-to-school pairing has emerged: businesses, educational institutions, and community organizations work together to create the academic conditions needed to educate the workforce of tomorrow.

Creating effective coalitions is time consuming and can be complicated, so new infrastructures, known as intermediary organizations, are being created to help bring businesspeople and teachers together. These third-party organizations increase the work-based learning opportunities that are available to students— real-world opportunities that match learning objectives, community resources, and business needs. Effective coalitions model a continuous-improvement process that involves all stakeholders in planning and development, implementation and management, monitoring and evaluation, and future planning.

Accountability and Authentic Assessment

Even as business educators focus on core indicators established in the 1999–2000 federal Carl Perkins Act, they must consider placement and retention rates at postsecondary levels. As noted earlier, if legislation directs that every student taking a career or technical course be classified as a Tech Prep or School-to-Work student, the impact of this legislation will be problematic and will make it difficult to garner support for continued School-to-Work legislation.

Steinberg, in *Real Learning, Real Work* (1998), has recommended teaching career preparation using school- and work-based learning as well as activities that bridge schools with communities. Every educational initiative must have some means of measurement; data collection and follow-up studies become the performance indicators that demonstrate a program's impact and justify its existence.

For career preparation to be useful, the work activities associated with it must be authentic. One of the most critical criteria for authentic work is that it have value and meaning beyond the instructional context. Therefore, prevailing testing instruments and techniques may not be the most suitable tools for authentic assessment. Curriculum specialists will need courage to abandon previous testing techniques and move to other assessment methods, such as portfolios (which document a learner's educational experiences and achievements), to authentically assess whether learning has occurred. If the curriculum changes but assessment techniques remain the same, school reform goals will become meaningless rhetoric. Assessment still drives instruction, not vice versa.

In *New Directions for High School Career and Technical Education in the 21st Century* (2000) Richard Lynch reported that authentic assessments based on specific workplace knowledge and skills were being developed. One option is to supplement and possibly replace the normal standardized ACT/SAT assessments with standardized Work Keys assessments of "applied" work skills. Work Keys assessments, developed by ACT, profile students' skills in applied mathematics, applied technology, listening, locating information, observation, reading for information, teamwork, and writing. These assessments also provide a job analysis system that determines the levels of skills required for competent performance in specific jobs, and give an assessment profile and evaluation of students' mastery of those skills.

After demonstrating mastery of the curriculum and the requisite career and technical skills, each student should earn a license or performance certificate. For example, the Cisco Networking Academy Program teaches and certifies high school and college students to design, build, and maintain computer networks. The certification is based on mastery of industry standards through various computer-based demonstrations, design and network management projects, and internships.

Authentic, work-related assessment has great potential to provide a deeper, more accurate portrait of student achievement and foster program accountability. With the number of certificate initiatives growing, it is important to ask whether students in these intensified programs also receive instruction that allows them to understand the business implications of, as in the example above, a technical network installation. Especially in a climate where workers not only change jobs but change careers, business educators must be more concerned about students' long-term educational interests than their short-term employment gains. Even though the business curriculum focuses on developing students who are capable of joining the workforce, it must not do so at the expense of preparing students to participate in society as fully capable citizens who—by virtue of their general educational knowledge and their acquisition of fundamental, life-based skills such as higher-level thinking and decision making—can rightly take their place in the future economy.

Summary

Evidence indicates growing support for work-based learning activities. Still, the challenge is not only to offer more opportunities but also to offer better ones by developing more intense workplace experiences that are connected to class work, thereby integrating business education and the core curriculum areas. Whether or not School-to-Career initiatives can be integrated with education reform and the push for higher academic standards will determine the longevity of these initiatives.

Integrating career education and the core curriculum areas takes time. Extra coordination and effort are necessary to develop block scheduling, facilitate joint lesson planning, and bring together teachers and employers to collaborate on curriculum.

Richard Lynch (2000) summed up the major purposes of career education:

- Provide career exploration and planning
- Enhance students' academic achievement and motivation to learn more advanced skills
- Help students acquire work competencies and skills useful for employment
- Establish pathways for continuing education and lifelong learning

If education in the 21st century can accomplish these objectives, students will enter the workforce with stronger skills and a greater chance of succeeding in their chosen careers. Business educators who can see their programs as potential areas of true school reform—with strong business and community involvement, solid evaluations of the opportunities available to diverse groups of students, and integrated academic and employment-related content—will offer leadership and provide momentum for making business education viable and fundamental for every student.

The development of curriculum frameworks for the work environment of the future and of models for authentic assessment of student achievement will result in a better-prepared workforce, and by extension, a citizenry that is better able to participate in a constantly evolving and global economy.

References

Abbott, J., & Ryan, T. (1999, November). Constructing knowledge, reconstructing schooling. *Educational Leadership*. Retrieved from the World Wide Web: http://www.21learn.org

Allen, L., DiBona, N., & Reilly, M. C. (1998). *A Guide to involving English language learners in school-to-career initiatives* [Abstract]. Washington, DC: U.S. Department of Education Office of Educational Research and Instruction. (ERIC Document Reproduction Service No. ED 426 284). Retrieved from the World Wide Web: http://oeri4.ed.gov/BASISDB/PUBLICATION/short/ DDW?W%3DTITLE%20PH%20WORDS%20%27school%20to%20career% 27%20AND%20PUB_YEAR%20%3E%3D%201996%20ORDER%20BY%20% 24RANK/Descend%26M%3D1%26K%3D25656%26R%3DY%26U%3D1

Gore, A. (1999). *Summit on 21st century skills for 21st century jobs.*

Lynch, R. L. (2000). *New directions for high school career and technical education in the 21ˢᵗ century* (Information Series No. 384). Columbus, OH: ERIC Clearinghouse on Adult, Career, and Vocational Education, The Ohio State University.

National Board for Professional Teaching Standards. (1997). *Vocational education standards for national board certification.* Arlington, VA: Author.

National Center for Education Statistics. (2000, May). *The digest of education statistics, 1999* (NCES No. 2000-0031). Washington, DC: Author. Retrieved from the World Wide Web: http://nces.ed.gov/pubs2000/digest99/

National Center on Education and the Economy. (1990). *America's choice: High skills or low wages.* Washington, DC: Author.

Secretary's Commission on Achieving Necessary Skills. (1991). *What work requires of schools: A SCANS report for America 2000.* Washington, DC: U.S. Department of Labor.

Steinberg, A. (1998). *Real learning, real work: School-to-work as high school reform.* Berkeley, CA: University of California at Berkeley, Graduate School of Education.

Work keys testing unlocks core of skills needed for job. *Activity, 37*(2), 8–9.

U.S. Department of Education Division of Vocational-Technical Education. (2001). *Tech Prep Education.* Retrieved from the World Wide Web: http://www.ed.gov/offices/OVAE/techprep.html

Voelkl, K., & Mazzeo, J. (1997). *Science achievement in Minnesota in the middle school years—results from IEA's third international mathematics and science study (TIMSS).* Washington, DC: U.S. Department of Education National Center for Education Statistics.

Program Management in Changing Times

Sharon Lund O'Neil
University of Houston
Houston, Texas

It has been said that the more we change, the more we stay the same. A paradox? Yes, a paradox of "static change," or really a truism that many individuals apply to varying degrees in their daily lives. "Static change" may be described as decision making that creates a pattern of actions based on certain perceptions, assumptions, and underlying principles that are believed and practiced by a person. As people change or consider how change affects them and others (and how it affects classroom instruction), they employ various elements of a foundation that drives and directs change. If the foundation provides a process that promotes positive action, useful change occurs. "Useful change," according to Kotter (1996), "tends to be associated with a multi-step process that creates power and motivation sufficient to overwhelm all the sources of inertia . . . this process is never employed effectively unless it is driven by high-quality leadership" (p. 20).

Although vulnerable to the paradox of static change, business educators have demonstrated leadership in meeting the many internal and external integrated, critical elements associated with change. For example, business educators face challenges every day that relate to (a) staying abreast of the broad-based and expanding breadth of information that the business education field encompasses; (b) keeping pace with rapid technological advances that affect every aspect of business; (c) assessing, projecting, and addressing the ever-fluctuating needs of the global marketplace; (d) evaluating, and as necessary, quickly and efficiently adapting programs based on supply and demand projections; and (e) advancing personal and professional development goals for lifelong learning in a competitive, changing environment.

Because these challenges are ever present, business educators must facilitate useful change by designing, developing, managing, and evaluating meaningful business programs. It is through this process that program management takes on added significance in business education.

The Significance of Program Management in Changing Times

Program management provides the foundation for effective, organized classroom instruction and learning. Every educator, in following an instructional plan (regardless of its source—whether self- or administration-imposed), provides the leadership for instruction and training via program management elements. The combination of elements and the extent to which the various characteristics are present and interact with each other form the basic plan. Thus, by identifying, as well as understanding, applying, and evaluating the basic principles of program management, teachers can more effectively meet the challenges that each new day brings and can increase their instructional effectiveness.

Most people, including teachers, can benefit from a general understanding of the elements of program management. Business teachers, as leaders of change, can maximize their leadership by applying the basics of program management. A discussion of the major elements of program management is provided in the section that follows.

Elements of Program Management

Most individuals channel their efforts into patterns that they follow fairly closely in nearly everything they do. In program management these patterns can be described by and linked to seven basic areas or elements. Before each element is discussed, it is helpful to consider the example of an individual or family buying or building a house. This example focuses on the importance of the seven elements in approaching any new project.

What are the considerations that must be given to an endeavor such as buying or building a house? What are the determining factors that will ensure that the result will be successful? Are there pitfalls that can be avoided to reduce stress during the process? What can be gained from a systematic application of the elements of program management? These and other questions can be addressed through thoughtful consideration, assessment, and application of the seven elements of program design:

1. Mission, goals, and objectives. A mission, identified early in any endeavor, will give more meaning to a project or program. A mission should be far-reaching, visionary, and creative. A mission may be a dream—frequently an intangible idea or cause that creates excitement and desire to pursue the mission. A mission should be the motivator and driving force that makes one reach beyond the norm and beyond reality. It is the over-arching element that keeps momentum going and gives rise to change and innovation. A mission gives purpose to life.

Although a mission may not be tangible, it is what drives goals and objectives. The goals and objectives are what move an individual toward a mission. Goals are the reachable elements of a lofty mission; and objectives are the smaller steps or processes that help one systematically achieve the goals. At each juncture, decision making takes place to help a person make progress toward reaching the desired result.

In the example of buying or building a house, the mission may be a "castle in the sky," a dream house, and all the valuable factors that make the house a home. The goal may be to provide a comfortable, beautiful environment for family members to enjoy. The objectives, or measurable steps to achieve the goal(s), may include identifying the various amenities that address the desires and needs of each of the diverse family members. A different mission for buying or building a house might be eventual resale, though the house will serve as a family shelter for an interim period.

Creating a mission for the classroom should be just as interesting and useful. A mission does not need to be developed by only one teacher, but it can be highly successful as an individual effort because compromise is not an issue. On the other hand, a business education department should derive significant benefits and rewards from devoting time to mission development and strategic planning. A "planning for the future" workshop or seminar focused on exploring issues, problem solving, or program development usually is well worth the time expended. Such an activity provides participants with the opportunity to give their best thinking and creativity to a collaborative effort. The combined effort can result in a better understanding of self and others, as well as in the formulation of a mission and in the development of goals and objectives. Taking time to talk about a mission for the business education program has considerable merit. When all the forces—administration, teachers, students, parents, and community—participate in and/or "buy into" a mission and, as a result, begin to move in the same direction, synergy is created and program management is on its way to a successful future.

2. Needs assessment, occupational analysis, and advisory groups. As with the development of a creative and motivating mission, business education program planners need good information upon which to build viable, quality, and meaningful programs. In the example involving selecting a home builder, a family would look for a person with knowledge of building a home or a person who knows when to employ the expertise of others such as architects, community planners, specialty master builders, subcontractors, a variety of craftspeople, and product/service providers.

Like the home builder, the business teacher must rely on other sources besides his or her own subject matter knowledge and pedagogy skills. Although the expertise of the business teacher is vitally important, it is imperative to take advantage of the many enhancements offered by community resources. Ignoring these important resources may cause a business teacher to lose the race against the ever-expanding society of specialized "knowledges." Drucker (1993) has suggested that as technology and other forces engulf us with more and more information, more people are forced to become specialists.

Business teachers need to tap the expertise and services of specialists such as business leaders; future employers; community planners; parents; and the wealth of resources represented by government and local, private, public, and volunteer organizations. It is just as important to periodically assess community and business needs and occupational changes as it is to learn students' needs, strengths, and weaknesses.

The vastness of our "knowledge society" dictates that business teachers must rely on as many sources as possible to get timely, accurate, and up-to-date information. It is an understatement to say that business teachers must stay abreast of technological changes, continually update their skills, rely on a myriad of resources, and constantly modify their curricula. Program relevance depends on the instructor having an exceptional ability to draw from many resources, because the nature of the business education discipline requires managing an ever-shifting program.

Successful business education program management is dependent on well-informed business teachers who capitalize on seeking out and using all available resources. Creating and fostering resources, such as is possible through active advisory committees and focus groups, should also be part of the program management plan. When business and industry employees provide significant input into the business education program, students entering and exiting it are exposed to the marketplace skills they will need for initial employment as well as for competing and succeeding in a competitive workforce.

3. Management principles: planning, organizing, leading, and controlling. Every business educator knows that it is necessary to practice, teach, and apply good management principles. A curriculum that has been well planned, is highly organized, has good leadership, and provides appropriate controls will weather most storms. The basic management principles that point to a successful curriculum also must be applied to other aspects of the instructional experience including classroom organization, curricula sequencing, instructional delivery, student involvement, supplementary activities, and relevant assignments, to name a few.

To be effective and efficient, every business education classroom needs a balance of management principles. However, the proper balance will depend on the course, its content and structure, the level and ability of the students, the teacher's personality and style, the instructional strategies employed, and a myriad of other factors that give character and substance to the instructional setting.

Management principles need to extend far beyond the business classroom. Most people, including home builders and teachers, realize that to be successful in life, it is necessary to plan, organize, and evaluate many different elements as each situation dictates. Business teachers who master management principles themselves and foster student development of the same skills will undoubtedly contribute to students' development of both work and life skills.

4. Instructional design model. Instructional Systems Development (ISD) is a widely accepted term for a variety of instructional design models. Most ISD models are composed of at least five major phases—planning and analysis, design, development, implementation, and evaluation. They are described in the following sections.

A. **Planning and analysis.** Planning, first and foremost, is critical to instructional design. Instruction must be well planned to ensure that lessons, units, and course content emphasize the appropriate concepts, skills, and knowledge areas and that each can be taught as well as learned. Planning encompasses the entire instructional design process, ensuring that the learning spectrum has a logical starting point and extends beyond the transfer of knowledge to stimulate the desire for lifelong learning. Applying management principles to each instructional process can effect a positive outcome.

B. **Design.** In the second phase of instruction—design—a plan is developed or "dissected" into a framework or model. The design phase takes the overall plan and breaks it down into smaller units or segments. To do this, the program designer must determine the assumptions and underlying base for a solid pedagogical framework that can be systematically constructed and developed into objectives and teachable components. In the design phase priorities are determined and alternatives selected to ensure that program ideas match program objectives. The design gives structure to the plan, which can then take shape and be expanded into teachable segments.

C. **Development.** The third phase—development—involves turning every aspect of instruction into a teachable form: learning objectives are developed into activities, instructional strategies and media are identified, materials and techniques are selected, content is sequenced and evaluated, and all program formats (the who, what, when, where, why, and how of instruction) are determined. Good curriculum development depends, to a large degree, on the extent of resources available as well as on the expertise of the curriculum designer. The success of the initial planning and design phases will be immediately evident when the development phase is started. If the outline is pedagogically sound, the curriculum developer will be able to expand it into an instructional plan that is ready to implement.

D. Implementation. The fourth phase of the ISD model—the implementation stage— truly reflects the effectiveness of all planning. This stage is vitally important to both instructor/facilitator and students/learners. A good curriculum can be enhanced with a master teacher's touch, and a superior curriculum in the hands of a solid, well-prepared teacher will become even better. The teacher/facilitator who is attuned to the total classroom environment will bridge the gaps from new learning to relearning to refocusing. Additionally, the teacher who draws from several models and theories of learning/teaching and employs a variety of programming methods and alternatives will promote high levels of learning.

It is always necessary to have balance among all the elements that contribute to the classroom experience. Balance is more easily attained by the teacher/facilitator who takes time to develop a good understanding of individual student needs. The teacher who possesses a positive attitude and imparts it to others, thus motivating learners to achieve their highest potential, has an advantage over the teacher who ignores this important element in implementing an instructional model.

The implementation phase of any ISD model is a tall order for one teacher. However, teachers/facilitators who are positive and maximize their "soft skills" (including communication, leadership, and human relations) see the benefits.

E. Evaluation. The last component of the ISD model is evaluation, but evaluation is not necessarily the final activity of the model. Assessment and evaluation must take place in each phase of the model—from the outset of the endeavor throughout the entire project. Ongoing evaluation is the only way modifications can be made before an inappropriate path is taken. Along with evaluation must come good decision making to determine when and what alternatives should be considered and implemented. The teacher who uses a variety of evaluation methods and techniques will be more apt to see the need for modifications before any major roadblocks appear.

The ISD model presented here, which focuses on five equally essential components, represents a well-accepted hybrid of several models and is popular in both educational and corporate training settings. Whether or not instructors use this model, they may wish to consider any one of the many program/curriculum planning processes and ISD models (with their many derivations, adaptations, and assumptions) that have been described in the literature (Bard, Bell, Stephen, & Webster, 1987; Caffarella, 1994; Craig, 1996; Dick & Carey, 1996; Goodstein, Nolan, & Pfeiffer, 1993; Knowles, Swanson, & Holton, 1998; Lewis, 2000; Mager, 1997; Munson, 1992; to name a few). Dick and Carey (1996), popular authors of a four-phase ISD model, probably come closest to the model presented above. Finding the best fit should not be a difficult task because most ISD models are well documented as to their adaptability and usefulness. To ensure successful implementation, it is advisable to take a systems approach to instructional design with an ISD model.

5. Organizational structure, controls, and political climate. In the example of building a home, it would not be wise to ignore the details of deed restrictions, permits, other planning commission policies, and inspections. Usually a builder must be licensed and bonded and follow the rules of the community. Similarly, it is important for the educator to understand the organizational structure, controls, and politics that govern the instructional setting. The teacher/facilitator should be aware of the internal culture that dictates what programs are offered and how, the hierarchy of priorities, why it is believed that certain programming models work better than others, and the key players (the real change agents in the system), to name a few.

Awareness of external factors, even those that may seem peripheral, will help the teacher/facilitator avoid pitfalls that can damage even the most success-ful program management efforts. It is important to get the facts about the existing organizational culture, to consider others' points of view about issues, to listen to ideas that may or may not appear to have any relationship to the task at hand, and to experience as many elements as possible that give insight on the perspective of an organization and community. Frequently, to gain a picture of the whole culture, it may be necessary to "brush shoulders" with people who operate in circles totally outside one's comfort zone. It is important to remember that working in a vacuum will cause entropy or, at best, slow progress and momen-tum. The effective change agent is one who thinks, plans, and consults beyond the parameters of the proverbial "box."

6. Resources and facilities. The availability and management of resources are important factors in nearly any endeavor. Key resource factors include funding, sources and availability of resources, financial stability, budgeting, accounting procedures, and oversight management. Several other considerations, whether building a house, modifying a curriculum, or rightsizing a program, should also be given serious thought when contemplating change. They include determination of the type and extent of facilities, materials, supplies, and services needed for the planning, implementation, maintenance, and management of the project.

Probably the most important factor in the overall schema of program management is human resources. Selecting the right people to do the right jobs at the right time applies to all facets of program management. People must want to change for change to take place. The benefits of change will be realized if facilitators can convey their vision to others and capitalize on human potential. Business teachers who accept and strive to meet this challenge every day will ensure that their instruction not only reaches their students but also has significant impact.

The five elements of the ISD model can also be applied to the management of resources that contribute to the operation of a program. That is, consideration should be given to each broad resource category—the elements related to planning, design, development, implementation, and evaluation. Business teachers who work collaboratively in cohesive teams will find merit in employing the expertise of advisory committees, conducting needs assessments, and learning about internal and external constituencies. Knowledge of as many facets of the program as can be gleaned from a wide variety of sources will, to a large degree, determine the success of a program.

7. Program marketing. Developing a solid program is essential; promoting and marketing it is just as critical. As Caffarella has stated, "many programs fail because of poor promotion" (1994, p. 172). Promoting the program to the intended audience with the right materials at the right time, price, and place should not be a haphazard process. Systematic marketing strategies should also follow the ISD model stages—planning, design, development, implementation, and evaluation—and should include finding the best answers to who, what, when, where, why, and how questions.

A marketing campaign that is well planned and well executed with good timing can enhance even the best program. This is not to say that a poor program should be packaged to overshadow its lack of quality.

Marketing may be one of the most difficult but also the most rewarding challenges. Business teachers should remember that "tooting one's own horn" is often an ideal starting point. Significant attention can then be given to finding out what works through a process of trial and error, and then identifying and using effective marketing strategies. To ensure the success of any program, marketing cannot be left to chance. Rather, it should be considered from the outset of the project and planned in tandem with the program to consider the competition and allow for adjustment.

The seven elements of program design presented in this section should be viewed as critical elements by anyone embarking on the development of new programs or the expansion of existing programs. Throughout this process it is important that change be modeled on an understanding of the past and present in order to facilitate a better appreciation of evolving issues and to better equip business classrooms to forge new paths. The sections that follow address additional program design elements and considerations.

Facilitating Learning for Diverse Populations

Meeting the needs of learners may be the most complex issue facing today's educators. It is intensified by the many technological advances, economic and political changes, and increases in specialized knowledge that accompany this era's information explosion. Today students are confronted with so many stimuli that the learning atmosphere can become a difficult maze. It is in this maze that some learners are lost if their needs are not identified and met early.

It is an understatement to say that technology has provided many opportunities for expanding our thinking, creativity, and options for the future. More and more information is becoming readily accessible in all subjects. Researching and sorting this information into useful and manageable "packets" has presented new avenues for exploration. Although general knowledge is valued for the balance it can give to individuals, specialized expertise, which changes frequently with technological advances, is a necessity in today's complex society.

For learning to be optimized in such a challenging environment, the definition of motivation must be expanded. To motivate learners, the business teacher must employ multifaceted approaches and strategies that are as complex as the learners themselves. Reaching students through creative approaches requires teachers to become facilitators of instruction. This involves moving from older lecture-based instructional strategies to experiential instruction that uses questioning, thinking, comparing, and "what-if" approaches.

Facilitation-based strategies require a teacher/facilitator to develop broad bases of knowledge where exposure to learning is greater than that of traditional instruction. The facilitator must also develop good questioning techniques to help him or her know when to stay focused on a topic and when to veer off on a related issue or to address a topic's applications. The facilitator's use of good questioning skills and techniques should encourage learners to be reflective, intuitive thinkers and discussants. It is extremely important that facilitators have sharp listening skills to enable them to pick up the signals for involving students in discussions that address their individual needs, strengths, weaknesses, and learning modes.

Scheduling Programs Within Complex Environments

In today's schools where learners are involved in many more activities than they were even a few years ago, educators walk a tightrope to offer both academic and enrichment opportunities—especially at the junior high/middle school and high school levels. Many students can easily add three or four hours to their academic day if they are involved in the arts and sports. Thus, planners and administrators must continue to focus on programming and scheduling issues.

Most junior high/middle school and high school schedules can be classified as traditional or block. The merits of these two basic approaches, and some of their modifications, are discussed in the following sections. With both approaches the mission is to find ways to motivate students to enjoy the enrichment of the many educational opportunities and social events that are associated with lifelong learning.

Traditional scheduling. In recent years many schools have experimented with ways to accommodate more students, maximize facilities, provide more course offerings, and meet the needs of nontraditional students who are actually no longer "nontraditional." These students, at whatever grade level, require more educational flexibility than students of a few years ago. Some of the alternatives to traditional scheduling, especially with respect to meeting the needs of junior high/middle school and high school students, are described here.

A. **Extended day.** Some schools have extended their traditional 6–8 class period days either before or after the regular school day to permit students to complete more units in shorter periods of time, giving them more options. For example, many schools have added a "zero" period, scheduled before school, mainly for enrichment and advanced classes, as well as for tutoring, private lessons, and sports programs. Even with this extension of the regular school day, the biggest complaint from teachers and students alike is that it is not possible to take more than one additional class each year. Frequently, students have to choose between sports and the arts, which does not give talented students ample opportunity to pursue their interests.

Extended-day programs that focus on evening classes have met with varying degrees of success. Even at the postsecondary level, the obstacles facing evening programs cause concern for program planners. Frequent assessment of programs is necessary to avoid the pitfalls that accompany such challenges as absenteeism, low enrollments, teacher availability, maintenance costs, security concerns, as well as how to schedule time for courses and determine which programs students want.

B. **Summer programs.** Another alternative to traditional scheduling is summer school (and year-round school in some school districts). Only a few years ago summer school was associated solely with remediation and makeup classes for K–12 students. Summer school now provides an option for students to sign up for elective courses during the regular school year and take required courses during one or more summer sessions, frequently in an accelerated time frame.

C. **Split schedules.** Some schools, usually private high schools and trade schools, have now implemented split schedules, in which two subsets of the student population can be accommodated during the day. A split schedule usually accommodates up to twice the number of students that would normally be served, because one group of students attends morning classes and another group attends afternoon classes. Running a split schedule does not necessarily mean that a school will employ different instructional staffs for their morning and afternoon programs. A split schedule frequently takes advantage of an overlap of classes to maximize teaching resources. That is, sections may be combined, where feasible, and fewer but larger classes may be offered. A split schedule may be staffed by extending each teacher's day, creating one or two large classes each day, and hiring aides or assistants for large classes or breakout labs. A split schedule class overlap usually spans a midday time frame of up to two hours.

D. Rotation schedule. A more liberally modified traditional schedule may include an 8–9-subject schedule, accommodating the extra class(es) by dropping one period each day or by rotating classes. For example, in such a rotation schedule, class one is the first period on the first day of the rotation, class two is first period on the second day, class three is first period the third day, and so on until the rotation is completed. While there are drawbacks to such a schedule, teachers and students alike enjoy meeting at different times of the day.

Block scheduling. Block scheduling is usually characterized by longer class periods and rotation schedules. In many junior high/middle schools and senior high schools, an eight-period schedule is a typical pattern with four classes meeting every other day with the entire rotation schedule being completed every two days. Block scheduling allows more time for classroom activities and assignments and requires teachers to explore varied instructional strategies. A distinct advantage of block scheduling is the acquisition of as much as 30 minutes a day for instruction because the "double blocks" cut in half the time needed to change classes. The resulting extra instructional time can be an advantage or disadvantage for some teachers.

An 8–9 period rotation schedule allows students to take more courses. Block scheduling also is credited with making possible a more rounded education for students, especially since some schools have added mandatory survey and exploratory classes. Survey classes, from junior high/middle school through grade 10, offer students a creative programming mechanism for exploring careers or sampling courses. A sampling course may be divided into two-to-three-week mini courses, with each segment introducing new subjects and teachers. Up to six or seven subjects could be "sampled" during a semester-long class. A real advantage for students who think they would like to take a certain subject (such as accounting) is getting a trial experience with a course within a short time frame. The two-to-three-week experience is a good alternative to signing up for a semester-length class and finding out that the course was not what was expected.

Some of the drawbacks of block scheduling may be rather obvious. Some students (and teachers) have difficulty adjusting to the long time frame associated with each class period. Also, students who are not motivated to take more than is required of them for graduation may have a greater opportunity to drop a course. Motivating students can be very difficult for teachers if students opt for a laissez-faire approach to completing their education.

Another frequently observed outcome of block scheduling is an unbalanced teacher-student ratio. That is, the best teachers usually end up with the most students, and the less-talented teachers appear to be rewarded with smaller classes and a lesser share of the load. Additionally, in schools where the two-day block rotation includes only one planning period, some teachers resent the loss of their daily planning period. Alternatively, in a recent survey of 55 business education teachers enrolled in instructional strategies and certification courses at the University of Houston, all but one of the junior high/middle school and high school teachers representing 25 Houston-area school districts expressed their preference for the double block of time for planning, even if it occurs only every other day.

As with traditional scheduling, block scheduling takes on many forms. An increasingly popular block schedule modification is the compression of the term length. That is, some schools offer 9- and 12-week as well as 18-week credit courses. Administrators and teachers who are proponents of the condensed credit system cite higher grades and course completion rates for students. Another variation of block scheduling is a one-day-a-week short day. The short day is a result of the other four days being lengthened. Many inner city and urban schools have implemented the short-day schedule for better use of facilities and resources. For example, the short-day schedule (also frequently referred to as the "extended-day" schedule because the weekly schedule has four long days and one short day) has contributed to daily expanded bus use. Bus schedules have been developed to optimize the utilization of resources by accommodating transportation of junior high/middle school and high school students as well as of elementary school children. The short-day schedule also has provided savings to school districts when lunch programs have been operated only on the extended four days each week. Teacher in-service training, special meetings, and other events (including student sports and competitions) can be held on the short day. Additionally, many school administrators have found that the short-day schedule makes the overall scheduling task somewhat easier and more streamlined. In general, they, along with students and teachers, feel morale is improved when the school week follows a less traditional, rigid format.

Block scheduling, with all of its advantages and disadvantages, is increasing in popularity with administrators, teachers, and students alike. For instance, the Houston-area teachers who were surveyed reported that the benefits of block scheduling outweighed any drawbacks. According to them, the longer blocks are good for reinforcing concepts, working more with individual students, and planning more effectively—with fewer lesson plans needed to accomplish the same result. Some teachers said that block scheduling is less confusing than traditional programming mainly because of less between-class movement. Others suggested that student learning is improved as a direct result of students completing assignments and homework in class, making up missed work, and getting needed attention and supervision. It was also interesting to note that while some teachers like direct contact with every student every day, others find it a nice break to see students on a rotational basis.

Common ground of traditional and block scheduling. The line between traditional and block scheduling is becoming dimmer and dimmer, even seamless in some cases, because of common areas found in most school programs. For example, the shortened day once a week is prevalent in junior high/middle school and senior high school traditional and block programs. Also, predetermined testing days are becoming the norm with both types of schedules, and alternate/rotating test schedules associated with subject areas and grade levels help to lessen overloads on students.

Many junior high/middle schools and senior high schools have found it particularly challenging to schedule a homeroom and/or study period in the daily or rotational schedule. Frequently, homeroom is an extended period, also on a rotational basis, at least once a week. Detention and disciplinary action pose additional challenges for most schools. Because students never seem to lack ideas that present new issues and challenges to school systems, finding creative and innovative ways to deal with these issues keeps meetings of administrators, teachers, and parents in vogue—even in schools that have moved study periods, review/reinforcement units, special testing, and detentions to Saturdays.

Program Challenges Pertaining to Adult Learners

As postsecondary programs are being designed and reengineered, additional challenges suggest that already complex environments must provide considerable flexibility to adequately serve adult learners. Program planners at the postsecondary level are being forced to be very creative in addressing the diverse, unique, and changing needs of their adult clients. In a manner similar to the ways administrators are addressing the scheduling challenges at the junior high/middle school and high school levels, program planners understand that adult learners are pulled in many directions. And the critical needs of adults are quite fundamental. For example, many of today's students work full-time, frequently while raising a family. Others are returning to school to complete their education after extended periods away from an educational institution.

For postsecondary planners, flexibility is a basic necessity, and one that presents articulation challenges as expanding program flexibility continues to migrate to lower educational levels. Serving diverse populations in an ever-changing environment at the postsecondary level requires institutions to be highly competitive as they vie for adult learner enrollments, offer quality programs that focus on skills that expand previously learned knowledge, provide a relevant curriculum based on current as well as future workplace needs, and deliver multimedia instruction in a variety of accessible formats and settings. Business education programs, in particular, must be continuously attuned to these challenges if programs are to survive, let alone grow.

Focus on the Client/Learner

The most successful programs consistently emphasize the learner and learner outcomes in all phases. Focus on the student must always be a priority in all seven elements of program management. Creative scheduling for the learner or client has become an art, especially when programs are offered away from a traditional school campus. A good example is the increase in programs, from the high school through university level, that are being delivered at nontraditional locations.

Technology has played a major role in expanding learning alternatives. Through distance learning, the Internet, taped programming, instructional television, interactive video, and similar methods, technology has provided innovative mechanisms to meet the needs of larger numbers of students. As the focus of program designers remains the learner, more and more doors for education and training will be opened to meet the needs of diverse populations who would otherwise find a traditional school environment to be a barrier.

Driving the Future

Innovation is the single most exciting factor driving change and the future of program management. Innovative and creative program designers are testing the limits of traditional programming. Government, industry, and the private sector have agreed that futuristic program design and delivery can no longer be dependent upon traditional settings and mechanisms that have been entrenched in the educational system. The past is important—it is a great teacher; but the future depends on change. Business educators should dwell on the past only long enough to forge new paths for meeting tomorrow's challenges.

What will programs look like in the future? How will they be developed? Who will benefit? Programs derived from creative thinking and experimentation are destined to become the norm. The norm must be continuously altered to encompass new delivery methods that will meet the changing needs of learners. Tomorrow's learners will be the benefactors of the efforts of program managers who consider the next-generation environment around them—an environment that includes boundless information and knowledge, innovative technology, creative partnerships and competition, social and economic challenges, and vast societal and political forces.

References

Bard, R. C., Bell, R., Stephen, L., & Webster, L. (1987). *The trainer's professional development handbook*. San Francisco: Jossey-Bass, Inc.

Caffarella, R. S. (1994). *Planning programs for adult learners: A practical guide for educators, trainers, and staff developers*. San Francisco: Jossey-Bass/ Pfeiffer.

Craig, R. L. (Ed.). (1996). *The ASTD training and development handbook* (4th ed.). New York: McGraw-Hill.

Dick, W., & Carey, L. (1996). *The systematic design of instruction* (4th ed.). New York: Longman Pub.

Drucker, P. F. (1993). *Post-capitalist society*. New York: HarperCollins.

Goodstein, L. D., Nolan, T. M., & Pfeiffer, J. W. (1993). *Applied strategic planning: A comprehensive guide*. New York: McGraw-Hill, Inc.

Kotter, J. P. (1996). *Leading change*. Boston: Harvard Business School Press.

Knowles, M. S., Swanson, R. A., & Holton, E. (1998). *The adult learner: The definitive classic in adult education and human resource development* (5th ed.). Houston, TX: Gulf Pub. Co.

Lewis, J. P. (2000). *The project manager's desk reference: A comprehensive guide to project planning, scheduling, evaluation, and systems*. New York: McGraw-Hill, Inc.

Mager, R. F. (1997). *Preparing instructional objectives: A critical tool in the development of effective instruction* (3rd ed.). CA: Center for Effective Performance.

Munson, L. S. (1992). *How to conduct training seminars* (2nd ed.). New York: McGraw-Hill.

Managing Curriculum Change

Linda G. McGrew
Middle Tennessee State University
Murfreesboro, Tennessee

For several decades business educators have learned to anticipate, accept, and adjust to changes in society, business, curriculum, and students. Each new decade presents the business educator with new challenges. Changes in the 21st century will increase the demands for business teachers to stay current in the profession. These demands occur as a result of anticipated changes, as well as issues even the most innovative visionaries have yet to imagine. Brandt (1996) has predicted, "Future changes will be bigger and come faster because the rate of change grows exponentially, not incrementally." This rapid change significantly affects the business curriculum and creates issues that must be addressed.

Incorporation of Standards and Competencies

As change infiltrates the curriculum review process, a comfort factor exists in that the primary mission remains the same—to educate students for and about business. Although many resources surfaced in the 1990s, the competencies and standards presented in the *National Standards for Business Education* (1995), the *Business Teacher Education Curriculum Guide & Program Standards* (1997), and by the Secretary's Commission on Achieving Necessary Skills (SCANS) (1991) provided a framework on which to build.

The *National Standards for Business Education* (National Business Education Association, 1995) redefined the parameters of business education by presenting a model for 12 basic content areas: accounting, business law, career development, communications, computation, economics and personal finance, entrepreneurship education, information systems, international business, management, marketing, and the interrelationships of business functions. The suggested educational and cognitive levels at which these core requirements should be taught provide a rational framework for basic business instruction.

The National Association for Business Teacher Education's *Business Teacher Education Curriculum Guide & Program Standards* (1997) followed with procedures for implementing the standards and refining a quality teacher education program. Further findings of the SCANS report (1991) identified eight broad competency areas needed by today's employee. Thus, the infusion of "soft skills" such as how to work with others, think critically, speak and write effectively, and develop lifelong learning habits surfaced as integral components of the business curriculum. These curriculum models and research findings created the foundation on which broader curriculum patterns and issues are built.

A "To Do" List for the New Century

Although a number of other issues emerge, selected curriculum components warrant action in the first decade of the 21st century. Four components are presented here for discussion:

- Expanding the content of basic business courses to encompass international business, entrepreneurship, personal finance, and business communication
- Incorporating technological innovations into the curriculum especially for keyboarding and word processing, distance learning, and e-business
- Influencing external entities such as accreditation agencies, legislation, businesses, and society
- Adapting to a changing student population's traits, behavior, and learning styles

Expanding the Content of Basic Business Courses

The mainstay of the business curriculum includes traditional courses such as economics, introduction to business, accounting, and business law. Expansion of the economy through globalization, small business activity, advances in communication technology, and subsequent financial planning activities has revitalized course content at all levels of education. Whether taught as separate courses or incorporated into existing basic business courses, the topics of international business, entrepreneurship, personal finance, and business communication are curriculum essentials.

International business. The number of U.S. firms that conduct business internationally increases each year. Accessibility to other countries through communication technology and trade agreements is a key factor influencing this growth. Such expansion contributes significantly to the diverse, multicultural workforce, and continued future development of the global economy appears apparent.

In all probability, students entering business careers will work directly with international firms that import or export goods and services or indirectly with suppliers or competitors. Regardless of the extent of the interaction, employees should possess a wide range of knowledge, especially of the countries most commonly involved in trade with the United States.

Currently, topics such as international trade, cultural differences, social and political differences, international finance, cross-cultural communication techniques, and marketing strategies comprise course topics. Increasingly, the social and political impact of global business warrants copious study. An interdisciplinary approach remains appropriate; and the infusion of foreign languages, geography, government, psychology, and the human sciences creates ideal integration units (Dlabay, 1998).

Entrepreneurship. Small businesses constitute a significant majority of U.S. companies and create millions of new jobs each year. Women are starting businesses at twice the rate of their male counterparts and employ more than 14 million people in cottage-based industries. However, the failure rate of small companies increases with this growth phenomenon.

A number of studies have shown that high school students want to own businesses and be their own "bosses." Nelton (1995) reported a Gallup Poll survey that sampled 602 high school students, small business owners, and the general public about starting their own businesses. The findings showed that 70 percent of high school students expressed an interest in becoming an entrepreneur. Additional findings indicate that all of these groups admitted that they need and want to know more about the requirements for starting and operating a successful business (Douglas & Adams, 1999).

Because of student interest in and the economic impact of small businesses, high schools are adding entrepreneurial education to their curricula. Likewise, a number of colleges and universities have launched courses as well as majors and minors in entrepreneurial studies. General-to-specialized instruction in management, accounting, finance, and marketing provides students with the basics for successful business operation. Capstone activities such as the development of a comprehensive business plan in which students conduct market studies, determine capital need, and prepare short-term and long-term proposals for a financial institution create awareness of the many facets of owning a business.

Organizations such as the Coleman Foundation, Inc., and the Kaufman Center for Economic Leadership provide support for the development of entrepreneurial studies (Kourilsky, 1995). Educational materials, seminars, and workshops are provided primarily through grants. Likewise, small business development centers and chambers of commerce assist new business owners.

Personal finance. Baby Boomers have learned that as they approach retirement age, managing finances is increasingly important. The outlook and debates about the solvency of social security, costs of long-term health care, and management of investments create challenges for Baby Boomers. Decisions about mutual funds, annuities, IRAs, and money market accounts often require the assistance of financial planners to maximize earning potential.

Many Net Generation students work part-time while attending high school. Also, each year college students appear to be increasing the number of hours they work each week in their full- or part-time jobs. Moreover, the majority of high school and college students report having checking and savings accounts. Descriptions of Net Generation consumption patterns prevailingly depict a group that has more, wants more, and has more from which to choose.

However, the 1999 Youth & Money Survey, conducted by the American Savings Education Council (ASEC), yielded some alarming findings. The youth surveyed were categorized as college-bound students. Four highlights from the report emphasize the need to promote personal finance courses to students:

- The vast majority of students ages 16–22 have never taken a class in personal finance, even though two-thirds admit that they should know more about money management.
- Nine percent of all students are rolling over credit card debt each month.
- Sixty-five percent of those who have had access to a personal finance course in school have not taken advantage of it.
- Eighty-two percent responded that they feel "fairly" or "very confident" about their level of understanding of financial matters. A misconception about the level of their financial understanding can hurt them financially in the future (American Savings Education Council, 2000).

A 1997 survey by the American Savings Education Council generated equally alarming results when on average students answered only 57 percent of the financial knowledge questions correctly, although 77 percent felt they were knowledgeable about managing money. Many of the questions were on terminology and not on reasoning ability or calculations. Survey questions included topics such as taxes, retirement, insurance, credit use, inflation, and budgeting. Savings and investment knowledge was reported as the weakest area for survey respondents, with an average score of only 47.3 percent (American Savings Education Council, 2000).

Business educators must seize the opportunity to introduce students to the world of finance and money management. Never before has so much contemporary information emerged from sources such as the Internet, journals, television, financial institutions, textbooks, and supplements. In their efforts to educate youth about money management, organizations such as ASEC, a coalition of public and private institutions, provide materials and support to business educators.

One of these initiatives, the Jump$tart Coalition (2000), has reported that teenagers account for a quarter of all credit card holders and that they spent nearly $10.9 billion in 1998. Recent research shows a direct link between financial literacy and personal bankruptcy rates. The Jump$tart Coalition cites as its purpose " . . . to evaluate the financial literacy of young adults; develop, disseminate, and encourage the use of guidelines for grades K–12; and promote the teaching of personal finance" (Jump$tart Coalition, 2000).

Modules and materials for use by students and teachers at all grade levels are available from other groups such as the National Council on Economic Education (NCEE) and the U.S. Department of Defense. Resources such as the U.S. Department of Agriculture's *High School Financial Planning Program*, NCEE's *Stock Market Game* and *Virtual Economics* CD offer teachers realistic hands-on activities and lesson plans in personal finance. Also, the September 1998 issue of NBEA's newsletter, *Keying In*, provides an extensive list of personal finance resources for students at all levels.

Business communication. Businesspeople increasingly cite oral and written communication skills as two critical skills that new employees lack. Therefore, some type of business communication course is a requirement in many International Association for Management Education, formerly known as the American Assembly of Collegiate Schools of Business (AACSB), accredited colleges and universities. In addition to the traditional theories addressed in business communication courses, content should include international, ethical, legal, and technological topics. Likewise, in high school business programs, critical writing skills and expanded topics may be included in a separate business communication course or presented as integrated units in other business courses.

Increasingly, the infusion of instruction in the effective use of e-mail and voice mail and the creation of online resumes prepares students to use the communication techniques practiced by businesses. Krause (2000) has stated, "Increasingly, employers are looking for individuals who communicate effectively, stay abreast of current technology, and display an understanding of key concepts necessary to make a substantial business contribution" (p. 7). Students taught to develop online resumes possess a competitive edge because they can utilize Web sites of large U.S. and international corporations (Wagner, January 1998). Business communication teachers will continue to be challenged to determine the appropriate mix of topics for their courses from this important, expanding area.

Incorporating Technological Innovations Into the Curriculum

The impact of technology on the business education curriculum can be overwhelming. Recent rapid growth in numerous technological domains supports many of the predictions for the next decade. The following are four predictions that business educators must consider when planning curriculum:

- The number of Internet users is expected to grow from 100 million in 1998 to more than 320 million in 2002. Access in 2002 will be 1,000 times faster than in 1998.
- The Windows 2008 icons will change considerably from those used now and will configure based on the individual and the intended use of the computer.
- Input from the keyboard will continue to be utilized; but additional input devices, such as voice command equipment, touch screens, and remote controls, will expand and become more commonplace in business and industry.
- Expanded security solutions including devices that read fingerprints or scan the eyes will be released to ensure individuals greater privacy (Brooks, 1998).

As these predictions become reality, the business education curriculum will continue to evolve its course content and instructional delivery systems. Specific areas, such as keyboarding and word processing, distance learning, and e-business, provide unique examples of curriculum expansion.

Keyboarding and word processing. While some of these predictions may appear radical, voice recognition software already available allows users to input information at 120 words per minute. IBM's software, ViaVoice 2000, includes an expandable 62,000-word dictionary for user dictation purposes. Yet, a major limitation for classrooms continues to be the technology's inability to accurately recognize different voices and the lack of funds necessary to convert to these systems. As the use of voice recognition software expands in business, keyboarding teachers will need to use input devices other than the keyboard. These devices raise questions about adjustments needed in future keyboarding applications courses. But regardless of input source, formatting, composition, and proofreading remain important aspects of application courses.

The expanded use of computers in classrooms and at home by individuals of all ages raises the question of when keyboarding instruction should begin. Curriculum planners are continuing to seek answers to this and other questions such as who is qualified to provide instruction at the elementary level and how business teacher preparation programs can assist in providing quality elementary keyboarding instruction.

A number of studies indicate that the most appropriate time to begin keyboarding instruction is at the middle/junior high school level. A recent study of business education in Tennessee high schools, however, found that 80 percent of the responding schools offered one to nine sections of keyboarding. Sixty-one percent of the Tennessee high schools responding to the survey reported a total of 33,306 students enrolled in keyboarding classes. Some high school teachers expressed concerns about the stability of their positions if keyboarding instruction is moved to lower grades because their certification does not include the middle school grades (McGrew, Sawyer, & Fann, 2000).

Of course, as rudimentary keyboarding instruction moves to lower grade levels, employment competencies of document formatting, editing, composition, and proofreading remain integral components of high school and postsecondary course content. Keyboarding software provides support for today's keyboarding teachers in addressing the placement of students at different skill levels. Expanded articulation agreements and skill assessment software provide additional alternatives to the problem of placement.

Changes in curriculum content and methodology should not occur without careful study and consideration. The Policies Commission for Business and Economic Education (1989) has cautioned curriculum planners stating, "We Believe That decision making and problem solving are best taught by presenting a balance of 'how' and 'why' in instruction. The 'how' will change as technology changes, but the 'why' will generally remain constant." Development of the skills required to format business documents correctly and to produce them at an acceptable rate remain the end goals of keyboarding and word processing courses. Application skill development (e.g., formatting, proofreading, composition, and editing) should not be replaced with a specific software's "click and drag" commands.

Distance learning. Expanding access to technology, changing demographics of higher education, and increasing competitiveness in delivering instruction propel faculty and administration to recognize distance learning as a top priority. Hsu, Marques, Hamza, and Alhalabi (1999) have referred to distance learning as a virtual classroom and defined it as "a system that provides the same opportunities for the teaching and learning process, beyond the physical limits of the traditional classroom's walls" (p. 96).

Alternative delivery methods expanded in the 1990s to include compressed video, cable television, desktop videoconferencing, interactive video, and online instruction. Currently, Web-based courses surface as the fastest growing method of alternative instruction. Teachers use the Web to deliver entire courses or to supplement courses taught in traditional ways.

Diverse audiences benefit from distance learning. Business executives, adults, students, homebound persons, and disabled individuals represent distinct groups that distance learning serves. Thus far, the greatest impact occurs in higher education; for example, a student at a New York university may enroll in a class at a California university. However, secondary schools are also beginning to embrace this option for students learning at home or in alternative schools.

Teacher certification/preparation programs at one or more universities can pool their efforts to help meet the need for business teachers, especially where programs have downsized or closed. Furthermore, businesses increasingly use intranets, videoconferencing, and closed-circuit television as cost-effective methods of delivering training to employees.

Issues arise in distance learning, especially in higher education, with regards to maintaining the integrity of course content, training faculty to use technology, articulating between educational institutions, protecting ownership of course material, and funding necessary technology. In addition, some faculty members and administrators find it difficult to shift paradigms away from traditional classroom instruction. These individuals contend that distance learning compromises course integrity and is another instructional fad like many others that have not prevailed.

A number of studies have been conducted comparing traditional methods of instruction with distance education. One study compared student outcomes of a computer applications course taught over the Web with outcomes of one taught in a traditional classroom setting. The findings indicated that students learn equally well regardless of the instructional delivery medium (Bartel & Bartholome, 1999).

A key factor in the continued growth of distance learning appears to be the training and incentives offered to faculty. Training instructors to use software and equipment such as microphones, cameras, projection systems, and two-way video, as well as developing required organizational skills to present these courses, remain priorities in the advancement of the virtual experience.

E-business. The rapid and phenomenal growth in e-business has caused business curriculum planners to develop instructional units or specialized courses, minors, and even majors in this subject area. The revenue earned from the rapidly growing number of individuals who purchase goods and services over the Internet is expected to reach $400 billion by 2002. The number of individuals making purchases will increase to 128 million in 2002, compared with 18 million in 1998. Recent reports suggest that 1.5 million new Web pages are created daily and that the number of Web sites doubles every eight months (Pritchett, 1999).

Two especially important trends—the increasing number of venture capitalists seeking to invest in innovative e-business ideas and the anticipated growth of global electronic markets—emerged as the new century began. Integrating traditional topics such as contract law and business ownership, as they relate to investors, into the e-business curriculum will help prepare students for this evolving field. In addition, knowledge of security, ethical, social, and privacy issues is essential for electronic entrepreneurs (Remp, 1999).

A course in electronic commerce should extend beyond Web page design and include concepts of management, marketing, advertising, selling, and technology. Increasingly, students are launching their own businesses and advertising routinely on the Internet. Business educators should continue to incorporate e-business into curriculum plans for the 21st century.

Influencing External Entities

A number of external entities impact business education curricula. Whether local, regional, or national, external agencies vary in mission and requirements. The myriad of influences provides mandates and standards that assist business educators in restructuring the curriculum to prepare students for business careers. Accrediting agencies, legislation, businesses, and society present opportunities and challenges.

Accrediting agencies. Regional accreditation can be earned by public and private secondary and postsecondary institutions. Specialized accrediting agencies, such as AACSB for college business programs and the National Council for Accreditation of Teacher Education (NCATE) for teacher education programs, provide standards from which curriculum content can be developed. For example, AACSB requires the infusion of such topics as diversity, globalization, legal and environmental issues, technology, and communication into business courses at accredited universities. Likewise, additional standards relating to the number of business and nonbusiness semester hours required for business majors influence program configurations.

Accredited business teacher education programs must meet NCATE standards and individual state requirements. Challenges continue for teacher preparation programs to maintain the integrity of their curricula while meeting general education, teacher education, and major content requirements. Because of the vast array of competencies and standards to be met, some programs now require five years instead of the traditional four years.

Legislation. Federal and state legislation influence curriculum decisions and impact funding of programs. The Perkins Act of 1993 and its subsequent amendments focused on vocational education and the preparation of students for careers. The 1998 Perkins III (Public Law 105-332) provided funding to high-quality vocational and technical education programs that met the following requirements.

- Integrated academic and vocational education
- Promoted student attainment of challenging academic, vocational, and technical standards

- Provided students with experience in, and understanding of, all aspects of an industry
- Involved parents and employers
- Provided strong linkages between secondary and postsecondary education
- Developed, improved, and expanded the use of technology
- Provided professional development for teachers, counselors, and administrators (United States Department of Education, 2000)

Although business education programs generally meet many of these criteria, specific restructuring of curricula includes Tech Prep initiatives, the integration of "general" and "business" courses, and the reconfiguration of cooperative learning and internship programs.

Teacher preparation programs can incorporate activities into existing courses and provide special seminars and workshops to assist business teachers in developing units integrating math, art, science, social studies, and language with business topics. Students will then have increased exposure to practical applications in the business world.

A focus on specific articulation agreements between the different levels of education emerged as a result of the Perkins Act and Tech Prep efforts. The goal of providing specific career direction to students and preparing them for postsecondary education programs requires extensive cooperation and improved communication between secondary and postsecondary educational institutions (Bottoms & Sharpe, 1996). Additionally, businesses will have an increasingly important role in determining the knowledge and skills necessary for success in the workplace.

Business and society. Businesses are downsizing, rightsizing, reengineering, and restructuring to gain the competitive edge. As changes occur in society, increased demands are put on educational institutions to prepare youth for a more complex, diverse workplace. Society calls for more from education; some people even feel that educational programs should be "everything to every person." Whether correct or not, educators are challenged to improve the work ethics, values, and knowledge and skill levels of students.

Businesspeople often provide input into curriculum development by serving as participants in focus groups and Developing A Curriculum (DACUM) processes. The DACUM process involves workers who serve as expert panelists for their occupations. Each panel works with a trained facilitator to determine the duties and tasks performed in the occupation as well as the general knowledge, skills, and resources required for success (Center on Education and Training for Employment, 1999). Subsequently, opportunities arise for garnering educational resources from corporations. Mutually beneficial interactions, such as advisory board service, classroom speaking engagements, field trips, internships, and mentoring opportunities, enhance collaboration opportunities between businesspeople and educators. At the same time, these partnerships support School-to-Career initiatives and career development activities for teachers that fall within the auspices of the Perkins Act.

Adapting to a Changing Student Population

Today's students, often referred to as the Net Generation, require a shifting of the paradigm of instructional strategies and curriculum content. Business teachers have a formidable task in striving to understand and meet the unique needs of this generation. Net Generation students have attended school in an era of shifting gender roles, expanding technology, increased diversity and globalization, and a widening gap in upper- and lower-income levels. Further, this generation has been exposed to more knowledge than students of previous generations. According to Pritchett (1999), "More information has been produced in the last 30 years than during the previous 5,000"(p. 9). He has further suggested that the knowledge base doubles every two years or less.

Developing critical-thinking skills. Such a knowledge explosion mandates the development of critical-thinking skills by educators and students. Business educators must first discern which topics and concepts are important and necessary in a course. Students must then be taught to analyze, apply meaning, and synthesize information to solve problems.

Collaboration in problem solving is a viable technique for teaching students how to succeed in the workplace (Sormunen & Chalupa, 1995). Critical-thinking activities can be incorporated into group activities that provide students with opportunities to brainstorm, communicate, negotiate, judge, reason, organize, and present thoughts as a team. The use of case studies for problem solving also promotes critical thinking. Of course, students need to be taught where to locate related information and that sound research is necessary to justify decisions and solutions. Armed with this knowledge students can apply critical-thinking skills to written assignments and to exam preparation, which will result in longer retention of subject matter.

Learning styles. One important aspect of teaching critical thinking is the reality that teaching and learning styles do not always mesh. Business educators will have to continue to study this area, analyze their teaching styles, and be aware that all students do not learn in the same way. Whether a student's learning preference is visual, auditory, tactile, or a combination of one or more of the senses, a shift from traditional methods of instruction (e.g., lecture) must occur for this generation. Teachers need to discern which students are more productive when they work independently and which students prefer to work in groups.

Learning styles are often associated with an individual student's dominant side of the brain. Often right-brained learners are more intuitive, social, impulsive, and creative. Left-brained learners are more analytical and structured and usually are more prepared and precise. Although teachers cannot change the basic style of a learner, they can assist the right-brained student in becoming more organized without squelching creativity. Likewise, assignments requiring creativity can help left-brained learners develop this area (Hopper, 1995).

Summary

As change occurs in society and the business environment, factors arise in curricular decisions arise that impact all business educators. As in the past, even the most innovative visionary cannot predict the extent of internal and external influences that may occur. Certainly, restructuring the basic business curriculum, meeting the challenges created by rapidly changing technology, integrating standards and procedures required by outside agencies, and adjusting to the needs of students emerge as critical issues.

Training for business teachers and attaining adequate resources to support programs will continue to be major issues for curriculum planners. Teacher preparation programs must meet the growing demand for new business teachers and prepare them with the knowledge and skills needed for 21st-century classrooms. Because of attrition over the next few years, many new teachers will replace experienced professional business educators across the nation. This new generation of business teachers will need training in innovative instructional strategies and classroom management techniques appropriate for a changing student population. Also, they will need to assume leadership roles in curriculum review and reform.

The mission remains to educate students for and about business. As global expansion continues in a diverse, technology-driven workplace, business educators face dynamic, new challenges. As in the past, business educators are expected to embrace the challenges and seize the opportunities with enthusiasm.

References

American Savings Education Council. (2000). 1999 youth & money survey. Author. Retrieved from the World Wide Web: http://www.asec.org/highlite.htm

Bartel, K., & Bartholome, L. W. (1999). University distance and on-campus learners: A comparison of beginning microcomputer applications students. *NABTE Review, 26,* 46–48.

Bottoms, G., & Sharpe, D. (1996). *Teaching for understanding through integration of academic and technical education.* Atlanta, GA: Southern Regional Educational Board.

Brandt, D. (1996). *Sacred cows make the best burgers.* New York: Warner Books.

Brooks, L. (1998, September). *Technology in the new millennium.* Presentation at the Delta Pi Epsilon Meeting at the Tennessee Business Education Association Conference.

Center on Education and Training for Employment, The Ohio State University. (1999). *The DACUM process.* Columbus, OH: Author. Retrieved from the World

Wide Web: http://www.interlynx.net/archway/ohio/dacumpro.htm

Dlabay, L. (1998, Summer). Integrated curriculum planning for international business education: Analysis of global business trends. *Delta Pi Epsilon Journal, 40,* 158–160.

Douglas, M. E., & Adams, M. E. (1999, October). Developing and teaching a high school entrepreneurship course part I: Rationale and content. *Business Education Forum, 54*(1), 32–35.

Hopper, C. (1995). *The study skills workbook.* Cincinnati: McGraw Hill.

Hsu, S., Marques, O., Hamza, M. K., & Alhalabi, B. (1999). How to design a virtual classroom: 10 easy steps to follow. *Technological Horizons in Education Journal, 27,* 96–108.

Jump$tart Coalition for Personal Financial Literacy. (2000, January). *What's new at Jump$tart.* Washington, DC: Author. Retrieved from the World Wide Web: http//www.jumpstartcoalition.org/whatsnew/shownews

Kourilsky, M. (1995, October). Entrepreneurship education: Opportunity in search of curriculum. *Business Education Forum, 50*(1), 11–15.

Krause, T. (2000). *Wired resumes.* Cincinnati, OH: South-Western Publishing Co.

McGrew, L. G., Sawyer, J. E., & Fann, N. J. (2000). *A suggested prototype for analyzing business education programs in the U.S.* Paper presented at Middle Tennessee State University, Murfreesboro, TN.

National Association for Business Teacher Education. (1997). *Business teacher education curriculum guide & program standards.* Reston, VA: Author.

National Business Education Association. (1995). *National standards for business education: What America's students should know and be able to do in business.* Reston, VA: Author.

Nelton, S. (1995, February). Help for teenagers. *Nation's Business, 83,* 50.

Policies Commission for Business and Economic Education. (1989). *The impact of change due to information technologies* (Statement No. 46). Montgomery, AL: Alabama Department of Education.

Pritchett, P. (1999, January). *New work habits for a radically changing world.* Dallas, TX: Pritchett and Associates.

Remp, A. M. (1999, October). E-commerce and emerging payment and privacy technologies. *Business Education Forum, 54*(1), 47–51.

Secretary's Commission on Achieving Necessary Skills. (1991). *What work requires of schools: A SCANS report for America 2000.* Washington, DC: Author.

Sormunen, C., & Chalupa, M. R. (1995, February). Strategies for developing critical thinking. *Business Education Forum, 49*(3), 41–43.

U.S. Department of Education. (2000). Carl D. Perkins Vocational and Technical Education Act of 1998 (Public Law 105–332). Washington, DC: Author. Retrieved from the World Wide Web: http://www.ed.gov/offices/OVAE/VocEd/InfoBoard.html

Wagner, J. G. (1998, January). Electronic resumes and online job searches: How computers are changing the job-seeking process. *Keying In,* 1–6.

Wagner, J. G. (1998, September). Teaching personal finance. *Keying In,* 1–7.

Diversity Today: Challenges and Strategies

Tena B. Crews	Alexa Bryans North	Sandra L. Thompson
State University of West Georgia Carrollton, Georgia	State University of West Georgia Carrollton, Georgia	Marietta City School System Marietta, Georgia

Tremendous changes are occurring in today's society, workplace, and classroom. For example, the workforce has changed in ethnic and racial composition, more women are now in business, older workers are keeping jobs longer, and people with disabilities are performing jobs once deemed impossible for them. As ethnic, racial, and social-class diversity increase in the United States, educators will be challenged to concentrate more intensely on what it means to be an educated person in our society (Banks & Banks, 1997). Diversity is multifaceted and encompasses more than ethnic differences. Therefore, diversity sensibility involves more than awareness; it requires incorporating diversity strategies into society, business, and education.

Diversity in society. The following statistics emphasize the changing demographics of today's society. For example, imagine that the 5.8 billion people on Earth are reduced to a single village of 995 people, it might include the following (Macionis & Plummer, 1996):

- 575 Asians
- 130 Africans
- 125 Europeans
- 100 Latin Americans
- 65 North Americans (Canadians, U.S. citizens, and Mexicans)

Society needs to be concerned with developing and enhancing the understanding of other cultures. All people need to feel respected and valued. Changes in society will dictate necessary changes in business and education.

Diversity in business. The varied backgrounds of workers have resulted in the need for businesses to seek effective ways to accommodate and utilize that diversity (Heggy, 1999). For example, the U.S. Department of Labor has projected that before the end of the first decade of the 21st Century, three-quarters of all workers will be women, minorities, and/or immigrants. "New jobs, new skill requirements, new ways of working, and rapid obsolescence are four trends contributing to change" (Morris & Massie, 1998, p. 6). Changes in the workplace have altered what workers do, how they do it, and with whom they work. King (1998) has noted that "most expect their work forces will be diverse in 20 years and that the ability to work in diverse teams will be critical."

Businesses feed an information-based economy that accelerates the pace of change. To remain on the forefront of change, businesses will continually need to improve, modify, and address change. Embracing diversity in the workplace will bring benefits to society, business, and education.

Diversity in the classroom. During the 1998–1999 school year, the U.S. student population in grades K–12 was approximately 50 million; postsecondary and college students numbered almost 15 million. Statistics show that the ethnic composition of the student population in American schools is changing. In public K–12 schools, approximately 20 percent of the children under 17 are minorities, including African Americans, Hispanic Americans, and Asian Americans (National Center for Education Statistics). By 2020, nearly half will be categorized as minorities (Ryan & Cooper, 1997). In order to understand and respond to increasing cultural diversity, teacher programs must not only raise questions about diversity but also develop courses of action that are valid for particular communities.

Since 1979 the National Council for Accreditation of Teacher Education (NCATE) has emphasized the need for diversity sensibility in the classroom, as shown by this statement from NCATE standards (1982):

> Provision should be made for instruction in multicultural education
> in teacher education programs. Multicultural education should
> receive attention in courses, seminars, directed readings, laboratory
> and clinical experiences, practicum, and other types of field experi-
> ences. (p. 4)

Teaching in the diverse classroom means more than addressing issues of diversity. Teachers must be aware of how they treat students, how students treat them, and how students treat each other. Students are dealing with not only their own cultures, but new cultures. Differences occur because of variations in ethnicity, socioeconomic status, race, gender, and regional and national origin. Thompson and Thompson (1996) have listed the following as the most difficult adjustment areas for students who are not natives of the United States: social isolation; language; norms, rules, and regulations; stereotypes; weather; food; oral presentations; and personal finance.

"Vast cultural differences among students in the nation's classrooms are primary factors in today's educational climate" (Drake, 1993, p. 264). Therefore, preservice, beginning, and veteran teachers must focus on understanding diversity in the classroom, integrating new instructional strategies into their curricula, and managing diversity. Diversity sensibility requires more than daily, weekly, or monthly activities; school- and work-based experiences should be ongoing throughout the year.

The National Council for Social Studies (NCSS) created the Task Force on Ethnic Studies to develop guidelines to help teachers implement multicultural curricula. The NCSS curriculum guidelines recommend that teachers and students accomplish the following (Regional Institute for School Enhancement, 1996):

- Understand the totality of the experiences of ethnic and cultural groups
- Understand the contrast between ideal and real situations existing in human societies
- Explore and clarify ethnic and cultural variations
- Promote values, attitudes, and behaviors that support ethnic pluralism and diversity
- Develop decision-making abilities, social skills, and a sense of political efficacy
- Develop skills for effective ethnic and cultural group interactions
- Present holistic views that are comprehensive in scope and a part of the total school curriculum
- Incorporate a continuous study of various cultures, historical experiences, and social realities
- Use interdisciplinary and multidisciplinary approaches in the curriculum
- Use comparative approaches in the study of ethnic and cultural groups
- View and interpret events, situations, conflicts, perspectives, and points of view
- Provide opportunities to participate in the aesthetic experiences of various ethnic and cultural groups
- Maximize use of local community resources to promote diversity

Meaning of Diversity

In its broadest sense, diversity includes the following: ethnicity; racial background; economic status; physical and mental ability; and the aspects of culture that include nuances of language, heritage, personal behavior, and self-identification. The complexity of the components of diversity can best be illustrated in the Dimensions of Diversity: The Prejudice Wheel (Figure 1). Diversity is a result of various differences among students. In many business education classrooms, the following areas from Figure 1 probably are part of student experiences with diversity: sexual orientation, geographic origin, race, ethnicity, gender, physical abilities/qualities, and age. In adult business education programs, income, marital status, education level, military experience, and work background may influence the classroom experiences extensively.

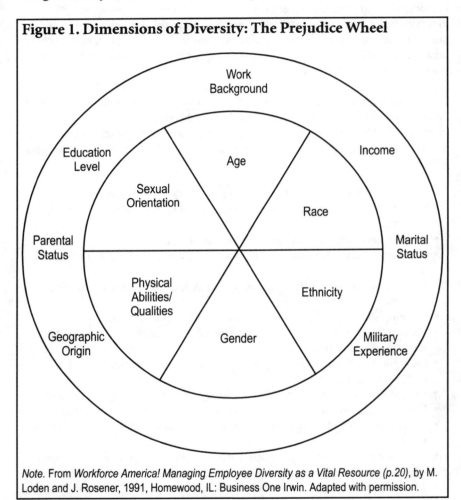

Figure 1. Dimensions of Diversity: The Prejudice Wheel

Note. From *Workforce America! Managing Employee Diversity as a Vital Resource (p.20)*, by M. Loden and J. Rosener, 1991, Homewood, IL: Business One Irwin. Adapted with permission.

Integrating instructional strategies that address these dimensions of diversity will create a more balanced curriculum. The Center for Research on Education, Diversity & Excellence (CREDE) has established standards for effective pedagogy. The CREDE rubric standards for effective teaching involve collaboration, assistance, questioning, complex thinking, conversation, and integration of activities for the diverse student population, as shown in Table 1. The rubric helps facilitate assessment of the presence of each standard at five different levels. For example, a teacher who has designed, enacted, and collaborated with students on joint activities that demonstrate skillful, simultaneous integration of multiple standards has applied a standard at its highest level: "integrating." The standards can be used as a guide for planning and incorporating activities that demonstrate cognizance of all kinds of diversity among students.

Diversity Curricula and Learning Styles

The Association for Supervision and Curriculum Development (Carbo, 1995, p. 22) has recommended the following foundational guidelines for teaching diversity:

- Give opportunities for discussion and understanding of meaning.
- Use project-based or team-learning activities.
- Incorporate explicit teaching of learning strategies.
- Provide supplemental instruction.
- Administer reasonable discipline.

Developing curricula and instruction that is culturally responsive provides students with opportunities to learn about diversity. Planning an effective diversity curriculum involves reviewing state and local curriculum guides, textbooks, and materials; altering classroom practices and assessment practices; and identifying teaching and learning styles.

> Business educators have a vital interest in the social and economic growth of our nation; therefore, they must take an active role to ensure that all students have equal access to and equal opportunity for a meaningful education. Business educators must define their position and responsibilities as they prepare students to enter and become productive in a diverse work setting. (Policies Commission, 1997, p. 105)

Diversity education must employ different instructional methods to prepare students of various cultural backgrounds for participation in mainstream American society. The key is for teachers to "begin educational efforts where their students are" in terms of their cultural awareness (Warren, 1992, p. 324). Doing so can be challenging because of the diversity of students' cultural backgrounds. Students' levels of cultural awareness vary based on the diversity of their communities, schools, and homes. Therefore, teachers should first determine where their students are by developing an awareness of the diversity in their communities and schools.

The impact of diversity on business and marketing education relates to how teachers help students learn most effectively. McEwen (1997) has stated,

> Research shows that the more diverse the student population, the greater the likelihood of a variety of learning styles. In fact, increasing

Table 1. Rubric for Assessing Enactment of CREDE Standards for Effective Teaching

General Definitions of Standards	Not Observed	Emerging: One or more aspects of the standard are enacted.	Developing: The teacher designs and enacts activities that demonstrate a partial enactment of the standard.	Enacting: The teacher designs and enacts activities that demonstrate a complete enactment of the standard.	Integrating: The teacher designs, enacts, and collaborates with students on activities that demonstrate skillful, simultaneous integration of multiple standards.
I. Joint Productive Activity: Teacher and students producing together	Joint productive activity is not observed.	Students are seated with a partner or a group, and (a) are encouraged to collaborate and assist one another, or (b) are instructed in how to work in groups, or (c) contribute individual work, not requiring collaboration to a joint product.	Students collaborate on a joint product.	Students work in a small group or on fully inclusive whole-class activities in which teacher and students collaborate on a joint product.	The teacher designs, enacts, and collaborates on joint product activities that demonstrate skillful integration of multiple standards simultaneously.
II. Language and Literacy Development: Developing language and literacy across the curriculum	Language and literacy development is not observed.	The teacher (a) listens and responds to student talk in ways that are comfortable for students; (b) asks questions; (c) rephrases students' answers; (d) connects student comments to content area knowledge;	The teacher assists students in expression and language development through incidental use of questioning, listening, rephrasing, or modeling, and provides structured opportunities for students to interact	The teacher assists students in expression and language development through questioning, listening, rephrasing, or modeling throughout much of instruction, and provides instructional activities to encourage	The teacher designs, enacts, and collaborates on language development activities that demonstrate skillful integration of multiple standards simultaneously.

	(e) explicitly models appropriate language; or (f) has students engage in reading, writing, or speaking activities using content vocabulary.	throughout much of instruction.	students to interact and use content vocabulary.	
III. Contextualization: Creating meaning by connecting school to students' lives	Contextualization is not observed.	(a) The teacher inquires about students' knowledge and experiences from outside school, or (b) parents or community members participate in activities or instruction, or (c) classroom activities are connected only by topic.	The teacher makes incidental connections between students' prior experience/knowledge from home, school, or community and the new activity/information, or some aspect of students' everyday experience or prior knowledge is included in instruction.	The teacher integrates the new activity/information with what students already know from home, school, or community.	The teacher designs, enacts, and collaborates on contextualization activities that demonstrate skillful integration of multiple standards simultaneously.
IV. Challenging Activities: Teaching complex thinking	Challenging activities are not observed.	The teacher (a) sets and presents standards for student performance, (b) accommodates students' varied ability levels, (c) connects instructional elements to academic concepts, or (d) provides students with feedback on their performance.	The teacher designs and enacts activities that advance student understanding to more complex levels, or connects instructional elements to academic concepts.	The teacher moves the activity forward, assists, and uses challenging standards to advance student understanding to more complex levels; connects instructional elements to academic concepts; and provides students with feedback about their performance.	The teacher designs, enacts, and collaborates on challenging activities that demonstrate skillful integration of multiple standards simultaneously.

V. Instructional Conversation: Teaching through conversation	Instructional conversation is not observed.	The teacher (a) converses with students or (b) uses questioning, listening, rephrasing, or modeling to elicit student talk.	The teacher converses with a small group of students about an academic topic and elicits student talk with questioning, listening, rephrasing, or modeling.	The teacher designs and enacts an instructional conversation with a clear academic goal; listens carefully to assess and aid student understanding; and questions students about their views, judgments, and rationales. All students are included in the instructional conversation, and students talk more than the teacher does.	The teacher designs, enacts, and assists in instructional conversation that demonstrates skillful integration of multiple standards simultaneously.

Note. From *Standards Performance Continuum: A Rubric for Observing Classroom Enactments of CREDE's Standards for Effective Pedagogy,* by Center for Research on Education, Diversity & Excellence (CREDE), 1999, Santa Cruz, CA: University of California Santa Cruz. Retrieved October 13, 1999 from the World Wide Web: http://www.crede.ucsc.edu/HomePage/Standards/SPAC/SPAC.html. Adapted with permission.

evidence supports the view that students from various culturally diverse backgrounds have different dominant learning styles. (p. 3)

It is important to understand the reality of diverse learners so educational myths are not perpetuated. The Secretary's Commission on Achieving Necessary Skills (1991, pp. 19–31) has identified learning myths and reality as shown in Table 2.

Table 2. Learning: Myths and Reality

Myths	Reality
Students resemble "blank slates."	Students bring their own knowledge and conceptions with them.
Learners are passive receptacles into which knowledge can be "poured."	Learning occurs when the student constructs, invents, and solves problems.
Skills are taught in isolation.	Learners must practice applying and combining skills for transference.
Knowledge, practice, and their applications should be separated.	Knowledge, practice, and their applications are intertwined and interdependent.
Knowledge and skills do not have to be taught in settings in which the work must be performed.	Teaching out of context impedes the transfer of training to new settings.
Education and training are based on individual performance.	Work occurs in the context of teams.
Problem-solving skills are too complex for early learning.	Human beings, even small children, are sense-making, problem-solving individuals.

The teaching standards and realities shown in Tables 1 and 2 emphasize the importance of using a variety of strategies to educate diverse student populations. To develop effective strategies to fit diverse learning styles, for example, an educator must first recognize that diverse learning styles exist. Education has consistently supported the notion that learning preferences or styles can be identified and categorized. For example, Vawdrey (1996) has defined learning preferences as follows:

These learning preferences influence communication style . . . For example, people who are visual tend to reveal themselves by using expressions like "I see" or "I get the picture." Auditory learners may say "I hear you" or "That doesn't ring a bell." Kinesthetic (tactile) learners talk about "getting a grasp" on things or "feeling" one way or another. (p. 67)

Motivating students to learn is a challenge for all educators. It does not necessarily depend on the ethnic or economic backgrounds of the class members. Instructional strategies that include peer teaching and small-group learning tasks can promote an attitude of success and enhance motivation. While motivation is not something teachers can automatically impart to their students, it should still be part of the equation when teachers endeavor to address the varying needs and learning styles of the diverse classroom. Students should be encouraged to find reasons to master the subject matter and become internally motivated.

Business educators may find that their biggest challenge is to identify additional effective teaching strategies for special education students who are mainstreamed in their classrooms. Currently "millions of students with disabilities are joining their non-disabled peers in mastering grade-level material" (Council for Exceptional Children, 2000, p. 1). Teachers must recognize the differences in students and develop instructional strategies to meet their needs. Research in special education has begun to highlight effective instructional strategies that must be implemented for special education students. These include providing intense, sustained instruction with a small teacher/student ratio; providing direct instruction; teaching for independent learning; using peer tutoring; providing training in phonological awareness; and providing early childhood intervention. With these instructional strategies, special education students can be successful (Council for Exceptional Children, 2000).

Activities and Strategies

Classroom activities should address learner preferences to provide diverse learners the opportunity to be successful. To develop curricula incorporating diversity training, teachers should begin by selecting materials and activities that show cognizance of diversity among learners. Next, educators should integrate these activities throughout the curriculum using what they know about race, class, ethnicity, gender, disability, and other diversity issues. Whenever possible, it is a good idea to build on instructional strategies that have worked in the past.

Diversity education does not involve a set curriculum, but a perspective that is reflected in all decisions about every phase and aspect of teaching (Ramsey, 1987). Four goals should be considered when developing diversity curricula:

1. Educate the entire school community through ongoing training.
2. Hold high expectations for all students.
3. Provide a rigorous curriculum that includes an appropriate amount of multicultural literature and history.
4. Identify underachieving students and strive to enable them to move to upper-level academic courses.

It is important to integrate diversity activities in both skills and cognitive courses as well as in student organizations. Table 3 shows sample diversity activities.

Table 3. Sample Diversity Activities

Skills	Activities
Word Processing	Diversity Report: In groups, students compile and present a list of gender stereotypes that they have encountered in society, business, or education. Mentoring: Students mentor either community elders or persons with disabilities in the use of technology.
Desktop Publishing	Diversity Newsletter: Collaborative groups create, design, and publish a newsletter highlighting or discussing important aspects of a specific culture. Intergenerational Project: Students record personal histories of their communities' elders and learn from their life experiences. Students then create Web pages to honor the elders' lives.
Keyboarding	Word of the Week: Each week a student provides a culture-related word list (5–10 words) for the class. Students key words and guess definitions. The student who provided the word list then shares the actual definitions with the class. Classroom Connection Project: Students key a message to a businessperson and transmit it via Internet, e-mail, or fax.

Cognitive Abilities	Activities
Business Management	Guest Day: Parents, relatives, friends, or businesspeople who have resided in other countries are invited to speak to the class. The guest speakers share information about specific management styles in other countries. Virtual World Travel: Students link with volunteers and service providers (e.g., the Peace Corps, Red Cross, military, or Salvation Army) around the world. Information is exchanged about dealing with diverse populations in various cultures/countries (e.g., use of nonverbal communication cues involving time, space, and dress, as well as cultural and business etiquette).
Basic Business	Diversity Logo: Students create a logo that expresses their ideas and feelings about diversity. This logo should be created on an 8-1/2 x 11" poster to be displayed in the classroom. Each student then writes a brief essay and prepares a short oral presentation.

	Service Project: Students undertake a service-related project designed to make a meaningful contribution to the health and welfare of diverse members of the community (e.g., design a park or community center to meet the needs of people of various age groups, with different physical capabilities, and/or from various socioeconomic groups).
Entrepreneurship	Access Plan: Students design the layout for a small business, making it fully accessible to people with disabilities—both customers and employees. Cultural Research: Students conduct research on a multiculturally owned company. Students search for the company address and compose a letter to the company explaining the research and asking for literature about the business. The students compile the information and give a presentation (possibly with a collage) about the company. Company representatives may also be present to answer any questions and talk about how they got started.
Travel and Hotel/Motel Management	Virtual Field Trip: Students research a vacation spot for a cultural experience. Given a travel budget, students are required to locate hotels and motels, restaurants, and sight-seeing locations; and present travel tips and information about other aspects of the trip related to diversity. Students present their findings to the class as if they were "selling the package" to a client. Down the Road: Students select an international landmark. They then plan a trip from their hometown to the landmark using preset criteria such as the most cost-effective route, most scenic route, or fastest route.
Student Organizations	**Activities**
FBLA/DECA/PBL	Community Diversity Panel: Students research a culture and develop questions about business and marketing strategies appropriate to that culture. Students invite community members of that culture to take part in a panel of diverse participants who will discuss international business and marketing strategies. Diversity Club: Students form a diversity club to promote unity and understanding through diversity education. Students start the club by writing about three commonly held cultural stereotypes. Each meeting highlights similarities and differences between U.S. culture and another culture. One objective of the diversity club is to debunk stereotypes.

Assessment Strategies

A change in activities to incorporate diversity necessitates a change in assessment strategies. Standard methods of assessment such as criterion-referenced quizzes and tests may be used. However, assessment alternatives noted by McEwen (1997) should also be included:

- Essay questions to elicit expression of thoughts and to encourage discussion
- Oral reports, sometimes in small groups, to enhance communication skills and allow for follow-up questions
- Portfolios, over a specific period, to give ample time to show progression of skills
- Videotaped performances enacted in the students' comfort zones (e.g., with peers in the media center or in a familiar business environment) to allow for self-evaluation
- Observations, individual or team, to facilitate real-world assessment processes
- Critical incident and other types of case studies to develop problem-solving and critical-thinking skills
- Peer evaluations to promote interaction
- Assessment centers, where students can select their peers for supporting roles while simulating a specific job scenario, to encourage peer interaction

To manage the diversity curriculum and assessment needs, it is important to keep these alternative strategies in mind:

- Grading: Do not put grades on everything a student does. Several presentations or writing samples can comprise a collection to be graded by peers, self, or teacher.
- Writing: Never grade the first draft. Have periodic draft reviews.
- Establishing criteria: Always develop clear criteria for grading. Discuss grading criteria with students.
- Self-evaluation: Have students check their own work. Provide answer sheets and have them find their own errors.
- Individual conferences: Initiate a short conference/conversation with each student once a week, if possible. Individual attention is good and allows the teacher to support students rather than always correcting them.
- Commendation to parents: Inform parents several times per year about at least one good thing their child has accomplished.
- Accentuate the positive: Focus on what students accomplish, not on what they fail to do.

Summary

Diversity sensibility involves more than simply becoming culturally aware (see Appendix A for a list of additional resources). Educators must adapt lesson plans and assessments to manage classroom diversity. Additionally, preservice, beginning, and veteran teachers can incorporate the following key factors into their planning for curricula and classroom experiences that are diversity sensitive:

- Develop a diversity knowledge base.
- Identify problems and issues that may need to be addressed.
- Guide diverse students by incorporating a variety of strategies.
- Serve as a facilitator and resource person rather than a lecturer and order-giver.
- Communicate high expectations for learning and behavior of students, regardless of the overall school culture.
- Create a workplace-like learning environment so students develop workplace skills in a diverse group.
- Require students to take much of the responsibility for their own learning.
- Individualize learning based on students' learning needs and styles, rather than being regulated by textbooks or rigid lesson plans.
- Use democratic instructional strategies such as role-playing/simulation, problem-solving exercises, and group discussion with students.
- Participate in professional development activities and/or enroll in classes that emphasize methods to teach diversity skills.

These factors enable a teacher to build skills in integrating diversity-sensitive activities in the classroom. As Josephs (2000) has commented,

> Teaching in the diverse classroom in a global economy means more than addressing issues of diversity or multiculturalism. We must be aware of how we treat our students, of how our students treat us, and of how our students treat each other. These kinds of issues span disciplines and professions. They are important in all classes, whether the format is lecture, discussion, or team projects. Each class, regardless of format or discipline, offers the opportunity to increase awareness of diversity and multicultural issues.

Business educators have an opportunity to assist their students in developing increased sensitivity to diversity among their peers. In providing classroom experiences that increase awareness of differences among students, educators also prepare students for the diverse workplace they will encounter later.

References

Banks, C., & Banks, J. (1997). Reforming schools in a democratic pluralistic society. *Educational Policy, 11*(2), 183–193.

Carbo, M. (1995). Educating everybody's children. In Cole, R. W. (Ed.), *Educating everybody's children: Diverse teaching strategies for diverse learners: What research and practice say about improving achievement* (pp. 1–7). Alexandria, VA: Association for Supervision and Curriculum Development.

Center for Research on Education, Diversity & Excellence. (1999). *Standards performance continuum: A rubric for observing classroom enactments of CREDE's standards for effective pedagogy.* Santa Cruz: University of California Santa Cruz. Retrieved October 13, 1999 from the World Wide Web: http://www.crede.ucsc.edu/HomePage/Standards/SPAC/SPAC.html

The Council for Exceptional Children. (2000). *How special education works!* Retrieved March 16, 2000 from the World Wide Web: http://www.cec.sped.org/nw/spedworks2.html

Drake, D. D. (1993). Student diversity: Implications for classroom teachers. *Clearing House, 66*(5), 264–266.

Heggy, P. (1999). Future resumes and diversity in the 21st century workplace. *Gonyea Career Marketing.* Retrieved December 9, 1999 from the World Wide Web: http://resumexpress.com/heggy.html

Josephs, S. L. (2000). *Teaching diversity.* Columbus, OH: The Ohio State University, Fisher College of Business. Retrieved January 20, 2000 from the World Wide Web: http://www.cob.ohio-state.edu/~diversity/teach.htm

King, M. (1998). Business poll stresses need for diversity education. *The Seattle Times.*

Loden, M., & Rosener, J. (1991). *Workforce America! Managing employee diversity as a vital resource.* Homewood, IL: Business One Irwin.

Macionis, J. C., & Plummer, K. (1996). *A sociological snapshot of our world.* Retrieved November 2, 2000 from the World Wide Web: http://www.hewett.norfolk.sch.uk/curric/soc/village.htm

McEwen, B. (1997). Teaching diversity and civility, Part 1. *Delta Pi Epsilon Instructional Strategies: An Applied Research Series, 13*(1), 3.

Morris, M. E. S., & Massie, P. (1998). *Cybercareers.* Mountain View, CA: Sun Microsystems, Inc.

National Center for Education Statistics. Washington, DC. Retrieved from the World Wide Web: http://nces.ed.gov

National Council for Accreditation of Teacher Education. (1982). *NCATE standards for the accreditation of teacher education.* Washington, DC: Author.

Policies Commission for Business and Economic Education. (1997). Policy Statement 50: This we believe about valuing cultural diversity in business education. In *National Business Education Association (NBEA) Policy Handbook.* Cincinnati, OH: South-Western Publishing Company.

Ramsey, P. G. (1987). *Teaching and learning in a diverse world.* New York: Teachers College Press.

Regional Institute for School Enhancement. (1996, January). *The teacher induction program bulletin (TIPS).* Kennesaw, GA: Kennesaw State University.

Ryan, K., & Cooper, J. M. (1997). *Those who can, teach* (6th ed.). Boston: Houghton Mifflin Company.

Secretary's Commission on Achieving Necessary Skills. (1991). *What work requires of schools.* Washington, DC: Author.

Thompson, H. B., & Thompson, G. H. (1996). Confronting diversity issues in the classroom with strategies to improve satisfaction and retention of international students. *Journal of Education for Business, 72*(1), 53–57.

Vawdrey, C. (1996). Principles of learning. In H. R. Perreault (Ed.), *Classroom strategies: The methodology of business education* (Yearbook No. 34, pp. 64–73). Reston, VA: National Business Education Association.

Warren, D. (1992). Teachers for the real world. *Education, 112*(3), 324–328.

Appendix A

PUBLICATIONS

- Banks, J., & Banks, C. (1989). *Multicultural education: Issues and perspectives.* Boston: Allyn and Bacon.
- Cole, R. W. (Ed.). (1995). *Educating everybody's children, diverse teaching strategies for diverse learners.* Alexandria, VA: Association for Supervision and Curriculum Development.
- Delpit, L. (1995). *Other people's children.* New York: The New Press.
- Tiedt, P. L., & Tiedt, I. M. (1995). *Multicultural teaching: A handbook of activities, information, and resources* (4th ed.). Needham Heights, MA: A Simon & Schuster Company, 40–41.

WEB SITES

- www.stolaf.edu/network/iecc/related-resources.html (Resources that promote connecting international classrooms via e-mail)
- www.cob.ohio-state.edu/~diversity/resource.htm (Bibliography list of writings addressing diversity issues related to various aspects of business, employment, and the classroom setting)
- www.rpcv.org/globaled (Newsletter by the National Peace Corps Association [NPCA]. Presents a brief description of fourteen projects)
- www.field-guides.com (Virtual field trips. Provides online field trips and allow students to discover the world. These sites have been arranged to build a story to follow with a series of "trail markers" that describe the site. Teacher's guides provide background.)
- www.diversitydtg.com/articles/diversity-web-resources.html (Compiled list of 20 favorite sites dealing with diversity by Calvin B. Ball III, senior associate with The Diversity Training Group. Selection was based on quality and breadth of information provided, ease of use, organization, and interest.)

Shaping the Elementary and Middle School Business Education Curriculum

Sharon A. Andelora
Upper Montclair, New Jersey

Business education is a natural for elementary and middle school learners: the curriculum is based in the "real" world of life and business, and therefore is intrinsically appealing—and it is hands-on, and therefore in keeping with the concrete operations stage of intellectual functioning that characterizes elementary and middle school learners (Sushkin, 2000).

Shaping the business education curriculum for these students involves

- Believing that studying business enhances students' work *and* life skills and that business education is as appropriate at the elementary as at the secondary level
- Choosing topics of study that enhance students' competence in five educational areas—basic skills, life skills, information technology skills, international business knowledge, and lifelong learning
- Planning a developmental approach (introduce, review/develop, reinforce, and master) to business education skills and content so that students are enticed and prepared to study business in greater depth as they advance in their education
- Working with professional colleagues and organizations, including community representatives such as business and education leaders, to determine and understand the mission, core content areas, and scope and sequence of the business education curriculum in its entirety in the community or school district
- Finding ways for students to use their newly developed business skills in venues inside and outside the school environment, so that other educators

and the community at-large see the relevance and importance of business education for all learners

This chapter explores the following questions: What is appropriate for business education at the elementary and middle school levels? How can business education best be managed as a unique part of elementary and middle schools? How should teachers address the more complex ethical issues that are by-products of the Information Age? What kind of planning is needed to design and implement a business education curriculum that is not only viable in itself but is also a valuable integrator of elementary and middle school academic content?

A Change in the American Dream

Perhaps more than ever before, business education is not only desirable but also necessary. Nearly everyone must earn a living, manage resources, and plan for the future. The new American dream has changed: some suggest that it involves not only owning a home but also owning a business. Others add that this dream must enhance their quality of life by making it possible for them to be self-supporting, more involved in their family or community life, and ultimately less stressed (Sapin, 2000).

The skill set required to achieve this lifestyle is becoming larger in scope and increasingly sophisticated. When business ventures fail, for example, generally it is because of lack of business acumen rather than lack of a good idea.

Today's students know and can do more with information technology than their parents, and sometimes more than even their older siblings. As a result, business education concepts formerly taught in secondary schools are commonly emerging as components of the elementary and middle school curricula. Parents and educators are realizing that as life and work become more complex and even overlap, the skills that may have been important only to those who wanted to succeed in business are even more appropriate for those who want to succeed in business and in life.

One Approach: Starting on "Home" Ground

Life and information technology skills offer a practical, relevant, and familiar starting point for introducing elementary and middle school students to business education. Many students have already used computers in their own or in friends' homes. Now that computers are more common, they are viewed as tools rather than as playthings. As tools, computers offer educators a mechanism that lets students appreciate how various business aspects are related to and impact one another.

Computers can also be a gateway to other business education concepts, such as career education, consumer education, personal finance, and entrepreneurship. For example, students can use computers to find consumer information and research potential business ideas, communicate that information for marketing purposes, schedule activities and appointments, develop budgets that show how increased costs of goods and services could affect the amount or kind of items a business produces, and create documents that connect a company to its customers. In some classes students design and create a product that they can sell. They learn about business functions by completing the project. Although this can be an introductory activity, students learn about project planning and development, budgeting skills, sales forecasts and reports, sales and advertising techniques, and profit and loss statements.

An example of an elementary and middle school curriculum consisting of keyboarding and information technology skills follows. When developing a curriculum for elementary and middle schools, it is important to weave the "introduce-review/develop-reinforce-master" thread throughout all grades in the school district. Appendix A offers a sample scope and sequence, and Appendix B presents an example of technology skills learning outcomes.

Keyboarding. Awareness of the importance of using proper keyboarding techniques should come first (sometimes as early as in the primary grades), followed by hands-on instruction whenever students possess the needed dexterity in their fingers (generally between third and fifth grades). Instructional content includes correct fingering, posture and technique, continuity practice, and word processing skills.

Scheduling regular class sessions (for this or any skill-based subject) is the most important factor in whether keyboarding is taught effectively, i.e., in such a way that students retain the skill from session to session with minimal backsliding. One-day-per-week sessions are better than none; however, this schedule can be counterproductive because it offers too little time for reinforcement.

Once students have learned the basics, it is important to create opportunities for them to practice and thereby retain their skills. For example, students can do periodic timed writings, review their posture and keyboarding techniques, and complete skill-building exercises from time to time. Too often students learn correct keyboarding techniques but lack the follow-up instruction that would prevent them from reverting to the hunt-and-peck method they used prior to the keyboarding course. Students should be held accountable for good keyboarding skills during any computer course they take.

Computer applications. Word processing courses offer a perfect opportunity for students to practice correct keyboarding skills and simultaneously learn computer application software. It is not only what students keyboard, but also how they keyboard that should be reinforced by the teacher. For example, once students learn formatting skills, the instructor can stress the need to keyboard and format correctly, and apprise other teachers of students' growing competence, so that students can continue to practice their skills when completing assignments for other courses.

Depending on how much time is available and how much emphasis is placed on computer applications in the business education curriculum, elementary or middle school students may be taught how to use the Internet for research and communication and/or how to create databases, spreadsheets, electronic media presentations, and Web pages. Students may also learn to draw and paint on the computer using computer graphics and to desktop publish, perhaps creating their own class or school newsletters and posters.

No matter which applications are taught, content should be relevant to students' experiences. Students tend to learn more when they see a need.

Cyber Ethics: Not for Technology Classes Only

The Digital Age brings ethical issues more complicated than the "simple" ones of copying homework or cheating on paper-and-pencil tests. Teaching cyber ethics involves the basics, such as instructing students to respect each other's work and not to copy or destroy other students' computer files (see Table 1). There are also issues involving intellectual property copyrights and software program piracy (which may seem like nonissues to students who have grown accustomed to copying music from Internet sites such as Napster). Then there are safety and privacy issues such as filtering (allowing only "approved" sites to be accessed from the Internet connection. There are also questions, such as whether filtering should be nationally mandated for schools receiving federal technology money or E-rate discounts, and whether and to what degree students should be "sheltered" from Internet access in schools.

When using systems with less intrusive forms of sheltering, such as filtered search engines and "safe harbors," *tech·LEARNING* e-zine recommends the following caveats for teachers (Crystal, Geide, & Salpeter, 2000):

- Work with faculty and school administrators to set standards for acceptable use.
- Make good, clearly defined, product-based assignments.
- Be clear with students about policies and consequences.
- Think carefully about room and computer setup.
- Provide education to interested parents.
- Inform students of safety practices such as not giving out personal information about themselves or where they live, and not arranging to meet someone they have met over the Internet.
- Institute safety practices among faculty. For example, student photos should be posted without names, or photos should be used only on protected Internet sites, and the school Web site should be password-protected and only first names should be used in bylines.

Role-playing is an effective way to teach ethics. Students can create different scenarios and discuss how they would handle them. Teachers and students can bring in news articles about cyber ethics issues and discuss how they would have handled the matter described.

Table 1. The Ten Commandments of Computer Ethics

These commandments should be adapted to the grade level being taught and posted in a prominent place.

  I. Thou shalt not use a computer to harm other people.
 II. Thou shalt not interfere with other people's computer work.
III. Thou shalt not snoop around in other people's computer files.
 IV. Thou shalt not use a computer to steal.
  V. Thou shalt not use a computer to bear false witness.
 VI. Thou shalt not copy or use proprietary software for which you have not paid.
VII. Thou shalt not use other people's computer resources without authorization or proper compensation.
VIII. Thou shalt not appropriate other people's intellectual output.
 IX. Thou shalt consider the social consequences of the program you are writing or the system you are designing.
  X. Thou shalt always use a computer in ways that ensure consideration and respect for your fellow humans.

Note. From "Ten Commandments for Computer Ethics," by R. C. Barquin, 1991. Retrieved from the World Wide Web: http://www.brook.edu/its/cei/cei_hp.htm. Copyright 1991 by the Computer Ethics Institute, 1815 H Street, N.W., Suite 1100, Washington, DC 20006, rbarquin@aol.com. Reprinted with permission.

Articulation of Business Course Content

Because business education topics are appropriate for elementary through postsecondary students, instructors must strive to avoid the major pitfall of duplicating course work. When subject matter is repetitious, students become bored and uninterested. Students should learn the basics and then reinforce their knowledge to a higher degree by taking courses that build on previous learning by introducing related, more advanced content.

Teachers can avoid duplicating course content in two ways:

- Teachers can pretest students to determine what they know and to find a suitable starting point that takes into consideration their prior experience.
- In the community teachers can work with professional colleagues, organizations, and business and education leaders to determine and define the mission, core content areas, and scope and sequence of the business education curriculum in its entirety (from the elementary to postsecondary

level). Consensus should be sought on which skills and objectives are appropriate for each grade level, and they should be clear enough to eliminate potential redundancy in content.

Articulation committee. Articulating curriculum expectations is important—not only in business education, but in all subjects (Wall, 1996). Articulation committees can be local (single school) or districtwide. When business education is taught in more than one district school, it is essential to create an articulation committee that includes representatives from each school. This committee should meet several times a year to discuss curriculum, set standards, and establish goals and objectives for business education classes.

It is important to begin with the big picture and craft a mission statement that articulates the focus, purposes, content, skills, and outcomes of the business education curriculum and marries these aspects to national, regional, and/or local school reform goals. Synergy can be created by dovetailing business education goals with existing academic curricula, and then determining the most effective way to achieve those goals. Strategic business-education partnerships can be formed that match an educational need (for example, experience in using databases) with a legitimate business need (surveying and compiling results of a marketing questionnaire). The next step is to establish benchmarks, evaluation mechanisms, and public relations devices that can measure progress and celebrate achievement.

This is a huge and potentially intimidating undertaking, so a reasonable timeline—perhaps spanning several years—is necessary to achieve desired results. Committees should be integrated horizontally (i.e., districtwide) and vertically (including teachers at all grade levels). Both are important for systemic change and to ensure that course content is deepened rather than duplicated. It is essential to build on small successes, working together to establish goals and objectives for various grade levels (see Appendix B).

The *National Standards for Business Education* include guidelines for quality in 12 curricular areas of business education at all levels (National Business Education Association, 1995). Although the standards do not mandate a specific curriculum, they do state what all students in grades K–14 should know and be able to do in business.

A subcommittee can be created to mark progress and handle administrative issues associated with curriculum, such as

- Matching schools and businesses in strategic partnerships or tapping into already-existing School-to-Career networks
- Creating professional development and continuing education opportunities for business teachers to address topics such as classroom management,

dealing with diversity, and upgrading technology skills

- Accessing resources from professional organizations and regional and national conferences such as the National Educational Computing Conference
- Positioning teachers as professional speakers at conferences and as experts about what works at various grade levels
- Making mentoring relationships available, especially to those individuals who have left the business world to create a second career as a teacher, and for those who may have taught high school business education but who are new to elementary or middle school classrooms
- Seeking projects that offer students opportunities to solve real-world business problems in the community
- Advising staff on current technology issues such as filtering, cyber crime, and computer virus protection
- Forming or providing teachers access to computer user groups
- Organizing districtwide business education days, technology and computer fairs, and similar events to showcase business education in the community

Certification at the elementary and middle school levels. The majority of states allow a certified business educator to teach at any grade level, but courses must be identified as business education courses. However, some certified business education teachers are restricted to teaching business education at the secondary level, designated as grades 7 through 12, and some certified middle school business educators have added a K–8 certification to their credentials, which allows them to teach a variety of courses in addition to business education.

Administrators welcome dual certification because it offers flexibility in teacher placement; however, dual certification may take the business teacher out of the business education classroom. A teacher who wants to teach only business education courses may consider forgoing dual certification.

Some school districts may see the value of including business education in the elementary or middle school curriculum but lack the resources or certified teachers to do so. To help solve this problem, business educators can mentor in schools that want these courses, participate in school-to-school partnerships, or initiate districtwide special-topic networking events for teachers.

Management of elementary and middle school classrooms. Structure and organization are the keys to success in classroom management, particularly in elementary and middle schools. Business educators set the standards and expectations for leadership, cooperation (team building), self-discipline, and other proactive work behaviors. Business educators also model these standards.

Issues such as organizing the physical space, establishing class routines, respecting the classroom and the equipment, and conducting oneself in a professional manner are critical to creating a functional and pleasant classroom. Guidelines should be posted to remind students of the behavior that is expected. It is also a good idea to rehearse routines with students and give them the opportunity to solve potential administrative and technical problems.

Table 2 lists tips for organizing a productive classroom environment. Chapter 13 of this *Yearbook* includes a more detailed discussion of exemplary classroom management strategies.

Extending Learning With Extracurricular Activities

Gaining community support for including business education in the elementary and middle school curricula is generally easier if teachers find ways to promote and celebrate their students' successes. The following extracurricular activities are ideal for showcasing students' competence.

- **School newspaper.** Skills: keyboarding, word processing, and desktop publishing. The school newspaper is a useful learning experience in and of itself, but it is also an effective marketing tool that can be used to inform the local board of education, parent groups, and other community members of school accomplishments.
- **School yearbook.** Skills: computer use, fact gathering, composition, publication design. Older students can make this a fund-raising project, thereby putting into practice what they have learned about entrepreneurship, marketing, finance, etc.
- **Competitions with students in other schools.** Skills: Varied. National student organizations such as FBLA-PBL enable students in grades 7 through 12 to compete locally and nationally in various activities such as keyboarding proficiency contests. The Partnership for America's Future (http://www.pafinc.com) integrates science and technology with business skills through its National Gallery for America's Young Inventors. The program lets students use their education now to solve real-world business and education problems for financial reward.
- **Computer and/or Web page clubs.** Skills: computer programming, design, electronic communication. Students can design, create, and maintain their school's Web page.
- **Schoolwide enterprises.** Skills: introductory business and/or marketing functions such as promotion, inventory control, etc.; computer skills; desktop publishing; and accounting. Students can staff, manage, and promote enterprises such as school supply stores and drama clubs.
- **Mock investment clubs.** Skills: personal finance, consumer education. Students can create fictional stock and bond portfolios and track their earnings (or losses) in the market.

Table 2. Organizing Elementary and Middle School Business Education Classrooms

Students in elementary and middle schools need as much guidance as possible in organizing themselves and their work. It is important for students to see the classroom as an organized place to work—one that is representative of the real world workplace, neat and clean without clutter.

- To avoid tripping over book bags around desks, students should store their bags on wall shelves. If shelves are nonexistent, a storage place within the room should be designated that does not block the exit or create traffic problems.

- It is a good idea to have students use a pocket folder for storing class assignments (if work folders are stored in the room, color-coding the folders by class will make it easier for students to find them). Students should place a pen or pencil in one of the folder pockets for use throughout the class period. If students use diskettes or CD-ROMs, they can place these in a second folder pocket, making them readily available for saving their work.

- As students complete their assignments, they should record their progress on a calendar or a checklist (also in their folder) and use the folder to hold printouts. Folders should be stored in a convenient spot, preferably in a file cabinet or storage box. Each drawer or box should be labeled with the class name. All folders and materials should be put away before students are dismissed from class.

- When outside resource materials are used in the classroom, they should be displayed in a place where students who need to access them will not disturb other students.

- Elementary and some middle school students are used to being dismissed from class by row number. This helps avoid congestion at the door, particularly as the next class tries to enter.

- To reinforce respect for the classroom and equipment, students should be instructed not to write on the desks or leave papers on the floor, and to put everything (such as chairs and software disks) in its place. It may be helpful to designate certain students in each class as equipment "proprietors," responsible for care and maintenance.

- It is critical to have a plan for enforcing classroom rules and to make sure students understand the consequences of failing to abide by them. Clarifying rules and consequences avoids the misunderstandings that arise when students are unaware of teacher expectations.

- Even the process of getting organized carries an opportunity for career education. For instance, many people have made careers out of organizing people and offices. (See Hemphill's *Taming the Paper Tiger: Organizing the Paper in Your Life*, and other such resources for information and examples of "personal assistant" careers.)

The Future of Business Education in Elementary and Middle Schools

Change is a fact of life, and the business education curriculum has been continually reshaped to meet business and industry needs (Hames, 1998). Surveying area schools and their business education offerings may provide information to help sell the idea of making business education part of the elementary and middle school curricula, if this is not already the case.

Business educators must be advocates for and practitioners of lifelong learning, continually upgrading their skills. Students are acquiring advanced technology skills at an increasingly early age. When shaping a curriculum that appears to evolve at lightning-speed, teachers may find it useful to follow the example of industries such as medical equipment manufacturing: to think in terms of overall mission, strategic partnerships, and core business functions. Resources should be used fluidly. It is also a good idea to build the "product"—curriculum—with modular components that can be retooled and reconfigured at will—and to be flexible, not to just teach the tools, but use the tools to teach.

References

Barquin, R. C. (2000). *Ten commandments for computer ethics.* Washington, DC: Computer Ethics Institute: The Brookings Institution. Retrieved from the World Wide Web: http://www.brook.edu/its/cei/cei_hp.htm

Crystal, J., Geide, C.A., & Salpeter, J. (2000, November 11). The concerned educator's guide to safety and cyber-ethics. *tech·LEARNING.* Retrieved December 1, 2000 from the World Wide Web: http://www.techlearning.com/db_area/archives/TL/112000/cyberethics.htm

Hames, R. (1998). *Integrating the Internet into the business education program.* Lawrenceville, GA: Author. Retrieved November 29, 2000 from the World Wide Web: http://www.crews.org/media_tech/compsci/pospaper.htm

Hemphill, B. (1992). *Taming the paper tiger: Organizing the paper in your life.* Washington, DC: Kiplinger Books.

National Business Education Association. (1995). *National standards for business education: What America's students should know and be able to do in business.* Reston, VA: Author.

National Educational Computing Conference. National Educational Computing Association. Retrieved from the World Wide Web: www.neccsite.org

Partnership for America's Future Inc. (2000). Akron, OH: Author. Retrieved from the World Wide Web: http://www.pafinc.com

Sapin, B. (2000, December 2). Discussion on entrepreneurship. Netwalkers meeting, Silver Spring, Maryland.

Sushkin, N. (2000). *Development theories.* Retrieved from the World Wide Web: http://www.wpi.edu/~isg_501/nsushkin.html

Wall, T. J. (1996, August). The computer: A tool for all subjects. *Curriculum Administrator*, pp. 54–55.

Appendix A. Keyboarding and Computer Applications Scope and Sequence for Grades 5–8

Content and Skills	Grade 5	Grade 6	Grade 7	Grade 8
Proper Techniques at the Computer	Review and reinforce concepts and skills.	Review and reinforce concepts and skills.	Review and reinforce concepts and skills.	Review and reinforce concepts and skills.
Computer Components	Introduce and review mechanical and functional components.	Review and reinforce concepts and skills.	Review and reinforce concepts and skills.	Review and reinforce concepts and skills.
Keyboarding	Present correct fingering (touch) system.	Review and reinforce concepts and skills.	Review and reinforce concepts and skills.	Review and reinforce concepts and skills.
	Conduct continuity practice, one-minute writings, class assignments, etc.	Conduct continuity practice, one-minute writings, class assignments, etc.	Conduct continuity practice, one-minute writings, class assignments, etc.	Conduct continuity practice, one-minute writings, class assignments, etc.
Word Processing	Introduce word processing concepts.	Review and reinforce concepts and extend skills to include producing	Review and reinforce concepts and extend skills to include producing	Review and reinforce concepts and extend skills to include producing an original research paper.
	Extend word processing practice to include • Themes • Reports	• Title pages • Bibliographies • Book reviews • Class notes • Outlines • Tables	• Reports with footnotes and bibliographies • Letters and envelopes • Graphics	
Databases			Introduce concepts .	Review and reinforce concepts and skills.
Spreadsheets				Introduce concepts.

Desktop Publishing		Introduce concepts.	Review and reinforce concepts and skills.
Telecommunications	Introduce concepts.	Review and reinforce concepts and skills.	Review and reinforce concepts and skills.
Presentations	Introduce concepts.		Introduce concepts.

Note: The curriculum is updated yearly to add more advanced concepts as students progress.

Appendix B. Student Technology Skills Learning Outcomes

Content and Skills	Grade 4	Grade 8	Grade 12
Use of Equipment	Develop an awareness of the proper use of equipment.	Demonstrate the proper use of hardware and software.	Assume responsibility for the proper use of equipment and resources.
Keyboarding	Develop an awareness of touch keyboarding.	Demonstrate touch keyboarding.	Maintain keyboarding proficiency.
Basic Operations	Recognize peripheral devices, access CD-ROMs, select and access programs from screen, output to a printer.	Reinforce operational skills and utilize available technology sources for research projects.	Continue to develop operational skills using research projects and learning activities.
Word Processing/Desktop Publishing	Create, edit, format, print, and save a document.	Enhance word processing documents in content areas through the use of advanced features.	Utilize word processing/desktop publishing skills in content areas.
Databases/Spreadsheets	Access data using a search and utilize a spreadsheet to view data.	Demonstrate database, spreadsheet, and graphing skills in content areas.	Employ database, spreadsheet, and graphing skills in content areas.
Multimedia Presentations	Use technology to create a project.	Create a multimedia presentation in content areas.	Design an interdisciplinary multimedia presentation.
Telecommunications	Access online information.	Work independently with online sources.	Apply global resources to learning activities.
Critical Thinking	Make appropriate choices of data in content areas.	Use appropriate selections of data and information in content areas.	Retrieve logical and appropriate choices of data for content areas.
Career and Technological Issues	Associate careers with technology and develop respect for technology.	Recognize the impact of technology on various occupations and explore ethical issues.	Explore career choices in technology and related proficiencies. Probe ethical and acceptable uses of technology.

Source: Pascack Valley Regional School District, K–12 Computer/Technology Articulation Committee in Montvale, New Jersey.

Managing the Learning Process for Postsecondary and Collegiate Business Education Students

Betty A. Kleen
Nicholls State University
Thibodaux, Louisiana

Never before have so many options existed to open the postsecondary/ collegiate learning process to so many students. Although the number one choice of the traditional college-age student remains a classroom setting with traditional teaching, the number of courses using nontraditional instructional methods is increasing each year (Neal, 1999). How the instructor manages the learning process plays a critical part in facilitating student accomplishment of objectives and mastery of course content, no matter what delivery method is selected.

Today's students are challenged to take responsibility for their own learning. To assist them, instructors must be effective facilitators of learning in any course delivery method. Business educators must keep the focus on the learners while developing a rigorous curriculum with relevant standards. Selecting materials and content, interacting with learners, and evaluating student progress are all key components that must be addressed in any course.

Postsecondary and collegiate institutions are using delivery methods such as self-paced learning in a traditional setting, traditional courses in nontraditional time frames, and courses or programs via business/community initiatives. Distance education courses are most often taught using Web-based, two-way audio-video, or videotaped instruction. Two- and four-year institutions alike are embracing distance education as a means of attracting students who do not have the time or the interest or are too geographically removed to enroll in a traditional course. These various delivery methods provide more flexibility for adults who want to earn a degree or receive training or retraining for a career.

Business educators must take an active part in identifying particular courses that can be offered using selected delivery methods. An effective combination of delivery methods will contribute to keeping business programs viable in the 21st century. Business educators should actively explore each of the methods included in this chapter.

Self-Paced Instruction in Traditional Classrooms

The traditional classroom with face-to-face instruction remains a dominant delivery method in most postsecondary/collegiate institutions. Large numbers of students under the age of 25 continue to prefer traditional on-campus courses conducted during the day and evening hours. For many students the social structure of the college or university, which provides interaction with their peers and faculty on a daily basis, is an important part of their learning experience.

Self-paced learning as a process in the traditional classroom is not new. Instructors can successfully employ a self-paced approach to learning in a variety of business courses. A self-paced approach can result in increased student satisfaction if managed well; this type of learning appeals to many adults. Any instructor who has ever attempted to keep an entire class together while working through software learning exercises has quickly realized that many in the class are frustrated with the pace. For some, it is too fast; for others, it is too slow. For adult students strongly focused on achieving course objectives and competencies, being able to work at their own pace may allow them to feel more in control of their learning.

Computer skills courses are examples of key courses for which self-paced learning can be used successfully. Self-paced learning is not necessarily appropriate for courses in which significant amounts of content need to be presented to all students simultaneously or in courses that use case studies, group projects, and a great deal of collaborative work.

Key challenges remain in managing the self-paced learning process successfully. Business educators teaching a self-paced course in a traditional classroom environment must address the following details.

- **Planning the course.** The entire course should be planned in detail prior to the first day of class. This includes such points as basic content and objectives, all exercises for class and homework activities, dates evaluations will be conducted, types of evaluations, quantity and quality requirements for various grades, and management procedures for student assignments and evaluations.
- **Informing students of deadlines.** A calendar suggesting satisfactory progression points and testing dates should be available on the first day of class. Adult learners like to be able to plan ahead. A calendar with the entire

term's deadlines can help them do this more effectively and may help lessen their stress levels.

- **Collecting student work and providing feedback.** Provisions must be established for organized receipt of electronic or paper-based work from students. These procedures should facilitate instructor monitoring of student progress and timely feedback to students. These procedures must be established on the first day of class.
- **Tracking student progress.** The instructor's record-keeping routines become crucial in a self-paced course. Adult learners often are very grade conscious. Being able to confirm that their individual progress records match the instructor's records is important to them.
- **Providing assistance to learners.** The instructor must be well versed in the content and/or tasks each student is working on during each part of the course. This means knowing where each student is in relation to the course content and objectives and being well prepared to provide effective assistance to individual learners.

With careful attention to management of the learning process, self-paced learning can be conducted within the traditional classroom environment, allowing students more individual control over their learning. Business educators who have facilitated self-paced learning recognize that the points presented in the previous list also apply to managing the learning process in a traditional paper-based correspondence course or a Web-based distance education course.

Distance Education

Distance education courses are growing in popularity each year. Neal (1999) wrote that the over-25 age group currently makes up the vast majority of students in distance learning programs. Matthews (1999) reported that 66 percent of the adult distance education market is female, and 80 percent of those women have children. Distance education offers numerous options. Discussion in this chapter focuses on three technological delivery methods: Web-based courses, simultaneous two-way audio-video instruction to students in geographically distant classrooms, and videotaped courses.

Western Governors University is probably the most widely publicized "virtual" university in the United States (Neal, 1999; Matthews, 1999). The Open University in England has also expanded vigorously on the Internet. Both the Open University and Western Governors use television, video and audiotape, videoconferencing, satellite broadcasts, and e-mail, as well as Web-based courses. While these "virtual" universities offer complete degree programs through electronic delivery of instruction, many traditional "brick-and-mortar" universities are systematically adding distance education courses to their traditional classroom offerings. Whatever the desired course, a student can typically find a distance education version of it through at least one university.

A few examples of schools offering various business education, office systems, and other business-related courses online are provided in Table 1.

Table 1. Sample of the National Association for Business Teacher Education (NABTE) Institutions Offering Distance Education Courses

Institution	Types of Courses	Method of Delivery
Black Hills State University	Undergraduate business methods and general business classes, graduate education courses	Web-based through WebCT
Colorado State University	Undergraduate business methods, graduate courses in vocational business	Web-based modules, threaded discussion chats, videotapes
Emporia State University	Various undergraduate and graduate business education courses	Web-based through Web in a Box or WebCT
Minot State University	Undergraduate and graduate information systems (software tools, programming, etc.) courses	Web-based through WebCT
Northwest Missouri State University	Various business education, office systems, and business administration courses	Web-enhanced and Web-based
Southeastern Oklahoma State University	Various leadership and business communication courses	Web-based through WebCT or Blackboard
SUNY Oswego	Undergraduate vocational education courses	Web-based

Note. From "Distance Education Courses for Business Teacher Education Programs Provided by NABTE Institutions," by D. LaBonty, 2000. Retrieved September 8, 2000 from the World Wide Web: http://grumpy.usu.edu/~labonty/nabte/webnabte/wpages/INDEX.HTM. Adapted with permission.

More specific information on online business education courses can be obtained by visiting an individual school's Web site, which often has a distance education or online classes link from the home page. While access to specific course materials is typically restricted to registered students, course titles and descriptions are usually accessible. Additionally, online course offerings on a regional basis may be found through such organizations as the Southern Regional Education Board's Electronic Campus (www.electroniccampus.org) or Governors State University (www.govst.edu).

Distance education changes the competitive environment in higher education, although conflicts remain between traditional principles of statewide coordination and those of competition. Johnson (1999) has identified distance education models in various states in his 1999 *NBEA Yearbook* chapter, "Distance Education: Learning in the 21st Century." Epper's (1997) comparative case study of statewide policies examined distance education in Minnesota, Maine, and Colorado. She concluded that coordination and competition can and must coexist, that careful consideration of the economic and organizational decisions needed is crucial to success, and that institutions and states are responding to new market demands.

"This We Believe About Distance Learning in Business Education," Policy Statement No. 65 from the Policies Commission for Business and Economic Education (PCBEE) (1999), included the following statement:

> Business educators should assume the responsibility for determining appropriate uses of distance learning to enhance program quality and facilitate learning. The competitive marketplace impels business educators to devise programs and offerings that attract learners while maintaining the quality and integrity of those programs. (p. 26)

In relation to distance education programs, Okula (1999) has further noted, "As the technology continues to improve, demand will continue to increase, and a better educated workforce will emerge" (p. 10).

Well-planned and well-presented distance education can be meaningful and interesting, while curriculum, course content, and quality standards are maintained. Distance education presents institutions with an opportunity to make postsecondary education more learner centered and possibly more cost effective as well.

Web-based instruction. One of the most recent growth areas in distance education is Web-based instruction at the postsecondary/collegiate level. Today two- and four-year colleges and universities, both public and private, as well as proprietary business schools, offer Web-based courses in many areas of business studies. These courses range from freshman-level courses in computer applications to graduate-level course work for education or business master's degrees. For example, Black Hills State University, Colorado State University, and Emporia State University offer both undergraduate and graduate courses in business education (see Table 1).

Business educators must maintain an active role when their institutions move into Web-based instruction to help ensure that their programs remain viable. The PCBEE has further identified the role business educators must play: "The role of business educators is to facilitate online learning by setting expectations, planning educational experiences, selecting materials, interacting with learners, and evaluating student progress by electronic mail or the World Wide Web" (Policies Commission for Business and Economic Education, 1997, p. 17).

Ryan (1997) has identified several issues relevant to a Web-based delivery system. These issues include desktop ergonomics, the criticality of testing to ensure skill/concept retention, the most effective use of media to deliver the training, the effect of the delivery system on the retention of content, and whether newer delivery systems affect users' ability to learn.

Adults of all ages enroll in Web-based courses. Students often sign up after being enticed by the prospect of not having to attend scheduled classes. Many times these students are not self-directed enough to meet all the demands of the course. Managing the learning process in a way that helps motivate students becomes a critical element of successful Web-based teaching. The very nature of Web-based instruction—time and place independence—may make it more challenging to engage students positively in the learning process. According to PCBEE Policy Statement No. 65 (1999), "Distance learning will require a change in the interaction between instructors and learners and will place greater demands on their time" (p. 26).

Numerous issues thus arise related to managing the learning process in a Web-based course. A typical assessment of instructors involved in Web-based instruction brings to light the extra preparation and training time needed to master the technology being used. Some type of training is typically necessary whether an instructor prepares and maintains his or her own Web pages or uses a commercial course management system such as WebCT, Web in a Box, or Blackboard. These software systems provide tools for communication and online testing and grading and an online architecture for conveying instructional content.

To manage the learning process effectively in a Web-based course, business educators must address the following issues, some of which are similar to those involved in self-paced instruction.

- **Designing the Web pages.** Web page hyperlinks (or documents posted using a course management software program) must be user-friendly. They should be designed to facilitate easy access to any materials a student needs to read and/or complete. Students should not feel that they are trying to make their way through a maze as they search for materials. Managing the learning materials can also involve legal and ethical issues. Copyright violations must not occur, and rights to ownership of materials must be addressed.
- **Planning.** Preparing a detailed online course syllabus is essential. While this online syllabus is typically very similar to a syllabus distributed in the

traditional classroom, additional management details may be necessary for the Web-based student.

- **Holding orientation meetings at the beginning of the term.** An orientation meeting should address the course description, objectives, and mechanical requirements. Additional issues such as instructional materials, assignments, deadlines, and test dates can be covered in the introductory session (Cooper, 1999). The institution may need to address technical or navigational training needs of students who wish to enroll in Web-based courses.
- **Planning and scheduling assessments.** Some Web-based courses include online testing. Others may require students to come to campus a few times during the term to complete tests or other key assessments. Students must know which option will be used when they sign up for the course.
- **Maintaining electronic materials.** The instructor must be timely in posting all materials for the course. Keeping the Web site up-to-date is imperative because students can access the site and work 24-hours-a-day, 7-days-a-week. Monitoring links to other Web sites is also important, as a link can disappear overnight.
- **Interacting with learners.** E-mail offers a convenient way for an instructor to communicate one-on-one with students. E-mail should be read and responded to in a timely manner. Frequently, instructors report heavy use of e-mail by Web-based students. This means more time will be needed to respond to these students. The communication time required to interact with 25 Web-based students on an individual basis is greater than comparable communication with 50 students in a traditional classroom. Timely feedback is important to the distance education student, and additional communication channels may be desirable to allow student exchanges with the entire class.
- **Maintaining grade books.** Grade books for a course can be maintained online. Course management software offers an easy way for faculty members to maintain grading records. Thus an individual student's current grade status can be available 24-hours-a-day, 7-days-a-week.
- **Establishing clear work submission procedures.** No school makes every software package available to faculty members. Web-based courses should specify appropriate submission methods and hold students accountable for meeting the requirements. Many schools identify standard hardware and software capabilities that students need for Web-based instruction and publish that information.
- **Establishing listservs or class electronic bulletin boards.** Listservs and electronic bulletin boards allow the instructor and all members of the class to share ideas, comments, and questions. If a specific class discussion exercise is desired, the instructor can simply post the discussion issue for students to address. Students and faculty can then monitor the discussion threads and contribute comments, ideas, and questions.
- **Establishing a chat room.** Private, course-specific chat rooms can be integrated with certain assignments to guarantee some interaction with other students enrolled in the class. Faculty often set a specific time each week

when they will be logged into the chat room. The instructor then blocks this time much as he or she would a traditional class meeting time so that other duties do not interfere. When the instructor distributes each week's discussion topics and related questions in advance, students can prepare for the discussion prior to logging into the chat room. Students can be required to participate in these scheduled chat room meetings a certain number of times during the term.

- **Conducting evaluations of Web-based courses.** Conducting a brief survey of student satisfaction with progress in the course at midterm can keep the instructor focused on continuous improvement of the course. A longer, mailed survey can be distributed at the end of the course (Cooper, 1999). Instructors can also develop and use HTML forms to collect data from their students and receive feedback on course materials, teaching style, and student progress (Hazari and Schnorr, 1999).

Schools often require the review of a Web-based course by a campuswide curriculum committee prior to listing the course as an official school offering, even though the same course taught in a traditional manner may have been approved previously. This review is done to help ensure the quality of the course and the commitment to maintaining the rigor and quality standards of the institution. With careful attention to managing the learning process, a business educator can present a Web-based course that maintains quality and offers the best of "anytime" education.

Two-way audio-video (compressed video) instruction. Two-way audio-video (compressed video) distance education provides students with a classroom teacher during the sessions, although that teacher may be hundreds of miles away. The faculty member typically teaches in a traditional classroom with special equipment to facilitate two-way hookups with remote sites. Although there are numerous motivational challenges facing the instructor, distance education students can succeed in such an environment.

Cutshall and Waltz (1997) reported on Vincennes University's two-way audio-video presentation of an introduction to business course. Analysis of end-of-term achievement showed that distance audiences performed better than the group of traditional on-campus students did. The course was presented via distance education to a group of employees at their work site and to a group of high school seniors at another distance site. The authors noted, "This success is most likely due to the added motivation of the students to succeed as indicated by their commitment to taking a class via nontraditional instructional techniques" (p. 20). Both distance groups appeared to adapt well to the technology.

Two-way audio-video (compressed video) education can work very effectively for various business courses including selected accounting, finance, economics, marketing, management, information technology, and office systems courses. The most dynamic, effective teachers should be chosen for these teaching assignments.

Instructors teaching such courses often go through training sessions to help them to be effective in this type of classroom environment. The training typically includes presentation skills appropriate for the camera, appearance, and mastery of equipment operation, as well as actual practice tapings that can be critiqued.

Effective management of the learning process in a two-way audio-video course should address the following issues:

- **Controlling equipment in the classroom.** The instructor needs to be able to control all equipment at a single control panel. An alternative to this approach is to provide a technology assistant during the entire session to handle such things as local and distant cameras and projection of class materials including computer graphics.
- **Acclimating students to the technology.** Students will need some time to master activating microphones, looking at cameras, and other routines unique to two-way audio-video instruction. Cutshall and Waltz (1997) have noted that this orientation is typically completed during the first class session.
- **Providing instructors/facilitators at remote sites.** Schools usually arrange to have someone on-site at each remote location to monitor equipment connections, distribute materials at the appropriate time, proctor tests, and address any classroom management concerns. These individuals often have some familiarity with course content.
- **Providing backup plans.** Technology problems occur. But with careful backup provisions, loss of connection with the remote site becomes the only technical reason to dismiss a session.
- **Collecting and returning student work.** Beginning the first week, clear-cut procedures should be established for distance students to submit assignments and to obtain feedback from the instructor.
- **Communicating effectively with students.** To manage the learning process effectively, e-mail and telephone consultation times must be adhered to for distance education students. While a campus student can physically come to an instructor's office, distance students do not have this option. With e-mail, voice mail, and Web-based chat rooms, contact can be effective.
- **Focusing on content and delivery.** Nelson (2000) has suggested 13 specific techniques related to content and delivery. Her suggestions include such things as providing a detailed syllabus, distributing assignments early to help students organize their time, maintaining consistency in class organization, establishing and displaying clear-cut objectives for each session, discussing the most important content early in each class session, using effective graphic aids, summarizing the lesson before closing the session, and allowing time for students to ask questions.

- **Involving students from all sites during the class session.** When the teacher focuses too much eye contact on the local class, it can contribute to an isolation effect in the remote sites. Use of seating charts allows an instructor to call on an individual student at any site when questioning techniques are being used. This procedure contributes to a feeling of involvement in the class.
- **Changing activities frequently throughout the session.** Cycles of 10–15 minutes of lecture, followed by some type of activity involving student teams with related class discussion, can go a long way toward maintaining student enthusiasm. Students often find it difficult to focus intently on monitors or screens for extensive periods of time.
- **Planning effective visuals.** Visuals that are simple in design, contain a minimum number of words on a slide, incorporate uppercase and lowercase letters for ease of reading, and appear in a sans serif typeface are best for two-way audio-video courses. These basic principles of computer slide show design are doubly important when distance students rely on monitors or projection screens as their only view of the materials.
- **Teaching sessions at the various remote sites.** By teaching at least one class session from each distance site, if equipment capabilities and travel funds make it feasible, an instructor can establish a higher level of rapport with remote site students. In this manner, the on-campus students also get to experience being at a remote site.

Addressing all of these issues will go a long way toward facilitating the learning process, not only for students at the remote sites but also for students in the traditional classroom.

Videotaped (one-way audio-video) instruction. Videotaping an entire course taught by an excellent, dynamic faculty member can allow a school to provide a videotaped course in future semesters. Videotaping may also allow a school to offer the course every semester, even if only a small number of students enroll. Some learners especially like being able to play and watch a tape more than once to help them understand the content of the materials being presented or observe demonstrations included in the taped class sessions.

When a videotaped course is prepared, it must be checked frequently to make certain that the content is up-to-date. While a human resources class on videotape may be usable for several semesters, a videotaped computer information systems course will have a shorter useful shelf life.

Some of the key issues listed in the sections discussing other delivery methods can also apply to videotaped courses. More specifically, business educators must address the following when planning an effective videotaped course.

- **Planning.** Careful design of lessons is important. Timing of classroom sessions should be planned so as little editing as possible must be done to ready the course for the distance education student. Although some editing will be needed to make materials flow well, careful planning can reduce the number of hours required to complete the editing. A detailed course syllabus and a listing of all assignments and accompanying deadlines are essential. Special attention should be given to clear, specific student objectives and expectations for quality. Dates and methods of submitting homework and projects must also be established.
- **Arranging assessments.** Arrangements must be made for testing. Students may be required to come to the college or university to take tests.
- **Providing timely feedback to students.** Providing effective feedback requires commitment on the part of the faculty. As with other nontraditional delivery methods addressed in this chapter, timely feedback is essential as students progress through the taped lectures and the various assignments and projects of the course.
- **Providing student-teacher interaction.** Once again, e-mail may offer a means of providing 24-hour-a-day, 7-day-a-week message-sending capabilities. Timely responses from the instructor are imperative.

For business courses in which content does not change significantly within one or two semesters, a videotaped delivery option can be a sound choice. Exhibiting teaching excellence and enthusiasm during the taped sessions and communicating with students to help maintain their motivation levels can help business educators succeed when using this type of course delivery.

Traditional Classes in Nontraditional Time Frames

To accommodate nontraditional learners, schools (especially those in metropolitan areas) may offer some classes on the weekend instead of at night during the workweek. Such courses can be scheduled in a number of formats such as the following:

- Classes meet all day on Saturday every other week for a semester.
- Classes meet all day Friday and Saturday or all day Saturday and Sunday every two weeks, providing a weekend off between class meetings.
- Classes meet three to four hours a day for a shorter number of weeks. Schools often refer to these sessions as "minimesters" or intersessions. Many colleges and universities offer such intersessions in the spring following the regular academic year and preceding summer school, or in the winter, immediately preceding the spring term.

Yet another approach receiving attention from colleges and universities can be referred to as a 4 x 4 program. In this type of schedule, a student goes to class four nights a week, attending classes A and B on Monday and Wednesday evenings, and classes C and D on Tuesday and Thursday evenings. To entice students to enroll in such an intense program that often follows a full day of work, the school often makes a commitment to offering a progression through an entire degree program via 4 x 4 offerings.

In each of the nontraditional time frames identified above, careful course planning and design remain essential. Motivation remains a key component within a program of this type. Maintaining standards in the curriculum, avoiding watered-down content, providing meaningful out-of-class projects, and providing students with timely feedback are significant course design and management challenges.

Business/Community Initiatives

With new delivery methods and thus greater competition for students, no school can expect past practices to guarantee success. Education leaders must become more responsive to their external stakeholders such as business and industry. These external stakeholders have become increasingly important clients of postsecondary and collegiate education institutions, especially community colleges. Business and industry spend hundreds of millions of dollars each year on corporate training. Established colleges and universities have the potential to supply many of these training needs if the education and business communities work together.

Computer literacy, supervision, management, and human relations are all popular training topics. On-site industry-specific training is also important. Many colleges and universities, especially community colleges, across the country provide contract-specific training to numerous companies in their service areas. Community college workforce-training partnerships began in the 1970s and have rapidly increased in number. Recent studies by the League for Innovation in Community Colleges and the National Center for Research in Vocational Education both found that over 90 percent of responding community colleges offered workforce training for employees of business, industry, government, and labor (King, 1997).

Riley noted in "Business/Industry Training Seminars" in the 1994 NBEA Yearbook,

> Establishing an effective liaison program requires expert communication skills. The client must have accurately assessed the needs of participants, set realistic expectations, and be committed to the goals of the seminar. Responsibilities must be negotiated so that both client and trainer share equally in the seminar outcome. (p. 114)

Riley's statements provide sound advice for a business educator involved in any industry-specific training or business seminars; no matter what course delivery method is used, the above points must be addressed to ensure that business is satisfied with the end results of the training. To effectively manage the learning process in business-education partnership classes, business educators should also address the following issues.

- **Maintaining communication.** Maintaining open, continuous communication between partners helps ensure agreement on course objectives.
- **Meeting the schedules of business and industry.** Business and industry training can be provided to groups of employees in numerous ways. Two-way audio-video course offerings for academic credit may fit a specific company's needs. Another company may need a much different delivery method. Distance education options make it more likely that educational institutions can meet the need for nontraditional training times.
- **Delivering quality training.** Competent instructors with strong delivery skills and soundly designed content and activities are imperative in maintaining a school's reputation for quality training.

Business/community initiatives are often an untapped option. Especially in a metropolitan environment, many opportunities may exist to provide employees of business firms with training and instruction. Large organizations frequently have training rooms on-site, which can be effective classrooms. Close cooperation between an organization and an educational institution may result in several semesters' worth of courses being taught on-site. In any postsecondary/collegiate business curriculum, the general education components of the curriculum can apply to many different programs.

The employer may designate time during the workday for class sessions. Or perhaps the class can be taught during the noon hour, on Saturday mornings, or after work hours. In a very large company, sufficient interest may exist in a single course to offer it on-site; in other organizations sufficient numbers of students may be working toward the same degree to merit on-site course offerings at one company for workers from several companies.

Work-based business and education partnerships include internship experiences, service learning, and community service. All these options support students' transition to work.

Internships, specifically, help students bridge the gap between classroom theory and actual practice within the work environment. Internships allow students, typically during either the junior or senior year, to gain real-world experience while earning university credit. Students are required to work a certain number of hours for each college credit. In addition to their employment hours, students may meet for seminars conducted by a faculty member. Many internships offer credit for the equivalent of one or two courses. Evaluations by on-the-job supervisors and postsecondary/collegiate internship coordinators represent most, if not all, of the course grade. While some interns may receive pay, others receive only school credit.

Service learning, as defined by Kielsmeier (2000), is a way of teaching and learning that engages students in active service tied to the curriculum. A creative instructor can incorporate service learning into virtually any course. Students in a computer applications course, for instance, can assist a nonprofit organization in setting up a database; students in a desktop publishing class can design brochures or prepare newsletters for a nonprofit organization; students in a management class can help organize a fund-raiser. Through service learning, students can achieve academically and personally in a project-based manner. Service learning can provide more realism and make a course more interesting.

Community service, like service learning, involves a student working for a nonprofit organization. In true community service, however, the student's volunteer work is not directly linked to a course project. Coplin (2000) has written that community service can provide students with a great way to explore careers, learn about the real world, and practice skills they will need in other settings. Coplin has also noted that students get an opportunity to experience the joy of helping others in a sustained way.

Training and Retraining

How many times will today's 18-year-old change careers in his or her lifetime? A significant portion of postsecondary/collegiate enrollment comes from employees training for new careers or retraining as technology and advancements necessitate additional education to keep up-to-date.

Businesses and industries throughout the country need a constant flow of skilled workers. New skills and occupations are constantly emerging; thus, business has an array of new job categories to fill. Conveying both current and projected needs directly to the schools is essential. Savvy companies are getting involved with schools. Savvy schools are getting involved with companies.

Credit Versus Noncredit

Traditional noncredit course offerings provide yet another option for the adult learner. For example, software skills courses are very popular noncredit courses. Other popular business noncredit offerings include supervision, time management, anger management, and diversity in the workplace. Not everyone wants to earn a degree. Certificates of completion are sometimes appropriate. Faculty members typically contract separately for noncredit courses. Thus, the courses are not part of their normal teaching loads. Schools usually offer such courses at a lower cost than traditional three- or four-hour credit courses.

By carefully planning content, handouts, visuals, and in-class activities, a business educator can successfully manage the learning process in noncredit courses. Many of the principles of organizing credit courses are applicable to noncredit courses. Often the only real differences are the shorter course length and lack of grades for noncredit courses.

Summary

Effective management of the learning process, coupled with sound curriculum and course planning, is essential for a successful course. Whether offering self-paced instruction in a traditional classroom environment, presenting a course using one of the popular distance education delivery methods, providing traditional instruction in nontraditional time frames, or working in a business and education partnership, careful course design and management of the learning process remain absolutes. The "instructor as a facilitator of learning" becomes a key phrase during the actual calendar term of the course.

Motivating students to complete courses presented via distance education provides additional challenges to business educators. By communicating with their students and providing effective and timely feedback on work, instructors help lessen the feelings of isolation students can sometimes encounter when working alone. Managing the learning process for these nontraditional delivery methods does take extra time, but the potential rewards are great.

Maintaining viable, quality programs that attract learners of all ages is critical in the 21st century. Are we managing the learning process most effectively in postsecondary/collegiate business education? As educators, are we moving our programs forward? How each of us chooses to answer the following questions will impact the success of our programs.

- What is the current status of distance education at my school? Within my department? Within my program? What is the status of distance education at competitor schools?
- Am I a leader in developing a quality distance education curriculum with relevant standards? If I am not a leader, am I a willing and eager follower?
- What business/community initiatives exist in the geographic area my school serves? What opportunities could develop? How can my department's courses fit into these initiatives?
- How can my program provide students with more business-education partnerships involving internships and service learning?
- Does my program provide a variety of delivery methods and time frames for adult learners?

The opportunities exist. How well will we meet the challenges?

References

Cooper, L. (1999). Planning an online course. *Business Education Forum, 54*(1), 45–46.

Coplin, W. (2000, August 8). Top 11 reasons for doing community service as an undergraduate. *Knight-Ridder/Tribune News Service,* PK2805.

Cutshall, R., & Waltz, D. (1997). Utilizing two-way interactive audio-video for distant audiences. *Business Education Forum, 51*(3), 19–20, 22.

Epper, R. (1997). Coordination and competition in postsecondary distance education: A comparative case study of statewide policies. *The Journal of Higher Education, 68,* 551–87.

Hazari, S., & Schnorr, D. (1999). Leveraging student feedback to improve teaching in Web-based courses. *T.H.E. Journal, 26*(11), 31–38.

Johnson, J. (1999). Distance education: Learning for the 21st century. In P. A. Gallo Villee & M. G. Curran (Eds.), *The 21st century: Meeting the challenges to business education.* (Yearbook No. 37, pp. 90–99). Reston, VA: National Business Education Association.

Kielsmeier, J. (2000). A time to serve, a time to learn. *Phi Delta Kappan, 81*(9), 652.

King, M. (1997). The relationship between community college education professionals' education and work experience and their professional development needs. *Dissertation Abstracts, 60-02A,* No. AAI9919788.

LaBonty, D. (2000, November 9). *Distance education courses for business teacher education programs provided by NABTE institutions.* Retrieved September 8, 2000 from the World Wide Web: http://grumpy.usu.edu/~labonty/nabte/webnabte/wpages/INDEX.HTM

Matthews, D. (1999). The origins of distance education and its use in the United States. *T.H.E. Journal, 27*(2), 54–67.

Neal, E. (1999). Distance education. *Phi Kappa Phi Journal, 79*(1), 40–44.

Nelson, S. (2000). The effective use of video in distance education. *Business Education Forum, 54*(4), 40–41.

Okula, S. (1999). Going the distance: A new avenue for learning. *Business Education Forum, 53*(3), 7–10.

Policies Commission for Business and Economic Education. (1997). *Policy statement no. 61: This we believe about the delivery of business education.* Reston, VA: National Business Education Association. Retrieved from the World Wide Web: http://www.nbea.org/curfpolicy.html

Policies Commission for Business and Economic Education. (1999). *Policy statement no. 65: This we believe about distance learning in business education.* Reston, VA: National Business Education Association. Retrieved from the World Wide Web: http://www.nbea.org/curfpolicy.html

Riley, D. (1994). Business/industry training seminars. In A. McEntee (Ed.), *Expanding horizons in business education.* (Yearbook No. 32, pp. 113–118). Reston, VA: National Business Education Association.

Ryan, W. (1997, Summer). Delivery systems reviewed. *Journal of Interactive Instruction Development, 10,* 18–24.

Student-Related Management Concerns

Gay Davis Bryant
Pellissippi State Technical Community College
Knoxville, Tennessee

Technological advances have brought about a revolution in education. The transformation that is taking place makes the profession of teaching more challenging and more rewarding. All aspects of the classroom are affected: the physical environment, the tools educators use, how and what they teach, how they manage students and the curriculum, how they grade. Management of resources—resources for faculty and student learning, curriculum resources that shape what students learn, and physical resources that make up the environment where students learn—must be addressed as teachers assess the impact of technology on their jobs, lives, and classrooms.

The printing press, books, computers, and the Internet are tools and products that were introduced over the course of 500 years. Yet all have had an immeasurable impact on learning, education, knowledge, and humankind. In the 15th century the printing press expanded communication and hastened the spread of information, making it possible to create many copies of a document quickly and inexpensively. The Internet is facilitating a giant leap forward in the same process by increasing the availability of information and the ease and speed of communication.

The computer and the Internet have also expanded the options for delivering education via distance learning. Distance learning is not new to business education. Education was being delivered via correspondence courses long before television and computers were invented. But now the spectrum of distance learning also includes everything from traditional classes in which students use the Web to find information to entire courses (and in some cases, entire degrees) that are delivered online.

With the growth of the Internet, closed-circuit television, satellite transmission capability, voice mail, e-mail, videoconferencing, and video and audiotape technology, educators have seen an unparalleled growth in distance education programs in the last decade (Okula, 1999). According to International Data Corp., a research firm based in Framingham, Massachusetts, the number of courses offered online doubled from 50,000 in 1998 to 100,000 in 1999. The firm has predicted that the number of Web learners will expand from 700,000 in 1999 to 2.2 million in 2002 (Berinato, 2000).

The number of schools offering online courses and degrees increases continually. Most experts agree that distance learning will not replace traditional classes and that students will continue to do well in regular classrooms surrounded by their peers and guided by teachers. However, distance learning makes educational opportunities available to millions of potential students who find it difficult to attend traditional classes (Okula, 1999).

Delivering material via distance education methods makes managing learning, curriculum, and the physical environment more complex. The use of the computer and the Internet in the classroom has created an entire subset of management issues for educators. Teachers must manage the security and maintenance of expensive equipment and software as well as the impact technology has on the curriculum and the structure of content and student evaluation. Students use technology to collaborate on assignments and communicate electronically via e-mail, discussion groups, and chat rooms. Teachers using distance education procedures must find ways to encourage participation and communication, create a comfortable electronic classroom experience, and make students feel that they are part of a group. New paradigms are being created to govern how participation, group work, communication, and assignments are graded and evaluated, as well as how testing is conducted.

Teachers have always been managers—managers of the resources used for learning (by students as well as by teachers for professional development), managers of the resources used to develop curricula, and managers of the physical environment used for learning. But the technology that has been incorporated into the classroom has broadened the spectrum of what a teacher must manage and has increased the complexity of day-to-day management. Teachers' concerns have shifted from primarily behavior and discipline to keeping up with technology, hardware, content, communication, and collaboration.

Integrating Technology at All Levels

A 40-year veteran educator, Howard D. Mehlinger, of Indiana University, has said, "the revolution has begun" (1999), referring to the transformation that has been brought about by the use of technology. This revolution is occurring in classrooms all over the United States and according to Mehlinger is eclectic and largely devoid of ideology. What schools do with technology varies widely. In elementary schools, much technology is used for remediation, providing drill and practice exercises for students. In secondary schools and colleges, technology is giving students the skills and knowledge they need to succeed in the workplace.

Schools also use technology to deliver instruction in alternative ways. Technology such as compressed interactive video can be used to broadcast an instructor's lesson to one or more school sites where it can be viewed on televisions. Students at other schools can take classes and pursue degrees entirely from their homes—using computers with connections to the Internet to access course content, tests, and communication tools. At all educational levels, the Internet opens windows of learning and cross-cultural collaboration and provides research opportunities (Mehlinger, 1999).

Elementary and middle schools. Distance learning is a factor in elementary and middle schools. While educators may primarily teach in a traditional manner, many supplement their lessons by incorporating Internet exercises into their curricula (Okula, 1999). Students can participate in live sessions on the Web with scientists and politicians, correspond with pen pals via e-mail, and use the Web for research. The National Center for Education Statistics reported that in 1999 elementary school teachers were more likely than secondary school teachers to assign students practice drills using computers (39 versus 12 percent) and to have their students use computers or the Internet to solve problems (31 versus 20 percent). Secondary teachers, however, were more likely to assign research using the Internet (41 versus 25 percent).

Secondary schools. Secondary school educators can incorporate distance education into their activities. For instance, in an introductory economics class, students can be instructed to visit various U.S. government sites to compare the data and analyses available and then summarize the information contained on the sites. The online edition of the *Wall Street Journal* (http://interactive.wsj.com/) and local newspapers are also excellent teaching resources. Students can be instructed to identify and print articles on particular economics topics. The articles can then be used to illustrate the applications of economic concepts and theories to real-world market events. The articles can also be used in presentations and as the impetus for class discussions. Additionally, online communication tools, such as discussion groups and chat rooms, can enable students to collaborate on economics projects (Shikha, 2000).

Not only are high school teachers incorporating Web-centric assignments into classes, they are also offering entire courses online. Some schools, such as the University of Nebraska-Lincoln's Independent Study High School in Lincoln, Nebraska (www.unl.edu./conted/disted), offer a complete high school diploma sequence online (Okula, 1999).

Postsecondary schools. In postsecondary education, the spectrum of Internet use runs from the inclusion of Internet exercises in courses to the delivery of entire courses and degrees online. At the community college level, several colleges have reshaped their curricula by dividing traditional three-hour semester courses into one-hour semester courses delivered online. This pattern provides flexibility for the learner and allows students who have already mastered some of the skills to enter and exit programs more smoothly (*Pellissippi State Technical Community College, 2000 Catalog*; *Sinclair Community College Catalog*, 2000).

Managing Faculty Use of Technology

Technology affects the work of faculty members by reshaping the teaching and learning processes, redefining the roles and authority of faculty members in organizing and overseeing curricula, and altering the bases for student evaluation (American Association of University Professors, 2000).

Teachers must deal creatively with the alterations that technology and distance delivery bring about in teaching and learning. These changes have created an environment of lifelong, continuous learning that serves students anywhere at any time (Society for College and University Planning, 2000). One change is that electronic instruction has a more one-on-one orientation than traditional instruction. Also, the teacher's role has shifted from center-stage lecturer to behind-the-scenes facilitator. To manage this shift, teachers must keep up with the latest technology and teaching techniques and learn to meet the demands that providing one-on-one, student-centered instruction makes on their time.

Technology has extended the boundaries of the classroom by connecting people and ideas around the world. It is now possible for students to engage in network-based projects and discuss issues (such as the impact of current news events on the stock market) with experts on a daily basis. New and exciting projects that incorporate the Internet into instruction are being developed and shared daily.

Managing design and development time. There are few hard-and-fast rules about the amount of time and resources needed to add a Web component to a course or to move a course totally to the Web. Faculty have reported working 60–80 hours a week while adapting a course to the Web. The ratio of 18 hours of Web course development for every hour of instruction is supported by research on the design and development of distance-learning programs and the development of computer-based programs. A study by Rumble (1997) showed hours of academic effort required to produce one hour of student learning in different media forms (see Table 1).

To transition a course from traditional to Web delivery takes time and support, and teachers must manage the time factor. Once the course is restructured, learning on the Web requires technical support as well as time to work

Table 1	
Media	**Hours of Academic Effort**
Lecturing	2–10
Small-group teaching	3–10
Teaching textbook	50–100*
Broadcast television	100*
Computer-aided learning	200*
Interactive video or CD	300*
*Requires support staff as well	

with students through e-mail on problems, assignments, and questions. The following suggestions apply to managing teachers in all Web-based and Web-enhanced courses:

- Provide a minimum of one semester of release time for development. Two semesters of release time over a year is better.
- Provide time for training and learning. This could be one to two weeks of concentrated time in the summer or a semester of release time to learn a subset of skills, such as a course management system or basic productivity tools.
- Provide support for changing the curriculum, if necessary.
- Provide funding for hiring content researchers to work with faculty to identify and review quality learning materials on the Web.
- Provide training in new Web course management tools (Boettcher, 1999).

Managing Student Use of Technology

An early study by Apple Computer in 1986 looked at classrooms representing a cross-section of K–12 schools and studied how the students learned and how the teachers taught. Apple has continued studying computers in classrooms for the last 15 years. In his 1994 follow-up to the 1986 Apple study, Dwyer noted the following:

- Teachers were not technologically illiterate. They could use computers to accomplish their work.
- Students using computers did not become socially isolated but showed more evidence of spontaneous, cooperative learning than did students in traditional classes.
- Students did not become bored with technology over time. Instead their desire to use technology for their purposes increased with use.
- Software selection was not a problem. Teachers easily found programs and productivity tools to employ in their classes.

Perhaps the most telling of the findings, however, was that observers noticed differences in the behavior of teachers and students. Students were taking more responsibility for their own learning, and teachers were working more as mentors and less as presenters. At the end of the fourth year of the study, classrooms were different from when they had begun and teachers were using a new variety of instructional methods. Each teacher seemed to have adjusted his or her style to the computer-rich environment and to be aware of the changes that had occurred in his or her professional outlook.

In terms of classroom management and discipline issues, the students had also changed. At West High School, in Columbus, Ohio, 21 freshmen were selected to participate in the Apple study in which they used computers as a resource tool. They stayed with the program for all four years until their graduation. All 21 graduated, whereas the student body as a whole had a 30 percent dropout rate. Ninety percent of the students involved in the study went on to college, while only 15 percent of the overall student body sought higher education. But the most important finding was the difference exhibited by these students in how they did their work. They routinely, without prompting, employed inquiry, collaborative, technological, and problem-solving skills (Dwyer, 1994). This study may not be representative of all students, but it does offer business educators some food for thought.

Another study commissioned by the Software Publishers Association in 1994 and conducted by an independent technology-consulting firm reviewed research conducted on educational technology from 1990 through 1994. The report was based on 133 research reviews and reports on original research projects. Even though this research was commissioned by private industry and could contain some bias, some of the conclusions related to classroom management in terms of what teachers teach and how they manage students bear consideration:

- Educational technology has a significant positive effect on achievement in all subject areas, in all levels of schools, and in regular classrooms as well as those for special-needs students.
- Educational technology has positive effects on student attitudes.
- The degree of effectiveness is influenced by student population, instructional design, the teacher's role, methods of student grouping, and the levels of student access to technology.
- Technology makes instruction more student-centered, encourages cooperative learning, and stimulates increased teacher/student interaction.
- Positive changes in the learning environment evolve over time and do not occur quickly (Software Publishers Association, 1994).

How are the learning needs of Net Generation students different from those of earlier groups, and what resources can be used to meet these needs? The Net Generation is the first to be surrounded by digital media. Computers with Internet connectivity, as well as cameras, video games, and CD-ROMs are found in homes, schools, factories, and offices. To members of the Net Generation, digital technology is no more intimidating than a phone or a toaster. With the technological savvy that these students bring to the classroom, a new set of classroom management issues and content delivery problems comes to the forefront.

Not only has the implementation of technology into learning affected how teachers manage resources, it has also impacted the student's role. Net Generation learners are more independent and practical. They want to be entrepreneurs, not employees of large companies like previous generations. According to Tapscott, this generation is looking for flexibility and freedom, "ownership," a highly collaborative environment, and continued skill building. This group uses technology such as e-mail, pagers, cell phones, and answering machines to communicate and to explore the world (Tapscott, 1998). By incorporating electronic communication and research resources into courses, teachers are using a familiar approach with which most students are comfortable.

Educators are also finding that a student-centered approach to instruction rather than an instructor-centered approach works well with Net Generation students. Many teachers must rethink the way they have delivered content. In order for teachers at all levels to manage these changes in learning preferences, they can implement strategies in presentation and course organization that take advantage of the student-centered instructional approach by including

- Assignments that allow students to learn through discovery and doing rather than listening to lectures
- Projects that have a real-world context and that strengthen such higher-order thinking skills as problem solving and decision making
- Activities that prepare students for constant change in the workplace by emphasizing their capabilities to learn and to acquire and use information (Jones, 2000)

According to Abigail Reynolds, state supervisor of business education in West Virginia, teachers are becoming facilitators of learning, changing their delivery methods from lecturing to activities and from single-subject to interdisciplinary approaches. She cited international business marketing and French I classes in which typical projects have involved researching product marketing in France, finding business articles in French newspapers, and translating the information. Teachers of these classes have cofacilitated and students have worked in teams (Glenn, 2000).

Will the "one-size-fits-all" approach that worked in the traditional classroom work online? Teachers have learned that online delivery of content brings a course down to an individual's level. The teacher is responding one-on-one, often through e-mail, to problems, questions, and concerns. Teaching this way is not easy. Constraints on teachers' time mean they must make choices about how that time is spent and managed as a resource (Glenn, 2000).

To what extent should the Web be used? There are basically three types of Web courses: (1) a Web-enhanced course, in which the course closely resembles a traditional course but is strengthened by the use of the Web; (2) a Web-centric course, in which the focus of the course is shifted from the physical classroom to the Web as classroom (using such electronic communication features as e-mail, discussion groups, and chat rooms to enhance learning); and (3) a Web course, in which learning is available anywhere at any time and electronic communication tools are used to conduct the class. The teacher must first decide at which level he or she is going to involve the Web, then adapt learning resources to that end in constructing the course (Boettcher, 1999).

Making students aware of expectations. Managing students' use of electronic resources in a lab or classroom has added a dimension of supervision to the teacher's role on the one hand, and a dimension of responsibility to the student's role on the other. Teachers must supervise thousands of dollars' worth of equipment and software and must be accountable for its security. Often, the delivery of entire courses depends on that equipment functioning properly and well. Students must respect the equipment/software in order to keep it functioning and to keep the environment productive. Teachers and school systems have developed procedures and documents, often called acceptable-use policies, that delineate the rules and processes governing the use of computers and the Internet in the classroom. Chapter 3 includes a thorough discussion of these policies.

Managing the Use of Resources for Curriculum

The business education curriculum is changing. The addition of technology to the classroom requires teachers to master not only what they are teaching but also the tools with which they are teaching. It is no longer sufficient, for example, to learn to do accounting and be able to teach accounting; accounting teachers must also learn to use computers, financial management packages, and spreadsheet programs, as well as the Internet. Teachers of distance education courses must master not only content, but also the delivery and management systems that serve as the interface between the instructor and students. Teachers must learn to manage constant, fast-paced changes and stay up-to-date in their respective content areas as well as in the technological areas. This means more study, more training, and more sharing among teachers.

Technology's impact on curriculum. Today 77 percent of the nation's classrooms are connected to the Internet (National Center for Education Statistics, 1999); and schools have an average of one instructional computer for every 5.7 students. The Software Information Industry Association's *1999 Education Market Report for K–12* indicated that the student-to-computer ratio had improved from 19:2 in 1991–92 to 6:3 in 1997–98. And for the first time, the installed base of instructional computers was higher in classrooms than in computer labs with 49.7 percent of installed instructional computers in classrooms compared to 41.1 percent in computer labs (Software Information Industry Association, 2000).

Teachers cannot escape the all-important questions of how to build a curriculum that uses computers as tools for processing ideas and information, what to put on those computers, and how to manage a computer-based curriculum. Fatemi (1999) has identified several critical questions: How do teachers judge the quality of software and Web sites? How do they find appropriate materials? When should such resources be used? How much should teachers rely on them? How should they be integrated into the curriculum?

It is up to teachers to review and evaluate software to include in their curricula. There is no lack of digital content available to teachers, but selecting which content to use for a particular lesson can be a daunting task. Complicating matters is the fact that many teachers lack the time and training they need to make the best use of digital content (Fatemi, 1999). A study in the third of *Education Week's* annual reports, *Technology Counts '99*, reaffirmed the importance of professional development. According to the study, teachers who had received technology training in the past year were more likely than other teachers to say they felt "better prepared" to integrate technology into their lessons. They were also more likely to use and rely on digital content for instruction and to spend more time trying out software and searching for Web sites to use in class. But despite the apparent need for curriculum-integration training, the *Technology Counts '99* survey shows that teachers are getting relatively little of it. Only 29 percent of teachers said they had had more than five hours of technology training in curriculum integration within the last year. More training and professional development for teachers is crucial if digital content is to be integrated into curricula.

According to the same survey, teachers seem particularly frustrated by the process of searching for software. More than half of the teachers who search for software to use for instruction say it is "very difficult" or "somewhat difficult" to find the kinds of products they want to fill their specific classroom needs. Teachers in grades 9–12 have the hardest time finding software, with 69 percent describing it as "very" or "somewhat" difficult. Numerous factors probably contribute to this sense of frustration, including the fact that many teachers do not know where to turn to find reliable evaluations of digital content.

Many teachers, particularly at more advanced levels, use productivity tools such as word processors, spreadsheets, and multimedia presentation packages in their classrooms, even though the tools were not specifically designed for education.

For the time being, sales of educational CD-ROMs far outnumber those of online materials. In 1998 schools spent $13 million on online subscriptions, compared with $340 million on stand-alone/modular software and $218 million on comprehensive software delivered on CD-ROMs (Simba Information, 1999). People in the industry say the focus on CD-ROMs will likely be short-lived. "I'm not sure CD-ROMs are going to be around long. Things are moving very, very fast to the Internet," Hurley, of The Learning Company said (Zehr, 1999).

Web sites have the advantage of being interactive and they are almost limitless in number and usually free. In addition, they can be updated far more frequently than CD-ROMs. From a content point of view, Web sites are excellent for education because they bring into the classroom countless primary sources and multiple perspectives, according to Cornelia Brunner, the associate director of the Center for Children and Technology in New York City. But this also raises new challenges for schools, she said. "The problem is that most teachers have not had the opportunity to prepare themselves to use these resources. For starters, they need to learn how to determine if the information on a site is valid and teach their students to do the same" (Zehr, 1999).

What types of equipment/software should be purchased to support technology in the classroom? Teachers who want to include technology in their classrooms are plagued by questions about what hardware and software to buy. Schools often do not have the funding to stay on the cutting edge of technology every year, and decisions must be made to try to get the longest use possible out of the equipment that is purchased today. The Knox County School System in Knoxville, Tennessee, considers the following when selecting hardware and software:

- Curriculum changes
- Advisory committee recommendations
- Articulation with postsecondary institutions
- Budget constraints
- Vendor recommendations
- Availability of support materials from textbook publishers
- Use by local businesses
- Networking capabilities (DeBord, personal communication, 1999)

Shifting to a student-centered curriculum. Technology can help move students to the higher levels of thinking required in a knowledge-based economy. "The bottom line," according to Kimberlee Bartel, assistant professor of business education at Central Washington University in Ellensburg, Washington, "is moving from a focus on our teaching methods to a focus on student learning methods" (Glenn, 2000). Student-centered learning puts responsibility on the learner. To be successful in distance-learning programs, students need to learn how to learn. They should be encouraged to be independent, self-directed, and able to learn from a distance. In creating courses and curricula, educators must realize that distance learning is not for everyone. Many students require the give-and-take of the classroom with both the teacher and their peers. Others are not disciplined enough to complete work on their own schedule, cannot read and comprehend well enough, or do not have other independent learning skills necessary to be successful (Okula, 1999).

Redefining evaluation. Teachers moving courses to the Web find that traditional ways of evaluating students may no longer work. Paper-and-pencil tests can no longer be used; face-to-face participation is being replaced by e-mail, discussion groups, and chat room assignments; and individual student work is being replaced with collaborative work.

Online course management systems have developed sophisticated testing capabilities whereby a teacher can deliver objective tests and instantly convey results. Students answer questions and are immediately notified if the answers are correct or not. One problem, however, with online testing is that the software is unable to ensure that the person taking the test is in fact the person enrolled in the class. Another issue of online testing is that of the open-book exam. When testing online, students have access to their books and notes and the temptation to use them. To validate identity and ensure test integrity, online teachers generally require students to take tests at a testing center under the supervision of a proctor (Carlson, 2000). Online tests have become a good way for teachers to structure drill material so the students can receive immediate feedback and then move on.

Collaborative learning with electronic communication tools. One of the problems with distance learning is the isolation the learner feels when working alone with course content and a computer. Many students miss the interaction with faculty and peers that takes place in a traditional classroom. Distance education teachers can incorporate curriculum resources into their Web classes to meet this socialization need. E-mail, discussion groups, and chat rooms have been used creatively to communicate with students and are used in group projects where students work with each other. The amount of time needed to read and organize e-mail messages, respond to questions and deal with problems, and evaluate collabo-rative assignments has added to the time it takes to teach classes online.

Converting traditional courses to Web courses has affected curricula in many ways. Issues of test taking, learner-centered instruction, group work, practical real-world assignments, and flexible restructuring of courses are being addressed in many creative ways by teachers all over the country.

Summary

It is impossible to deny the tremendous effect that computers and technol-ogy have had on classrooms and learning around the world. The explosion of new technologies is truly a revolution in education (Mehlinger, 1999). Technological advances drastically affect the way teachers teach and students learn. The business world demands that schools prepare educated workers who can use technology effectively in the global marketplace. Educators hold the key to the effective use of technology to improve learning. If they do not understand how to employ and manage technology in the classroom effectively to promote student learning, billions of dollars being invested in educational technology may be wasted.

The technology of computers, video, and telecommunications is changing the sources of expertise and approaches to acquiring knowledge. There is no longer a question of whether new technology will be used in schools; the question is how to manage what is available and how to employ the technology as an extension of the classroom.

More questions are being raised than are being answered about the management of educational resources as impacted by technology. These questions include issues related to

- The equity of access to education
- The costs of developing and implementing distance education programs
- Changes and challenges facing faculty
- Pressures on existing organizational structures and arrangements
- Accreditation of and quality assurance in distance education programs
- Copyright and intellectual property rights issues (Lewis, et. al., 1999)

The opportunities and challenges that technological innovation brings make this a dynamic time for educators. To meet these challenges, business educators need an attitude that is fearless in the use of technology, that allows them to take risks and think "out-of-the-box," and inspires them to become lifelong learners. Technology has transformed the role of the teacher as thoroughly as the introduction of printed textbooks did. Business educators must seize their opportunities, capitalize on the impact of technology, and manage all the resources available to them for lifelong learning.

References

American Association of University Professors. (2000). *Special Committee on Distance Education and Intellectual Property Issues.* Washington, DC: Author. Retrieved from the World Wide Web: http://www.aaup.org/spcintro.htm

Berinato, S. (2000, March). Coming after you. *University Business.* 29–33.

Boettcher, J. (1999). *Faculty guide for moving teaching and learning to the Web.* League for Innovation in the Community College.

Carlson, R. (2000, March). Assessing your students: Testing in the online course. *Syllabus,* pp. 16–18.

Dwyer, D. (1994, April). Apple classroom of tomorrow: What we've learned. *Educational Leadership, 51*(7), 4–10.

Fatemi, E. (1999, September 23). Building the Digital Curriculum. *Education Week*. Retrieved from the World Wide Web: http://www.edweek.org/sreports/tc99

Glenn, J. M. (2000, February). Teaching the Net Generation. *Business Education Forum, 54*(3), 6–14.

Jones, C. L. (2000, February). Reaching and motivating N-Gen students. *Business Education Forum, 54*(3), 4.

Lewis, L., et.al. (1999, December). *Distance education at postsecondary education institutions, 1997–1998* (NCES 2000-013). Washington, DC: National Center for Education Statistics.

Mehlinger, H. D. (1999). *School Reform in the Information Age*, p. 117.

National Center for Education Statistics. (1999). *Teacher use of computers and the Internet in public schools* (NCES No. 2000-090-1). Washington, DC: Author. Retrieved from the World Wide Web: http://nces.ed.gov/

National Center for Education Statistics. (2000, May). *The digest of education statistics, 1999* (NCES No. 2000-0031). Washington, DC: Author. Retrieved from the World Wide Web: http://nces.ed.gov/pubs2000/digest99/

Okula, S. (1999, February). Going the distance: A new avenue for learning. *Business Education Forum, 53*(3), 7–10.

Pellissippi State Technical Community College, 2000 Catalog. (2000). Knoxville, TN: Pellissippi State Technical Community College. Retrieved from the World Wide Web: http://www.pstcc.cc.tn.us/community_relations/catalog/

Rumble, G. (1997). *The costs and economics of open and distance learning*. Sterling, VA: Kogan Page.

Shikha, D. (2000, February). Integrating the Internet into economics courses. *Business Education Forum, 54*(3), 22–24.

Simba information. (1999, December 29). Retrieved from the World Wide Web: http://www.simbanet.com

Sinclair Community College Catalog. (2000). Dayton, OH: Sinclair Community College. Retrieved from the World Wide Web: http://www.sinclair.edu/

Society for College and University Planning. (2000, January 15). *Why are learner-centered environments imperative?* Retrieved from the World Wide Web: http://www.scup.org/tomorrow/why.htm

Software Information Industry Association. (2000, January 20). *Education market report: K–12 education market division*. Washington, DC: Author. Retrieved from the World Wide Web: http://www.siia.net/pubs/education/emrkl228.htm

Software Publishers Association. (1994). *Report on the effectiveness of technology in schools 1990–1994*. Washington, DC: Author.

Tapscott, D. (1998). *Growing up digital—The rise of the Net Generation*, pp. 1–2.

Technology counts '99: Building the digital curriculum. (1999, December 15). *Education Week*. Retrieved from the World Wide Web: http://www.edweek.org/sreports/tc99.htm

Zehr, M.A. (1999, September 23). Screening for the best. *Education Week*. Retrieved from the World Wide Web: http://www.edweek.org/sreports/tc99

Setting the Stage for Successful Learning

Donna J. Cochrane
Bloomsburg University
Bloomsburg, Pennsylvania

Preservice and first-time teachers are especially concerned with creating classrooms that set an appropriate tone for learning. Education and work and life experiences have given these teachers extensive knowledge of their specific subject matter. Knowledge alone, however, does not guarantee classroom competence. Rather, one's classroom management skills determine whether one succeeds or fails as a facilitator of learning.

This chapter

- Addresses the relationship between classroom management and student learning
- Examines popular approaches to classroom management and related principles and practices
- Describes management strategies designed to create environments that allow learning—and students—to flourish

Classroom Management: The Key to Student Learning

Good classroom management helps students understand where they are to go and what they are to do, with minimal confusion (Danielson, 1996). In well-managed classrooms, discipline problems are few and student achievement levels are high. In fact, a meta-analysis of 50 years of research revealed that when compared with other factors such as cognitive processes, home environment, school culture, and curriculum design, classroom management had the greatest effect on student learning (Wang, Haertel, & Walberg, 1994, cited in Cummings, 2000).

Approaches to Classroom Management

While all teachers want to teach well and help students learn, misbehavior often prevents teachers from doing so (Charles, 1999). Thus, the fundamental question for teachers becomes one of discipline—that is, what can they do to promote attention, cooperation, and civil behavior among their students?

A number of researchers have provided workable approaches to classroom management. Three such approaches are described below.

Assertive discipline. This model, popularized in Marlene and Lee Canter's training series of the same name, is a concrete system of communicating expectations and establishing consequences for students' positive and negative behaviors. The model received wide acceptance from teachers in the late 1980s and early 1990s because its simplicity, structure, and specificity made it relatively easy for teachers to implement and for students to understand.

Canter and Canter (1992) have stated that students need to

- Know teachers' behavioral expectations
- Have limits
- Receive positive recognition and support
- Learn how to choose responsible behavior

Clarifying teachers' expectations of student behavior and what students can expect from teachers in return (Canter and Canter, 1992) involves

- Stating the rules that students must follow at all times
- Creating the system of positive recognition that students receive for following the rules
- Establishing the consequences that result when students choose not to follow the rules

For example, one experienced business educator established the following system of rules and consequences:

- Follow directions the first time they are given.
- Raise your hand and wait to be recognized before speaking.
- Use appropriate language. Appropriate language does not include swear words, put-downs, or a loud tone of voice.
- Keep hands, feet, and objects to yourself.
- Be in your seat with all your materials when the bell rings.

Breaking a rule means being faced with the following consequences:

- First offense: warning

- Second offense: remaining after class
- Third offense: detention
- Fourth offense: parental contact
- Fifth offense: removal from class (Sorg, 1994)

This teacher's rules adhere to the Canters' (1992) guidelines: they specify which behaviors are appropriate, and they contain a limited number of observable rules. Canter and Canter posit that classroom rules must apply at all times throughout the day and that teachers should consider involving students in choosing some of the rules. Teachers can give individual students positive recognition by praising them, calling or writing complimentary notes to parents or guardians, and offering special privileges and tangible rewards.

Some educators have criticized the assertive discipline model for its reliance on praise and other rewards, which some authorities believe reduces intrinsic motivation (Charles, 1999). This model, however, continues to enjoy widespread popularity, which suggests that it provides educators effective skills that they have not been able to find elsewhere.

The quality school: managing students without coercion. This concept, described in William Glasser's 1992 publication of the same name, is an appeal to teachers to emphasize high-quality work and create a discipline plan that is concerned with classroom satisfaction rather than one "that demands . . . doing something to or for students to get them to stop behaving badly in unsatisfying classes . . . No matter how much coercion we use, we cannot consistently control other people" (p. 56, 73).

Glasser has differentiated between "boss" teachers and "lead" teachers. Boss teachers, as he has described them,

- Set tasks and standards
- Talk rather than demonstrate, and rarely ask for student input
- Grade students' work without involving them in the evaluation process
- Use coercion when students resist (Charles, 1999)

Conversely, lead teachers realize that genuine motivation to learn must arise within students. Glasser has advised teachers to spend most of their time on two things: organizing interesting activities and providing assistance to students (Charles, 1999). Lead teachers, for example,

- Discuss the curriculum with their classes in such a way that many topics of interest are generated
- Encourage students to identify topics that they would like to explore in depth
- Discuss with students the nature of the schoolwork that might ensue, emphasizing quality and asking for input on criteria of quality

- Explore, with students, the resources that might be needed for quality work and the amount of time such work might require
- Demonstrate ways in which the work can be done, using models that reflect quality
- Emphasize the importance of students' continually inspecting and evaluating the quality of their own work
- Make evident that everything possible will be done to provide students with good tools and a good workplace that is noncoercive and nonadversarial (Charles, 1999)

Too often, teachers dealing with discipline problems use the boss approach because it is quick and decisive (Glasser, 1992). Yet, Glasser has written,

> ...kicking disruptive students out of class, keeping them after school in detention, or suspending them may control the immediate situation, but it does not deal with the basic problem: how to get them involved in quality learning. In the quality school, lead teachers must learn how to handle a disruptive student in a way that is not punitive yet gets the situation under control and, at the same time, opens the student's mind to the option of beginning to work in class. (p. 135)

Creating a learning community. Carol Cummings' book, *Winning Strategies for Classroom Management* (2000), describes what she considers the first winning principle: the importance of connecting and bonding with each student. Person-to-person connections create a more engaging and motivating classroom environment; an engaging environment creates engaged students and fosters a learning community that nurtures each learner's strengths and recognizes (and accommodates) each learner's weaknesses (Cummings, 2000).

Forming healthy connections with students involves the following strategies:

1. Connecting with students. Teachers can send postcards to incoming students in late summer welcoming them back to school and into the classroom; place welcoming letters to students on their desks with envelopes for their responses; or take students' photos and write each student's name on his or her photo, then review the photos before each class arrives and greet as many students by name as possible.

2. Using appropriate self-disclosure. This can be accomplished by sharing feelings, attitudes, or experiences in ways that are helpful to students.

3. Having high expectations and faith in students' abilities. Students will perform and behave exactly as expected. Expecting students to be the best will help ensure that they will be the best (Etterman, 1986). High expectations for success can be built on by allowing students to demonstrate learning in different ways such as by

A. Having them work in groups or pairs
B. Having them do real-world problem solving
C. Partnering with local businesses on activities that are relevant to what students are learning in the classroom, such as designing a menu for a local restaurant in a desktop publishing course
D. Using rubrics, or scoring guides
E. Evaluating problem-solving or teamwork skills
F. Giving and then rating project presentations
G. Assessing the quality of ideas
H. Providing feedback about classroom projects

4. Networking with students' families and friends. Cummings has cited a 1996 study by Laurence Steinberg that found one in three parents "seriously disengaged" from his or her adolescent's life and especially from the adolescent's education. It also found that only one in five parents ever attended school programs. It is important to find ways to connect with students' families, such as by attending community events, inviting parents to speak about their careers, or by sending home monthly newsletters.

5. Building a sense of community in the classroom. School shootings, such as the one that occurred at Columbine High School, confirm that too many students in today's classrooms think they are "zeroes" or outcasts. Noticing each student and encouraging him or her personally and academically builds strong teacher-student connections.

6. Using rituals and traditions. Students find security and comfort in traditions (Cummings, 2000). Using journals; work-study logs; class photo albums with captions; newsletters; seasonal projects, such as a theme-based work portfolios or student-led conferences, can help create a sense of tradition in the classroom.

Communication skills and talking with students to better understand their backgrounds are vital to constructing a safe, connected learning community. Cummings (2000) has recommended creating multiple opportunities to poll students by using active listening techniques.

Teaching Strategy—The Most Effective Classroom Management Tool

Lang (1986) has suggested that "a teacher who is genuinely interested in effecting high-quality student performance knows that efficient utilization of classroom time is a must" (p. 4). Teachers must devote out-of-class time to the organization and development of activities that are appropriately challenging for students at various ability levels, thus making the teaching strategies themselves classroom management tools. "A well-managed classroom makes it possible for the teacher to concentrate on the *teaching* process [rather than on administrative or disciplinary processes]" (Etterman, 1986, p. 5).

Organizing and planning curricula and instructional strategies help teachers interpret discipline as a positive—rather than negative—word that signifies self-control in behavior and work performance. Using an array of methods, teaching styles, and resources that facilitate learning is the key to maintaining a stimulating learning environment (Ladd & Ruby, 1998).

No matter which concepts or subject matter the curriculum addresses, teachers must identify desired learning objectives before selecting the teaching strategy or strategies appropriate to achieving those objectives. A certain flexibility is called for as well—if teachers have spent time connecting with individual learners, then strategies can be modified, adapted, or combined to accommodate students' learning styles or, in some cases, the temperament of a given mix of students.

Whole-group methods. Lecturing has been a prime delivery method in classrooms for centuries. While different teaching strategies other than lecturing are encouraged, one could argue that lecturing has its place. Lectures put the control directly into the hands of the teacher, who has the expertise. Laird (1985) has described lecturing as a nonparticipative medium, but has contended that it is an efficient way to deliver instructional material.

In the training and development field where learning objectives are very specific, many trainers successfully apply the "mini-lecture" format. High school instructors can also use this format. O'Connor, Bronner, and Delaney (1996) have described mini-lectures as instruction delivered for 10–15 minutes followed by reinforcement activities. Such a structure maximizes students' involvement by catering to their attention spans and having students move quickly from one activity to another (Schrag & Poland, 1987).

To use mini-lectures, it is important to think in terms of "segments." Dividing class time into a series of segments that may be relatively independent or that may build sequentially is an effective strategy. A typical high school class period should include no more than three to four segments. In block scheduling (longer periods of 70–90 minutes), segments of 10, 15, or 20 minutes can be used, with up to six or seven segments per period.

Each segment should have three parts: explanation, student activities, and summary (Smith & Delahaye, 1987). The explanation and student activities should take up most of the time, whereas the summary should be quite brief.

It is a good idea to begin the class with an introduction that explains how the particular lesson fits into the total curriculum and what objectives students will accomplish during the class. Posting the agenda on the board or on a flipchart may help save time and assist students who are hearing impaired or who have difficulty following directions. Listing learning expectations will enable students to check their own progress. During this introduction, the pattern for the explanation, activity, and summary steps may be also shared with the students (Smith & Delahaye, 1987).

The next step is to deliver the mini-lecture and any information needed for follow-up activities. For example, in a business law class the mini-lecture may introduce information about the nature of contract law. Basic definitions and cases can be used to illustrate the points of law under discussion. It is a good idea to use visuals as well as speech. Visuals can be created simply by writing key vocabulary words on the board or displaying important information on transparencies, handouts, poster displays, or computer-based presentations. Giving the class copies of the visuals lets them follow along and note the major points of the presentation, thus reinforcing the concepts.

In the activity stage of the mini-lecture, students learn by doing. A teacher may choose to help students apply relevant concepts, or if students cannot correctly apply the concepts to their activities, then the explanation may be repeated in another format. To test students' understanding of contract law, for example, they can be instructed to apply what they have learned to several case studies. Students can work by themselves, with partners, or in small groups.

Finally, teachers can bring all the pieces together and tie up loose ends by summarizing and soliciting questions from the class before going forward (Smith & Delahaye, 1987). The explanation, activity, and summary format should be continued until all learning segments are covered.

It is important to allow time near the end of the class for a wrap-up. Reinforcing major topics and key points will create closure. Some type of evaluation may be appropriate to demonstrate that learning has taken place (see step 3 of the Creating a Learning Community section, above). For example, students can be asked how they can apply what they have learned to what they are doing now. The wrap-up also lets the teacher link concepts to the next class session. Building a sense of continuity of the material is vital, regardless of whether the class is skill- or content-oriented.

Small-group, cooperative, and team methods. Using these types of learning activities in the business education classroom make sense. Businesses today use teams to solve problems, and small-group strategies in business education classes allow more active learning to occur. For example, suppose a teacher wants students to share reports on articles they have read about a particular topic. A large class makes this activity seem impossible. However, a team approach allows students to learn from other students' reports and to summarize their group readings in a meaningful format.

Consider the following strategy: the teacher reads and categorizes student reports before assigning small-group work. The teacher can individually grade student reports, if such evaluation is suitable. Because reports will probably fall into broad subject categories, the teacher can identify each category by number and place a number (representing the category to which the report belongs) at the top of each paper. When papers are returned, the students can group themselves according to the numbers their papers were assigned. The groups can then share their articles with each other, find the common themes that bind the reports together, and summarize major points. Each group can then assign a member to present the common themes and major points, with examples, to the rest of the class.

A variation of this teaching strategy is to assign students to a particular category, and once they find a common theme, have them interact with the other groups to see if there are any links. This strategy works well with readings on technology topics because the topics are so interrelated.

One way to generate interest in a basic business or introduction to business class is to undertake an ongoing group project. At the beginning of the semester, students can form groups and choose a type of business they would like to organize. Information about ways in which business firms are organized should be made available to the students. Each group can then work on one organizational aspect and apply it to the business. For example, if the topic is marketing, groups can formulate their firm's business marketing strategy. The end product, after all aspects of the course are completed, will be a plan for forming and managing a business firm. The projects can be submitted as a report at the end of the course, and the groups can present their business plans to the rest of the class. (For an example of how students can use mentors to help them launch "live" businesses, as two students did in Rialto, California, see Glenn, 1999.)

Individual learning activities. Many individual learning activities, such as having students research community leaders or businesses and create posters, interview-based reports, field-based projects, book reports, and case studies, allow students to combine textbook knowledge with real-world experience.

These activities and teaching strategies can vary from "tried-and-true" methods. Field-based projects, for example, encourage students to interact with the business world. Basic business or entrepreneurship classes are appropriate for student–to–business owner interviews that culminate with written reports that are shared orally with the rest of the class.

Educational trends impacting teaching strategies. Alternative scheduling patterns (for example, the movement away from the traditional 45- and 55-minute class periods to intensive, block, or block-of-time scheduling) directly impact how classes are organized for learning. Unfortunately, some teachers naively assume that they can successfully force two "old" lessons into this restructured time frame (Hackmann & Schmitt, 1997).

No matter which scheduling pattern predominates, students must engage in authentic and challenging learning activities. Hackmann and Schmitt (1997) have suggested planning three to four activities during the instructional block, with at least one activity involving direct and substantial engagement of students in the learning process.

For example, a block-of-time lesson could be structured in the following manner:

1. Review previous learning by checking homework, asking students questions, and having students work in pairs for self-assessment. (Supply guidance, such as a performance matrix, to assist students in the self-evaluation process.)
2. Deliver new materials and concepts to students by using a variety of instructional strategies: direct teaching, demonstrations, multimedia presentations, inquiry learning, etc.
3. Organize students for group activities that promote hands-on learning so that they can fully comprehend and apply the concepts presented.
4. Incorporate guided practice in order to assess all levels of student understanding (Hackmann & Schmitt, 1997).

Mansfield and Echternacht (1999) have noted that some school districts are modifying curriculum by integrating business education course work with other subjects. This trend is based on the principle of combining the best subject matter, pedagogy, and practices of business education curricula with those of other disciplines. This combination helps ensure that students learn both the theory and the application of specific content areas.

A number of integration models exist. The following are some examples for business education teachers to consider:

- All business teachers can be encouraged to include writing assignments that help them assess students' writing deficiencies and take steps to remedy them.
- Business teachers and teachers from other disciplines can work in teams to enhance the business program's content and to develop additional integration activities.
- The overall curriculum can be made more relevant to the workplace through the incorporation of more hands-on and interdisciplinary content.

- Curricula can be aligned by modifying business and other courses. Integrating additional workplace competencies into a nonbusiness course and additional nonbusiness content into a business course will make both courses more relevant.
- A senior project can be used as an integrator that allows students to apply information from previous course work and demonstrate multiple skills and competencies.

Summary

Teaching remains a challenging profession. (See Appendix A for elements of effectively managed classrooms.) The concepts and strategies described in this chapter represent just a few ways teachers can set the stage for successful learning. Attending professional conferences, collaborating with other teachers, reading professional journals, visiting Web sites that contain already developed lesson plans, and adapting previously used teaching techniques can help teachers recycle and reinvent strategies that will enhance their classroom management skills and develop more active and engaged learners.

The following Web sites can assist business education teachers who want to build their repertoire of classroom management strategies:

- http://www.fbe.unsw.edu.au/learning/instructionaldesign/strategies.htm
- http://www.tedi.uq.edu.au/teaching/TertiaryToolbox/glossaryTeaching.html
- http://www.gmu.edu/facstaff/part-time/strategy.html
- http://faculty.necc.mass.edu/frizvanov/TeachStrateg.htm
- http://www.unet.maine.edu/Faculty_Services/TeachLearn.html
- http://u.arizona.edu/ic/edteach/strategy.html

References

Canter, L., & Canter, M. (1992). *Assertive discipline: Positive behavior management for today's classroom.* Santa Monica, CA: Lee Cantor & Associates.

Charles, C. M. (1999). *Building classroom discipline* (6th ed.). New York: Longman, Inc.

Cummings, C. (2000). *Winning strategies for classroom management.* Alexandria, VA: Association for Supervision and Curriculum Development. Retrieved November 14, 2000 from the World Wide Web: http://www.ascd.org/readingroom/books/cumings00book.html

Danielson, C. (1996). *Enhancing professional practice, a framework for teaching.* Alexandria, VA: Association for Supervision and Curriculum Development.

Emmer, E. T. (1984, June). *Current research on effective classroom management.* Austin, TX: Texas University Research and Development Center for Teacher Education.

Emmer, E. T., Evertson, C. M., & Anderson, L. M. (1980). Effective classroom management at the beginning of the school year. *Elementary School Journal, 80,* 219–231.

Etterman, C. L. (1986, April/May). Classroom management techniques for the effective business education teacher. *Business Education Forum Yearbook Issue, 40*(8), 5–7.

Glasser, W. (1992). *The quality school: Managing students without coercion* (2nd ed.). New York: Harper Perennial.

Glenn, J. M. (1999, October). Business spotlight: Hewlett-Packard telementors help launch the "cappuccino connection." *Business Education Forum, 54*(1), 12–13.

Hackmann, D. G., & Schmitt, D. M. (1997, April). Strategies for teaching in a block-of-time schedule. *NASSP Bulletin, 81*(588), 1–9.

Ladd, P. A., & Ruby Jr., R. (1998, October). Observation: Key to successful classroom management. *Business Education Forum, 53*(1), 40–41.

Laird, D. (1985). *Approaches to training and development* (2nd ed.). Reading, MA: Addison Wesley Publishing Company, Inc.

Lang, M. J. (1986, April/May). Factors that determine success for the new business education teacher. *Business Education Forum Yearbook Issue, 40*(8), 3–4, 7.

Mansfield, J., & Echternacht, L. (1999). Curriculum integration: Optimized learning for high school students. In P. A. Gallo Villee & M. G. Curran (Eds.), *The 21st century: Meeting the challenges to business education* (Yearbook No. 37, pp. 47–58). Reston, VA: National Business Education Association.

O'Connor, B. N., Bronner, M., & Delaney, C. (1996). *Training for organizations.* Cincinnati, OH: South-Western Educational Publishing.

Schrag, A. F., & Poland, R. P. (1987). *A system for teaching business education* (2nd ed.). New York: McGraw-Hill Book Company.

Smith, B. J., & Delahaye, B. L. (1987). *How to be an effective trainer: Skills for managers and new trainers* (2nd ed.). New York: Wiley Professional Development Programs.

Sorg, B. (1994, October 9). *Effective classroom management and discipline.* Presentation at the Eastern Business Education Association Convention, Cherry Hill, NJ.

Appendix A. Elements of Effectively Managed Classrooms

Effective classroom management sets the stage for successful learning by addressing five distinct elements:

- Management of instructional groups
- Management of transitions
- Management of materials and supplies
- Performance of noninstructional duties
- Supervision of volunteers and paraprofessionals

Emmer (1984) has described classroom management as a three-phase activity; phase one, preactive, prior to the start of the school year; phase two, beginning of the school year; and phase three, remainder of the school year. Each phase involves conceptualizing classroom activities in terms of the five elements listed above.

Preactive phase. In this phase, teachers concentrate on arranging physical facilities, identifying expectations for student behavior, and establishing work requirements and routines (Emmer, 1984).

The arrangement of physical space is the first concern: Emmer (1984) has recommended leaving a clear line of sight from small-group work areas to the rest of the class; avoiding "blind spots" where students can drop from sight, such as behind tall bookcases or filing cabinets; and arranging furniture so that teachers can easily move about the room to monitor individual students. Many distractions and disruptions can be prevented with careful attention to the room arrangement.

Rather than identifying expectations for student behavior as simply a list of rules, Emmer (1984) has recommended that teachers conceptualize the nature of activities that will occur in the classroom and specify how students should behave in these activities in order for the classroom to function smoothly. For example, when students are engaged in small-group work, what should they do if their group has a question and the teacher is working with another group?

Teachers must establish routines for distributing work assignments, returning graded assignments, and monitoring makeup work. This allows teachers to concentrate on instruction rather than on administrative duties. In a computer applications class, for example, a folder can be prepared for collecting, storing, and returning each student's assignments. Rather than wait for teacher direction, students can access their folders at the beginning of each class. "Road signs" placed prominently around the room can be used to remind students of work routines.

Beginning of the school year. In this second phase, teachers communicate expectations, norms for behavior and work, and routines and procedures for conducting activities (Emmer, 1984).

Well-managed classes are the result of effective leadership from day one. Successful teachers tend to be "front and center" and to maintain personal contact with students. They are the main source of information about what students are to do and they stay actively involved, either by providing directions and instruction, or by monitoring (Emmer, 1984). Emmer, Evertson, and Anderson (1980) have found that the level of order created during the first few days of school reliably predicts the degree of student engagement or disruption for the rest of the year.

Remainder of the school year. In this phase the emphasis is on maintaining behavioral and work norms and designing and conducting activities in ways that keep students actively engaged in learning. Providing for student success and adapting instruction to meet individual student needs (especially for lower-achieving students) are critical in this stage (Emmer, 1984).

One key to maintaining behavior norms is dealing with inappropriate behavior promptly instead of ignoring it (Emmer, 1984). Dealing with inappropriate behavior when it occurs prevents this behavior from escalating in duration and in frequency and therefore from continually interrupting instruction. Teachers who are good classroom managers tend to have created interesting and engaging curricula, quality standards for student performance, and relatively simple and unobtrusive procedures for inappropriate behavior (see the Approaches to Classroom Management section above).

Classroom Management Theory and Practice

Cora Lytle
Coastal Georgia Community College
Brunswick, Georgia

The educator's idea of classroom management is constantly evolving. In the past an effectively managed classroom was a quiet, orderly environment with compliant students and a teacher who was able to cover the entire textbook in the allotted semester. Teachers reacted with sharp discipline measures to students who failed to conform. Today classroom management theories place an emphasis on creating an adaptable, effective learning community (Brophy & Alleman, 1998; Evertson & Harrison, 1992). A proactive approach to potential classroom problems is taken.

The concept of keeping order in a classroom has changed from developing rows of silent, passive students to encouraging active, involved learners who readily participate in an educational environment that respects peer, community, and teacher needs and sensibilities. Educators and administrators alike recognize the importance of managing classrooms using an approach that increases the likelihood that learning will take place. Concepts of what that approach should be vary from state to state, district to district, even teacher to teacher. Each business education teacher must determine what management results those who set school policy expect and what management techniques best serve students as individuals. A successful classroom atmosphere requires a holistic approach that encompasses the management of classroom space and equipment, the establishment of rules and procedures, and the preparation of lessons and activities that engage all students. In every phase of classroom management it is essential that teachers take into account the interactions among the students and between the students and the teacher.

Managing Classroom Space and Equipment

Although space limitations, classroom environmental variables, administrative demands, and allotment of books and materials may leave teachers feeling powerless to control the physical aspects of their jobs, the ability to adapt can put them in charge. First, instructors generally know ahead of time what they will have to work with, and second, they can be prepared to use what they have creatively, even if it is a classroom with only one computer. Effective physical management of the classroom not only decreases management problems but also increases learning (Williams, Alley, & Henson, 1999).

Seating arrangements. The physical layout of the classroom is the first management area for which the teacher must plan. Are there single desks, long tables, or some other combination of seating arrangements? Are there windows in the room? Where are whiteboards or blackboards located? If an overhead projector is used, which seating design best facilitates viewing? How can the materials be arranged to create the most productive learning environment? The number of students in a class and the age of the students will also impact seating arrangements. In some instances, research has shown the conventional row system to be most productive, whereas other research finds the circle pattern least disruptive and most encouraging to student participation (Kauchak & Eggen, 1993). It is helpful to try a variety of seating schemes with each class to determine what works for those particular students.

Teachers should be especially observant at the beginning of the year if they allow the students to choose their own seats when entering the classroom for the first time. Although much seating choice may be socially dictated, some may reflect learning styles or physical needs. For instance, if a student chooses to sit near the window, he or she may feel more comfortable learning in a well-lit area. Students who choose to sit near the front may be eager for teacher-student interaction or may be accommodating a hearing or vision problem. As with many aspects of classroom management, careful observation is a powerful tool for enabling the teacher to create an environment that will be most conducive to learning for each student (Ladd & Ruby, 1998).

How classroom space and seating arrangements are managed will also be dictated by the course of study. What works well in a business communication course where considerable discussion is desired may not be ideal for a business math class where peer-to-peer assistance is helpful. The circle arrangement enhances participation and works well in discussion-oriented courses like introduction to business or business law. In any class the circle offers a comfortable alternative to standing in front of the room for student presentations. Knowing they may present from their seats may encourage students who are fearful of standing before an audience to concentrate on report content rather than on report length, resulting in longer, more in-depth papers. The number of students in a class and the size of the room can be prohibitive when creating circles. Age and achievement level also have an effect on the circle approach. Younger students may see a circle as an opportunity to make faces at each other or mouth answers—added distractions that are not present in a row arrangement (Kauchak & Eggen, 1993). Trying out different desk arrangements in an empty classroom can eliminate the lost learning time that would occur should the first attempt be done with a room full of middle school students. Sometimes only trial and error will afford the teacher the best layout for a conventional classroom.

Group work may require arranging and rearranging of seats during a class session. With planning, an instructor can eliminate much confusion and loss of learning time. Development of classroom routines early in the semester can reduce the transition time from one activity to another. Prearranging the seats before students enter the room or placing the group activity toward the end of the period can eliminate lost on-task time as well. Any rearrangement of furniture requires clear and precise instructions. Indecisiveness on the teacher's part about which seats should go where will result in classroom chaos. Whatever the arrangement of seats, the teacher should make certain that he or she can move easily around the room and student safety is not compromised by blocked exits (Fenwick, 1998). Seating arrangements that eliminate or minimize physical interaction or touching between students also alleviate problems (Williams, Alley, & Henson, 1999). Additionally, teachers must accommodate all students with special needs without giving the appearance of differential treatment (Williams, Alley, & Henson, 1999).

Computers. Computers add a new dimension to seating problems. If one or two computers have been put in a conventional classroom, the instructor must take into consideration how he or she plans to use them. If the computers are used to demonstrate ideas or concepts with all the students observing, and no projection device is available, sufficient room must be allowed for students to gather around and view the monitors. If a small group of students will be using a computer for an activity, such as a stock market game, while the rest of the class works on other projects, there must be sufficient space for the group to access the computer without distracting nearby students.

In computer labs often little, if anything, can be done to change predetermined equipment setups, and teachers must work within the confines of workstations and wiring. Students often develop a sense of computer ownership if they sit at the same computer for a number of class periods (Bayless, 1995). Disruptions then develop if one day a student chooses to set a new seating pattern. Also, computer rooms with close workstations and shared resources frequently allow for more social interaction throughout a class session than might result in a conventional class. Keen observation is again the teacher's best tool to determine if a revised seating arrangement would eliminate the unnecessary social interaction (Ladd & Ruby, 1998).

Whether the teacher assigns the seats or the students determine the arrangement, requiring consistency and maintaining a seating chart can be helpful management tools. In a computer room with potential security and equipment problems, individual student responsibility is encouraged when students know the teacher can account for who sat where and when he or she sat there. Also, depending on the lab arrangement, students in computer labs often work with their backs to the teacher or their faces screened by a monitor. It is difficult to learn student names when the back of someone's head is the only point of reference. Adding name cards to the tops of the monitors in easy view can eliminate this problem.

Computer labs are often created in preexisting conventional classrooms that are not well suited to a computer environment. The teacher should determine ahead of time how visible the whiteboard or overhead projector screen will be from all seats. If it is difficult for some students to see without rearranging their chairs, alternative ways of presenting information should be sought. Handouts are one option. Another is presenting instructional information and directions at the beginning of the period rather than throughout the period to eliminate the need for students to rearrange their seating more than once during class.

Even if initially there is a computer for each student, the teacher still needs a plan for breakdowns, particularly if no backup equipment is available. Creating learning partner teams at the beginning of the semester gives students advance notice of the computer sharing that will take place if needed (Bayless, 1995).

Printers. Sharing printers is another potential area for classroom chaos. The printer-to-computer ratio must be taken into consideration. Determining exactly what has to be printed to permit effective assessment is important. A plan in which all students print at the end of the period is predestined for mass confusion (Bayless, 1995). One solution may be to assign one student from each work group to obtain and distribute printouts, thus eliminating the problem of having groups of students congregate around the printer. If students save to disks, assignments can be checked without being printed. If the computers in a classroom are networked to a main server, students can create individual folders, and the teacher can correct the assignments from his or her workstation. A combination of printouts and assignments saved to disk or server varies the demand on the printer, especially if each student is working at his or her own pace. It is important to remember that printers seem to malfunction precisely when they are needed most, so an alternate plan is necessary when tests or projects are involved.

Organization. The key to effective management of the physical aspects of the classroom is organization: knowing what is to be used, when, and where it is. Shuffling through piles of papers, arranging and rearranging chairs, or setting up equipment only to find it does not work wastes time and allows the students an opportunity to seek diversions elsewhere, resulting in management problems.

Helping students manage their materials. When students learn to manage themselves, their possessions, and their classroom environment, the teacher's job is easier. Students should know exactly what their responsibilities are as far as the maintenance of their work areas, where and when disks or other materials should be stored, where the printer paper is located, and where completed assignments should be placed. Students should know what is expected of them when they move around the classroom. Often simple changes in the physical environment can prevent opportunities for misbehavior or chaos (Phelps, 1991).

With the unfortunate increase in school violence, many schools have eliminated the use of backpacks and other bags in which to carry books. Students with many books to lug between classes may need help developing a plan for remembering to bring their materials to every class. A class discussion early in the session about where lockers are located or where in the school building their preceding classes are located can help students plan for class preparedness. Students who feel that the teacher empathizes with their predicament may be more likely to respond positively. The teacher could institute a token reward system as an added incentive for coming to class prepared.

Laying the Foundation for Learning

Williams, Alley, and Henson (1999) have stated, "A learning community can serve as a proactive means of diminishing discipline problems in the classroom" (p. 11). Although it takes the effort of both teachers and students to create a sense of community, it falls to the teacher to develop the foundation and establish guidelines that enable a dissimilar group of individuals to evolve into a learning community. Participants in the community must respect each member's approach to the common goal of learning. The teacher serves as the model to the students. When teachers treat students with respect, consistency, and fairness, they demonstrate the behavior they expect from their students (Tierno, 1996). Emmer (1994) has emphasized the effect the teacher's emotions have on classroom management, noting that inappropriate student behavior arouses negative emotions in teachers that in turn affect their reactions to students. When a teacher reacts in a confrontational manner or uses an approach that embarrasses a student, the teacher is modeling the very behavior he or she hoped to eliminate (Tierno, 1996). A teacher who shouts at a disruptive student loses the respect of the entire class (Williams, Alley, & Henson, 1999). Jones (1996) has pointed out that "You'll never control a student, much less a room full of them, until you are first in control of yourself" (p. 26).

To facilitate the creation of a learning community, the instructor must first know the students and the culture or environment of the school as a whole. A teacher must recognize what social problems will be impacting the classroom every day. Are gangs an issue? Do the students divide themselves into well-defined cliques? These issues can be significant factors in group projects.

Williams, Alley, and Henson (1999) have suggested using a "count-off" technique to create work groups, to avoid the appearance of singling out students to work together.

Taking any opportunity to show an interest in or speak one-on-one with each student throughout the semester can demonstrate true interest in the students (Dollard & Christensen, 1996). Although an instructor may feel that he or she does not have a minute to spare for a personal conversation with a student, research shows that time spent building positive relationships reduces time lost dealing with management problems later (Korinek, Walther-Thomas, McLaughlin, & Williams, 1999).

Teachers must understand the social environment of their students. What music are they listening to, what movies are popular, how are the school teams doing, and who is involved in which activities? What's "in" and what's "out" in clothing can spark classroom management problems. One secondary school had "color day" with the various grades assigned a specific color to wear on that day, such as blue for eighth grade, green for ninth, and so on. Unwittingly, the administration had assigned one grade a color that was traditionally taboo among the students on that particular day of the week. Students in that grade became extremely anxious and distracted trying to decide what they were going to do on the assigned day. It is important for teachers of adolescents to remember that their students are trying to "maintain their membership simultaneously in many communities" (Fenwick, 1998, p. 624). There are events and problems in students' lives that they consider more important and that exert more pressure on them than schoolwork (Matus, 1999).

Teachers must be aware of the emotional obstacles that may impede student learning and create classroom management problems. Peer pressure, family difficulties, work demands, relationships, or harassment by other students can be everyday occurrences for many teenagers (Williams, Alley, & Henson, 1999). Creating an atmosphere of positive reinforcement in the classroom can emphasize that the teacher has high expectations for each student regardless of the outside support he or she may or may not be receiving. Exhibiting zero tolerance in the classroom for bullying or harassment will communicate clear standards of the behavior that is expected of every student (Williams, Alley, & Henson, 1999). Being aware of group dynamics can prevent a teacher from unintentionally forcing a student into a "choice" situation that runs so counter to peer pressure that it is nearly impossible for the student to choose to respond as the teacher would wish.

Rules. Creating a classroom environment where every student feels he or she belongs, has something meaningful to contribute, and can learn using his or her own individual style requires a shared responsibility between students and teacher. Rules and discipline procedures play a big part in creating this atmosphere. Students are generally made aware of school rules through student handbooks, and many of the rules involve legal issues beyond the immediate control of the classroom teacher. However, every teacher needs to incorporate specific rules of behavior that he or she expects in the business classroom. Many experts and discipline models suggest that instructors involve the students in the creation of classroom rules (Hardman & Smith, 1999; Morris, 1996; Wasicsko & Ross, 1994; Williams, Alley, & Henson, 1999). Whether the teacher designs the rules or the students are involved, the rules should be stated in positive rather than negative language (Dunton, 1998; Hardman & Smith, 1999). The number of rules set should be limited to less than seven (Hardman & Smith, 1999; Williams, Alley, & Henson, 1999).

Rules need consequences, and if punishment is necessary, it should fit the crime (Wasicsko & Ross, 1994). Enforcement of rules needs to be done with consistency and fairness. Schoolwork should never be used as a punishment (Wasicsko & Ross, 1994). Often teachers stipulate a punishment for an entire class if one student fails to comply with the rules. When using this classroom management technique, "the teacher is modeling a value system of injustice and unfairness" (Romeo, 1998, p. 131). And the teacher may be creating a hostile classroom environment that sets students against each other and breaks down any sense of community (Romeo, 1998). Rules and consequences should be a means for the teacher to establish a positive learning environment (Thompson, 1994).

Reinforcing rules. The business instructor must realize that his or her physical presence directly impacts the dynamics of the classroom. The way an instructor moves around the room and his or her position when presenting materials affects students' reactions and interactions. Simply moving toward an offending student while continuing direct instruction is often enough to counter a potential problem. Taking center stage establishes authority early on, but moving to the rear and around the classroom throughout a lesson gives the teacher a new perspective, and the students recognize the teacher's increased opportunities for observation (Department of Education and Professional Studies, University of Limerick, 1999). Physical presence is further emphasized by voice, gestures, posture, and eye contact. A teacher must handle himself or herself in a positive, assertive, but nonaggressive manner. A timid voice and apologetic posture will undo any advantage careful furniture arrangement and mental preparation may have afforded. On the other hand, an aggressive attitude can encourage an aggressive response from many students. A teacher's eye contact and physical demeanor can project "withitness" to the students. Withitness, or being aware of classroom dynamics and student behaviors, allows teachers to anticipate and preempt potential problems (Gordon, 1997). By making eye contact with every student in the room at some point during a class, the teacher projects to each student that he or she is seen as an individual and not just a part of a faceless crowd.

When instructors assume a teaching position near the front center of a classroom, research has shown an "action zone" is created (Williams, Alley, & Henson, 1999). The zone includes the students in the front row and those in a receding wedge-shaped area directly in front of the teacher. The teacher is more aware of the actions and interactions of students seated in this zone, and the students in turn are more involved in the learning process. Having more than one teaching spot can create different action zones at different times. In a classroom with moveable furniture, changing desk positions frequently can also help vary the action zone. In classrooms where it is physically impossible to change the furniture layout, changing the student seating arrangements can serve the same function. For instance, a specific date such as the first of each month could signify "seat-changing day." Students could draw numbers for their seat assignments for the upcoming month.

Teaching students self-management. The desire in today's school systems to create a learning community in the classroom where students are given choices and a voice in their learning increases the responsibility of the students to manage their own behavior. If students are to participate effectively as members of the learning community and subsequently of society as a whole, they must be individually responsible for their reactions and interactions. The teacher's role has moved beyond controlling student behaviors to creating an environment that facilitates learning by engaging students productively (Evertson & Harrison, 1992). The establishment of classroom rules gives students guidelines of which appropriate outcomes are expected. Often, however, students lack the background or self-management skills to know how to attain those outcomes. Teachers must help students understand that a conflict of opinions and ideas is a normal outcome of human exchanges (McGuire, 1998). Students need to be taught compromise and to respect themselves, as well as others (Hawkins, 1997). The rules developed for the classroom should be structured to help students develop responsibility for their own actions (Ross & Bondy, 1993).

The wired classroom with access to the Internet and e-mail has significantly added to the need for students to exercise self-management. Although it is the teacher's responsibility to set clear standards, constant monitoring and observation of every student is not always possible, even if Internet management software is installed. Computer use rules in the form of a classroom acceptable-use policy, which every student and his or her parent sign, can help students set guidelines for their responsibilities and behaviors (O'Donovan, 1997). Involving students in an active discussion about Internet etiquette and dangers can also prevent problems.

Lessons in self-management can become an integral part of classroom activities. Teaching students to set goals with assignments is a start (Alberto & Troutman, 1999). If an accounting instructor allows time for students to work on homework, the students could be asked to estimate how many problems they think they will be able to complete before the bell. At the end of the period, the teacher should ask the students to evaluate whether they met their goal, and why or why not. Topics such as talking or "so-and-so was bothering me" open the door for a brief discussion of self-management issues.

Students need to know that the teacher is aware of each of them as an individual. Assuring them through eye contact, comments about successful school activities, or sincere expressions of personal concern can go a long way in building a bridge of respect between the student and teacher.

Procedures

While rules, which state specific do's and don'ts, are guidelines for acceptable behavior, (Williams, Alley, & Henson, 1999), procedures are the systems the teacher and students develop to ensure that learning takes place through a smooth transition from one activity to another. They are generally numerous and unwritten and specify the methods for dealing with classroom tasks (Kauchak & Eggen, 1993). Where homework or completed papers are placed; the steps to follow when borrowing school equipment; how a hall or library pass is obtained; and by whom or when supplies can be accessed are all examples of procedures that lessen wasted time and reduce classroom confusion.

Evertson and Harrison (1992) have pointed out that a classroom environment requires students not only to mentally process new academic knowledge, but also to understand how to respond to, present, or participate in the sharing and gaining of that knowledge. Classroom procedures guide students in this pursuit. Students expect some classroom participation procedures based on all their previous school experiences. However, each business teacher must determine ahead of time which procedures should become second nature in each classroom. With both verbal and nonverbal cues, the teacher can establish routines that allow students to become self-monitoring and reduce the potential for discipline problems. A teacher may use an orientation period at the beginning of each year to outline specific procedures (Zeiger, 1996). All students expect established procedures, and the lack of knowing how to proceed detracts attention from learning. The expected behavior entering and leaving a classroom, how absences affect tests and assignments, and how participation in discussion is initiated are all necessary classroom procedures best developed in the first days of a semester (Kauchak & Eggen, 1993).

Procedures are particularly important in a computer lab where requests for teacher assistance can become backlogged and overwhelming. Using colored plastic cups set on top of the monitor or workstation—red signifying "I need help before I can proceed further," yellow signifying "I need help, but I can keep working," and green signifying "I am working successfully"—is one way to allow the teacher to be more effective (O'Donovan, 1997). The use of learning teams in which the teacher is asked a question only if the team cannot solve the problem also helps the students become more self-reliant.

Beyond knowing ahead of time what procedures students will be expected to follow, the instructor must know what procedures he or she will use for routine tasks. When and how will attendance be checked? How will students' names be learned? Will the teacher need name tags or cards on the desk, or is he or she good at associating names and faces? Which observation methods best reveal the activities that engage students in learning most of the time? How will observations be recorded for future reference when designing lessons? The routines for tracking grades, absentees, and incomplete assignments can be time-consuming (Holzberg, 1995). Business teachers, with their knowledge of computers, can easily make use of a wide array of software programs to track this information. One common program, Microsoft Works, has an education package that includes a grade book and test setups.

Being prepared with systems to handle a variety of situations saves valuable learning time in a classroom. For instance, it is useful to have an assortment of ways to divide a class into groups, such as using a deck of cards, counting off numbers, or using birth dates. Having predetermined strategies not only saves time but also projects the image of a prepared, in-charge teacher.

Homework. Teachers must have a plan for handling homework. Will homework or outside projects be assigned? How much and how often? What will be the consequences for late homework or incomplete projects? Similar approaches must be taken with regard to class work and tests missed due to absenteeism. Matus (1999) has emphasized the difficulties that can be encountered in this area, particularly in urban high schools. Punishing students for failing to complete homework when home factors create an impossible study environment only serves to promote the type of classroom management problems associated with uninvolved students. Additionally, it may be unrealistic to assign homework that requires use of a library when transportation is a problem, or streets are unsafe after dark (Matus, 1999). By creating situations in which students know ahead of time that they will fail because of circumstances beyond their control, the teacher creates classroom management problems. One solution suggested by Matus (1999) is to allow students several days to complete a homework assignment. Another option is to allow class time for projects and class trips to the school library. Williams, Alley, and Henson (1999) have emphasized that well-planned homework is essential to academic achievement. Business teachers need to develop homework systems that serve academic and curriculum goals but do not impede classroom management efforts.

Technology. The use of computers for assignments is another factor that must be addressed. Many students may have neither technological know-how nor easy access to a computer outside of school. Students lacking computer resources will be at a disadvantage if they are expected to compete with peers who have desktop publishing software and computer-literate parents. Grading criteria must be designed so as not to penalize students who lack home computer access,

but at the same time, not to discourage other students from using their technological expertise. A teacher must find a way to level the playing field when one
student has the resources to produce a multimedia presentation and another must
resort to a handwritten paper. For example, a grading rubric that places specific
values on creativity, appearance, effort involved, organization, content, and
demonstration of learning allows the teacher to judge each project on its own
merit. A student could successfully fulfill all of these requirements with or without
using a computer. Unfortunately, placing a point value on spelling or grammar
would give an edge to students with access to a recent version of word processing
software.

Depending on the region in which they teach, instructors will often find a
wide diversity of technological ability in their students. O'Donovan (1997) has
suggested taking advantage of the "experts" in a class by making them technology mentors. Once certain students have demonstrated their expertise, the
teacher can have them act as troubleshooters and helpers for other students. As
the year progresses, their jobs might include training other mentors, so that
eventually all students have an opportunity to be one of the classroom experts
(O'Donovan, 1997). This can be a useful strategy for a computer class. For
noncomputer classes, pairing "techies" with "nontechies" to work together on
projects or for trips to the computer lab can accomplish the same objective.

Keeping Students Engaged

Most importantly, teachers need to know what they want their students to
be able to accomplish and how the students will demonstrate those accomplishments. Sharing those goals with the students during an orientation period helps
create a positive atmosphere in the classroom (Zeiger, 1996). Having clearly
defined goals allows the teacher to choose instructional paths that take into
consideration each student's learning style and level of learning readiness. By
accommodating a variety of student learning profiles in his or her lesson plan,
the teacher is better able to keep students actively involved and interested in
learning. Teachers should also be aware of students' postures and body language.
Do students look bored, inattentive, or asleep? Engaged students are less likely
to become bored, and student boredom is the root of many classroom management problems (Department of Education and Professional Studies, University of
Limerick, 1999).

Research has shown that using activities that present opportunities for
movement around a classroom can actively involve students in learning (Gibson
& Govendo, 1999). Although the learning centers concept is more commonly
found in the lower grades, it can be used at all levels. Stations or "departments"
of a business such as sales, purchasing, or manufacturing could be set up in
different areas of a room. An accounting assignment could require students to
move among the departments to gather information from the papers or materials
placed there to complete the assignment.

The need to involve students motivates teachers to design programs that allow students to construct knowledge rather than receive it (Hand & Vance, 1995). When designing these programs, teachers must create flexible lesson plans that take into account a variety of learning styles and approaches. For instance, in a business law class one group might want to present a mock trial or debate to illustrate how a law applies, another group may want to make its point with a videotape or clip of a movie or TV show, whereas yet another group may be more comfortable and more productive using a PowerPoint presentation. Accommodating learning styles allows students to create a final product that involves and excites them. Giving students choices of assignments or projects within the framework of what the teacher wants to accomplish engages students in their learning by allowing them to use their particular skills or explore areas of interest to them (Hawkins, 1997). Options provide all students a better chance for success, and successful students present fewer classroom problems.

Group work. Group work is frequently used in classrooms to encourage students to become active participants rather than observers. Before instituting group projects, teachers must prepare students to interact in groups so that none of them are held back by a lack of social skills. The failure of a student to interact effectively with others adds to the difficulty of classroom management. One way to prevent this problem is to provide examples of how a group discussion or a group project might be approached before setting the students out on their own. It is also important to demonstrate brainstorming, emphasizing acceptance of the ideas of others to help create a comfortable sense of community with fewer classroom management problems. In the middle grades, in particular, it is essential to introduce students to the idea of roles in the group. This is equally important in teams in which two or more students share a computer. Having the students develop a specific plan for who will be responsible for what in a group project involves them not only in their own learning but also in the management of their learning environment and their association with others.

Research has shown that a group size of three to five generally works best (Hand & Vance, 1995). A group of three learners has been found to force the most student participation (Simplicio, 1999). Although smaller may appear to be better, research has shown that discussion groups of two tend to deviate to personal issues and waste time (Simplicio, 1999).

Facilitating active learning. Often when students complete group projects for class presentations, they are far more concerned with their own presentation than with learning from or discussing the presentations of other groups. Classroom interruptions occur when students are focused on what their group is planning to do rather than on the presentation in progress. When asked for comments after a presentation, they may have little to offer. One way to ensure that students are mentally involved during presentations is to institute a peer assessment or review process (Black, 1999). Providing students with an outline of specific evaluation items, such as those a teacher would use in grading, encourages active listening during presentations. For instance, in a business communication class, voice level, grammar, development of the topic, vocabulary, and presentation manner could be listed.

Another approach to peer review suitable to upper grades involves more detailed and critical reviews. For example, a class presentation project in an accounting class might include analyzing the financial statements of different companies. Directing students to compare companies on points such as degrees of profit or loss, marketing techniques, or growth potential requires students to take notes and create written or oral responses, which can serve as the basis for class discussions.

Instructing students ahead of time in what they should listen for and providing examples helps students develop the listening skills needed to gather necessary information. It also gives students a concrete purpose for listening and eliminates the type of distractions that occur when students are inattentive.

A variety of other methods can be used to help students manage their own learning procedures. One is to give students an outline on which to write information they should glean from materials. Students should also be taught to do their own outlining. In preparation for a test, each student could be assigned a different section of material to outline and share with the class. This activity helps students gain insight into the learning processes of others and see new ways to address their own learning. Students who can then illustrate their own train of thought may choose to use graphic organizers, less structured than outlines, to allow for more freedom of expression and serve as a memory aid (Barton, 1995).

Students should also be taught how to approach different test types and test questions. As an icebreaker at the beginning of a business math class, a deceptively simple-looking quiz can be used to emphasize the importance of reading directions. The problems are printed clearly with the symbols to add, subtract, multiply, or divide. However, the brief instructions at the top of the sheet indicate that the plus symbol means to subtract, the multiplication symbol means to divide, etc. Students seldom forget to read directions again.

Teaching students how to set goals and apply time management techniques to learning activities and assignments gives them a sense of control that reduces frustration and feelings of being overwhelmed (Korinek, Walther-Thomas, McLaughlin, & Williams, 1999). It is important never to assume that a student has learned how to learn simply because he or she has completed a given number of years of education.

Questions. Research has shown that the questioning strategies a teacher uses to maintain active student participation can have a significant and positive effect on classroom management (Wang, Haertel, & Walberg, 1994). Questions can be used in a variety of ways to encourage learning. In classroom discussions, the teacher can use students' questions to reinforce or introduce concepts (Barton, 1995). Further development of an idea voiced by a student assures members of the class that their participation is meaningful. They can stay on task and involved when they know their opinions have value and their questions are not dumb. Students who fear being judged will simply withdraw mentally and see no purpose in exploring different aspects of the problem at hand.

When students are actively engaged in developing and answering questions, classroom management is easier. However, teachers frequently have problems getting students to either ask or answer questions. Lack of participation may lead a teacher to answer his or her own questions, and students in turn to simply cease thinking of possible responses (Higgins, 1999). Providing sufficient time for students to develop answers, particularly to higher-level questions, can be useful. A minimum of a three-to-five second wait is suggested (Williams, Alley, & Henson, 1999). Higgins (1999) has proposed allowing students to write out answers and then switch the answers with a partner for comment. Answers can then be discussed in class. The process encourages all students to mentally engage in working through to an answer. Collecting the answers helps ensure participation.

Students who understand what questions to ask are better prepared to conceive answers. Modeling example questions teaches students how to ask questions. Assignments that require students to develop a list of questions about a topic can also be useful. For instance, introductory computer classes frequently involve new concepts and terminologies. Here, a team approach can be used with each student developing a list of questions. Team members can then take turns asking and answering each other's questions (Weisz, 1990), adding to a student's perception of how to develop appropriate questions that are understood and answered correctly by others.

Conclusion

Research by Wang, Haertel, and Walberg (1994) has shown classroom management to be one of the most significant influences on student learning. The current trend toward creating a sense of community in the classroom gives students both an added voice in and an added responsibility for their own learning and behavior. Teacher responsibility has moved from a focus on discipline to a need to understand all the facets involved in classroom management. Understanding the social demands on today's students and using a positive approach to maintaining authority and establishing rules will ensure that both the educators' and the learners' individual needs are met. A win-win situation in a business classroom is one in which each student feels involved and challenged, and the teacher's management style focuses on learning as the key to a successfully managed classroom.

References

Alberto, P. A., & Troutman, A. C. (1999). *Applied behavior analysis for teachers* (5th ed.). Upper Saddle River, NJ: Prentice Hall.

Barton, J. (1995). Revitalize classroom discussions. *Education Digest, 60*(9), 48–52.

Bayless, M. (1995). Redesigning the classroom to reflect technology's impact. In N. J. Groneman & K. C. Kaser (Eds.), *Technology in the classroom* (Yearbook No. 33, pp. 106–116). Reston: VA: National Business Education Association.

Black, J. (1999). Get them involved, keep them interested. *Techniques: Making Education & Career Connections, 74*(7), 58–59.

Brophy, J., & Alleman, J. (1998). Classroom management in a social studies learning community. *Social Education, 62*(1), 56–58.

Department of Education and Professional Studies, University of Limerick. (1999). *Critical incidents: Classroom management.* Retrieved December 5, 1999 from the World Wide Web: http://inset.ul.ie/cm/index.html

Dollard, N., & Christensen, L. (1996). Constructive classroom management. *Focus on Exceptional Children, 29*(2), 1–12.

Dunton, J. (1998). The four b's of classroom management. *Techniques: Making Education and Career Connections, 73*(1), 32–33.

Emmer, E. T. (1994). Towards an understanding of the primacy of classroom management and discipline. *Teaching Education, 6*(1), 65–69.

Evertson, C. M., & Harrison, A. H. (1992). What we know about managing classrooms. *Educational Leadership, 49*(7), 74–78.

Fenwick, D. T. (1998). Managing space, energy, and self: Junior high teachers' experiences of classroom management. *Teaching and Teacher Education, 14*(6), 619–631.

Gibson, B. P., & Govendo, B. L. (1999). Encouraging constructive behavior in middle school classrooms: A multiple-intelligences approach. *Intervention in School & Clinic, 35*(1), 16+. Retrieved December 1, 1999 from EBSCOhost (Masterfile) database on the World Wide Web: http://www-us.ebsco.com/home/default.asp

Gordon, R. L. (1997). How novice teachers can succeed with adolescents. *Educational Leadership, 54*(7), 56–58.

Hand, B., & Vance, K. (1995). Implementation of constructivist approaches within the science classroom. *Australian Science Teachers Journal, 41*(4), 37–43.

Hardman, E., & Smith, S. W. (1999). Promoting positive interactions in the classroom. *Intervention in School & Clinic, 34*(3), 178+. Retrieved December 1, 1999 from EBSCOhost (Masterfile) database on the World Wide Web: http://www-us.ebsco.com/home/default.asp

Hawkins, D. L. (1997). It's more than teaching history. *Social Studies, 88*(3), 108–112.

Higgins, P. (1999). Promoting students' responses to questions. *College Teaching, 47*(3), 101.

Holzberg, C. S. (1995). Classroom management at your fingertips. *Learning, 23*(4), 57–59.

Jones, F. H. (1996). Did not! Did, too! *Learning, 24*(6), 24, 26.

Kauchak, D. P., & Eggen, P. D. (1993). *Learning and teaching: Research-based methods.* Needham Heights, MA: Allyn and Bacon.

Korinek, L., Walther-Thomas, C., McLaughlin, V. L., & Williams, B. T. (1999). Creating classroom communities and networks for student support. *Intervention in School & Clinic, 35*(1), 3+. Retrieved December 1, 1999 from EBSCOhost (Masterfile) database on the World Wide Web: http://www-us.ebsco.com/home/default.asp

Ladd, P. D., & Ruby, R. (1998). Observation: Key to successful classroom management. *Business Education Forum, 53*(1), 40–47.

Matus, D. E. (1999). Humanism and effective urban secondary classroom management. *Clearing House, 72*(5), 305–307.

McGuire, J. V. (1998). Building teams in the classroom. *Techniques: Making Education & Career Connections, 73*(6), 52–53.

Morris, R. C. (1996). Contrasting disciplinary models in education. *Thresholds in Education, 22*(4), 7–13.

O'Donovan, E. (1997). Back to school checklist: Making your technology user friendly. *Technology and Learning, 18*(1), 23–27.

Phelps, P. H. (1991). Helping teachers excel as classroom managers. *Clearing House, 64*(4), 241+. Retrieved December 1, 1999 from EBSCOhost (Masterfile) database on the World Wide Web: http://www-us.ebsco.com/home/default.asp

Romeo, F. F. (1998). The negative effects of using a group contingency system of classroom management. *Journal of Instructional Psychology, 25*(2), 130–133.

Ross, D. D., & Bondy, E. (1993). Classroom management for responsible citizenship: Practical strategies for teachers. *Social Education, 57*(6), 326–328.

Simplicio, J. S. C. (1999). Some simple and yet overlooked common sense tips for a more effective classroom environment. *Journal of Instructional Psychology, 26*(2), 111–115.

Thompson, G. (1994). Discipline and the high school teacher. *Clearing House, 67*(5), 261+. Retrieved December 1, 1999 from EBSCOhost (Masterfile) database on the World Wide Web: http://www-us.ebsco.com/home/default.asp

Tierno, M. J. (1996). Teaching as modeling: The impact of teacher behaviors upon student character formation. *The Educational Forum, 60*(2), 174–180.

Wang, M. C., Haertel, G. D., & Walberg, H. J. (1994). What helps students learn? *Educational Leadership, 51*(4), 74–79.

Wasicsko, M. M., & Ross, S. M. (1994). How to create discipline problems. *Clearing House, 67*(5), 248+. Retrieved December 1, 1999 from EBSCOhost (Masterfile) database on the World Wide Web: http://www-us.ebsco.com/home/default.asp

Weisz, E. (1990). Energizing the classroom. *College Teaching, 38*(2), 74–76.

Williams, P. A., Alley, R. D., & Henson, K. T. (1999). *Managing secondary classrooms: Principles and strategies for effective management and instruction.* Needham Heights, MA: Allyn & Bacon.

Zeiger, A. (1996). 10 steps to a happier classroom. *Teaching Music, 4*(1), 38–39.

Facilities Management

Dawn E. Woodland
Indiana University of Pennsylvania
Indiana, Pennsylvania

Linda F. Szul
Indiana University of Pennsylvania
Indiana, Pennsylvania

A facility is defined as "something that is built, installed or established to serve a particular purpose" (*Merriam-Webster's Collegiate® Dictionary*, 2000). Facility management, as discussed in this chapter, refers to the configuration of learning environments for business education. The learning environments include general-purpose classrooms, computer classrooms, and computer labs. This chapter is not intended to be a comprehensive how-to manual for every aspect of the classroom-teaching environment. Rather, it focuses on planning and configuring new or remodeled educational facilities.

> Institutional classrooms of the 21st century must be designed and developed to leverage technology. Technology is not a panacea for all training; however, when properly used it can increase training efficiencies while maximizing training effectiveness. It is neither desirable nor economically feasible that all classrooms have maximum technological capabilities. Schools must direct their modernization efforts to those classrooms [in] which technology can provide the greatest return on effectiveness and efficiency. (Sullivan, 1994, p. 3)

Rooms filled with computers are a common sight at all levels of education—elementary, secondary, postsecondary, college, and university. A fine line distinguishes computer classrooms from computer labs from classrooms equipped with technology. Many teachers and technicians see rooms with computers where instruction takes place as computer labs. According to Leamy (1997, p. 2), "computer classrooms are specifically designed for instruction [while] computer labs are designed to meet the remaining needs, i.e., access to class software, access to specialized hardware and software, and general access for students who do not own computers." Classrooms equipped with technology are designed to enhance a teacher's traditional delivery of instruction.

Initially, administrators of various ranks served as technical support for implementing computers in schools. But their backgrounds provided them with no preparation for designing classroom facilities, either for teachers using technology to deliver instruction or for students using technology to enhance learning. Later, schools entrusted the responsibility of designing these facilities to individuals with computer training. However, technical personnel in many cases did not understand classroom/teaching procedures (Stenzel, 1996). Consequently, the design of computer facilities did not support effective instruction. Today this flaw is overcome by employing a team approach to design, which invites the input of teachers, technicians, engineers, and interior designers. "Satellite uplinks, microwaves, and fiber optics and the merging of television and the Internet [have] implications beyond both technology and curriculum change. Educational design must include changes in how we build and use educational facilities" (*Designing the Electronic Classroom*, 2000, p. 1).

Whether in a lab or classroom, teachers use the same computers for different areas of instruction. Because computers can be configured to do many different things for many different users, they frequently end up not being optimally configured. Teachers and students find themselves using equipment that is either too powerful or not powerful enough to complete their tasks. Purchased computers often run the latest software with all of the "bells and whistles," when the bottom line for teachers and for students continues to be the efficient production of structured assignments. A critical element of the design process is conducting a needs analysis to determine the projected uses of the facility and appropriate hardware and software. "Based on the needs analysis, [the design team] can make recommendations to purchase or update a system to meet the users' needs and improve productivity" (Beisse, 1999, p. 32).

When faced with the costs associated with upgrades and/or new purchases, the design team must take a creative approach to securing funding. The majority of educational institutions do not have the budget to meet the recommendations made by their design teams. One source of outside funding is Cisco Systems. The innovative program, Cisco Networking Academies, is designed to teach and certify secondary and postsecondary students to design, build, and maintain computer networks capable of supporting national and global organizations. "To kick-start the program, Cisco Systems [plans] to contribute approximately $18 million dollars in curriculum, equipment, and resources" (Cisco Systems, 1998, p. 1). In addition to monies, Cisco is addressing the critical need for network administrators within schools themselves. Students who participate in the Networking Academies not only fill their own schools' networking needs but also can be "loaned out" for building and supporting the networks of other nearby schools.

An added element in designing computer facilities is the incorporation of an essential instructional component—the computer—that can be an irresistible distraction to students. In the past, facility design included caveats, for example, about the distracting nature of windows in the classroom. Computer classroom design should concentrate on using configurations that enable the teacher to effectively control computer use.

Planning for New or Remodeled Facilities

Room configurations present opportunities and challenges for instructors. Business education teachers can provide valuable input on design decisions based on their experiences. A classroom configuration that fosters good teaching using computers is different from a configuration that fosters good teaching without computers. General-purpose classrooms include several common design guidelines that cover acoustics, accessibility, electrical outlets, lighting, instructional media, and telecommunications.

- Acoustics. Design should focus on reducing noise.
- Accessibility. Rooms should be easily accessible to the disabled and at least ten percent of the seating should be equipped with left-handed tablet arms.
- Electrical outlets. An adequate number of outlets should be available to support instructional media.
- Lighting. Controls should be simple and easily accessed by the instructor. Note taking should be possible with dimmable lights.
- Instructional media. Classrooms should be equipped with standard equipment including a computer, ceiling-mounted data/video projector, screen(s), VCR, and overhead projector. Ideally, an equipment closet should be located in the room.
- Telecommunications. A network port should be included in the instructor's area to provide Internet access.

Traditional classroom design may not be appropriate for computer classrooms. Computer classrooms that are configured for effective learning allow for both lecture and demonstration. Facility planners of computer classrooms, in particular, and of all classrooms, in general, should incorporate the following important design considerations to facilitate learning:

- Open architecture
- Projection with suitable sight lines for all
- Desk space and seating suitable for seminar-type discussions
- Capability to follow lectures and/or demonstrations without distractions
- Ability to collaborate with peers or instructors without impediments

Facility layout. Three layouts typically found in educational settings show how design considerations may or may not be incorporated into a final configuration. The advantages and disadvantages of these computer classroom designs are discussed below.

Layout I, according to Stenzel (1996, p. 5), has been nicknamed "the boxcar." It consists of rows of computers that run perpendicular to the side aisle where the teacher and the chalkboard are stationed. All of the students face the same direction with their backs to the projection screen. This design has few advantages and several disadvantages.

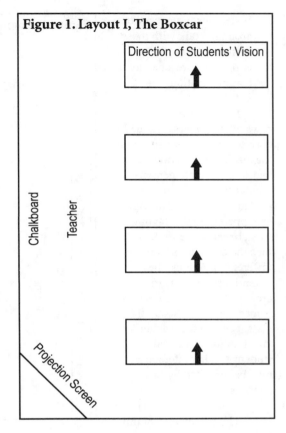

Figure 1. Layout I, The Boxcar

- Impediments to teacher and student interaction. The narrowness of the aisles prevents the teacher from moving freely around the room. Student interaction is limited by seating that offers only a view of other students' backs.
- No sight lines. Students have difficulty in viewing the projection screen, which is placed behind them.
- No facilities for seminar sessions. The lack of space prohibits the use of a seminar table for collaborative projects and interaction between teacher and students.
- Difficulty in monitoring workstations. Because the teacher cannot easily walk around the classroom and students face their computer screens, they have an opportunity to focus on activities other than those related to instruction.
- Severely limited opportunity to view demonstrations. Because the projection screen is at the students' backs, they have difficulty viewing and following any demonstration.
- Limited opportunity for collaboration. The lack of a seminar table and the arrangement of computers contribute to a limited opportunity for collaboration.

If students in one row turn around to talk with those in the next row, the computers are a barrier to communication.

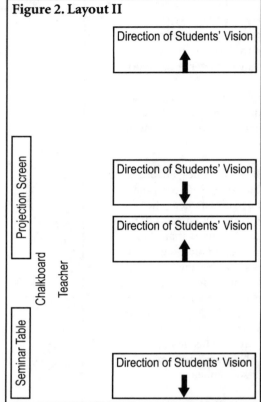

Figure 2. Layout II

Direction of Students' Vision

Direction of Students' Vision

Direction of Students' Vision

Direction of Students' Vision

Projection Screen

Chalkboard

Teacher

Seminar Table

Layout II consists of rows of computers arranged between two wide aisles with the teacher, projection screen, and seminar table perpendicular to the rows of students. Two disadvantages are apparent in this layout. First, because the students face the computers from different directions, the potential for glare is increased and lighting the room is more difficult. Second, the distance from the teacher's area is significant, and student-teacher interaction may be inhibited by that distance.

The advantages of this layout outweigh the disadvantages.

- Wide aisles. Wide aisles encourage student-teacher interaction and give the teacher unencumbered access to all parts of the room.
- Good sight lines. Students have good access to the projection screen when it is used for demonstrations.
- Seminar table. A seminar table gives students the opportunity to interact with the teacher and other students.
- Fewer distractions. Students in the outside rows face away from their computer screens when viewing demonstrations or participating in discussions; this position minimizes the temptation to surf the Web or view e-mail at inappropriate times.
- Greater collaboration. Students have increased opportunity for collaborating with their peers next to them, and students in the middle two rows have the opportunity to work with peers across the table.

Layout III is a modified multiple-horseshoe layout with wide aisles and relatively easy access for teacher and students. Workstations are arranged in semicircles with the teacher and projection screen at the hub of the semicircles. The advantages of this layout consist of the following:

- Teacher accessibility. This layout allows the teacher to stand anywhere in the room and quickly scan the room to observe students while making each student easily accessible.
- Seminar table. A seminar table can be placed anywhere in the room, most advantageously at the back.
- Configuration. This layout represents a configuration that enhances teaching effectiveness and student collaboration while it minimizes distractions.

For additional information on classroom layouts, refer to the following:

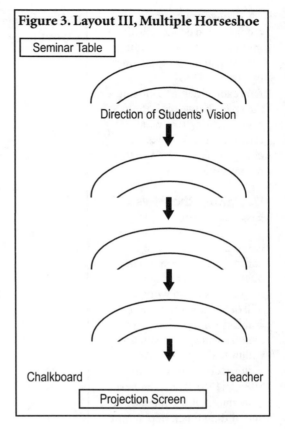

Figure 3. Layout III, Multiple Horseshoe

- http://www.cit.cornell.edu/computer/instruct/classtech/labguide/labguide.html
- http://www-dcst.monroe.army.mil/crxxi/annexe.htm

Classroom reconfiguration. Existing computer classrooms can be reconfigured within budget to meet ergonomic standards and disability requirements and to enhance learning. It is important to note that the Americans with Disabilities Act (ADA) requirements apply to reconfigurations as well as to new construction.

Simple physical changes to the facility may include painting the walls a light color and replacing window treatments with light-colored blinds. When new computer systems are purchased, it is a good idea to consider a flat-screen monitor and a mini-tower rather than a desktop configuration. These changes will reduce space requirements and minimize glare. Simple racks that attach to workstations can hold student books. Obtaining adjustable keyboard trays will also help save space and prevent repetitive strain injury (RSI).

Layout I can be reconfigured economically into Layout II by relocating the workstations of the inner two rows so those students face each other, and closing the space between those two rows, creating two wide aisles. Figure 4 shows the changes that result from that reconfiguration.

Designing the Physical Environment

Space is obviously of paramount importance in a computer classroom. "The quality of the interface between user and workstation will determine the general comfort [of the students] and the efficiency of production within the...space." (*Architectural Graphic Standards*, 1994, p.175). Thus, the basic workstation is the fundamental building block in planning and designing the computer classroom. When designing a computer classroom, the key is to make the work area "task-specific"; in other words, to choose those aspects that support computer use as opposed to other uses.

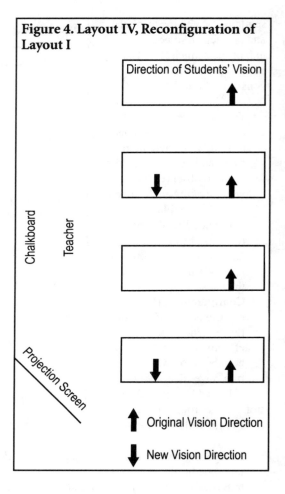

Figure 4. Layout IV, Reconfiguration of Layout I

The basic workstation "must be large enough to accommodate paperwork, equipment, and other accessories that support the user's function" (*Architectural Graphic Standards*, 1994, p. 176). Computer workstations should be at least 48 inches long (Michael, 1995) to hold a mouse, monitor, keyboard, and document holder, while allowing for working room.

Ergonomic concerns. One of the most important considerations, however, is the adjustability of the workstation. Workstations should be of a height to avoid neck and back strain, RSI, and poor posture. An added benefit of higher workstations is that the teacher can view the students' progress from a standing position.

The key to selecting a workstation chair is its adjustability. A nonadjustable chair can contribute to neck, back, and leg pain. "A chair with both back and seat adjustment levers, sufficient back support, adequate cushioning, and a 'waterfall' (slope to the chair's front) seat design that takes pressure off the backs of a student's legs and promotes better circulation will help to eliminate back and/or neck muscle pain" (Beisse, 1999, p. 119). Furthermore, students need to be able to adjust seat height to avoid leg pain caused by feet that are too close to or too far from the floor.

Other ergonomic factors influence good computer classroom design. The physical appearance of the room must convey an atmosphere of serenity, quiet, and comfort. For maximum performance, walls should be painted a light color, and window treatments should be light-colored to reflect heat. Carpeting and acoustical tiling should be used to minimize noise. Traditional fluorescent lighting casts a glare on computer screens and is tiring to the eyes. Glare can cause the monitors to appear washed out and may increase the time needed to read text. Traditional lights should be replaced with nonglare fluorescent lighting, and computer monitors should be equipped with antiglare screen covers. Ergonomic problems and possible solutions (Beisse, 1999, p. 121) are summarized in Table 1.

Table 1. Ergonomic Problems and Solutions

Ergonomic Problems	Possible Solutions
Back or neck muscle pain or numbness	■ Replacing nonadjustable chairs with adjustable chairs ■ Adjusting keyboard heights ■ Installing adjustable keyboard shelves ■ Recommending frequent breaks
Leg pain or numbness	■ Replacing nonadjustable chairs with adjustable chairs ■ Placing footrests on the floor
Eyestrain or headaches	■ Reducing screen glare ■ Adjusting lighting ■ Installing antiglare filters on screens ■ Recommending frequent breaks
Wrist and finger pain or numbness	■ Adjusting keyboard heights ■ Supplying keyboard wrist rests ■ Recommending frequent breaks

While certain rules apply to traditional classroom density, in computer classrooms density is an even greater concern. According to Stenzel (1997), when students are crowded, elbow-to-elbow, they are less likely to edit their work and think critically. Overcrowding increases frustration that, in turn, increases computer-related anxiety. Furthermore, the aisle that separates rows of computers should be no less than 30 inches to provide adequate space for chair clearance. However, such a distance may not conform to ADA requirements for wheelchair clearance. It also may not provide adequate clearance for the teacher to walk between rows.

Cabling and wiring. Cables are the backbone of the network and carry all information in the form of electrical radio frequency transmissions or light (fiber-optic) transmissions (Campbell, 1996). Planning for cabling is one of the most important and most frequently neglected components of network planning. When choosing cabling, planners should be cognizant of the purpose of the network, not just of cost or technology.

Three types of cabling are available: twisted-pair, coaxial, and fiber-optic. Twisted-pair cabling is made of two to four pairs of wires intertwined throughout their entire length of cable. The more twists per foot, the greater the efficiency of the cable. Twisted-pair cabling is identified by categories; the higher the category number, the more twists per foot and the less chance of interference. For use in a classroom, Category 5, the highest category, is the best choice because it provides maximum transmission speed and the lowest chance of interference.

Coaxial cable, often called Bayonet-Naur Connector (BNC) cable, consists of a single copper wire encased in insulation and then covered with a layer of aluminum or copper braid (Campbell, 1996). This type of cable provides more noise protection and greater transmission speed than twisted-pair cabling. Coaxial cable is a high-bandwidth medium that can carry thousands of signals at once.

Fiber-optic cabling is the most expensive type. It conducts photonic signals, or light, and is indifferent to interference. The light is conducted along a slender plastic or glass fiber covered with a thin insulating coating surrounded by a plastic sheath that protects the delicate fiber. Fiber-optic cabling has advantages over coaxial and twisted-pair cabling in its speed and lack of interference. The disadvantage is cost; fiber-optic cabling is expensive and difficult to install. More information on twisted-pair, coaxial, and fiber-optic cabling can be obtained at http://www.scsite.com/bdc2e/ch03/ (Shelly, Cashman, & Serwatka, 1998).

Once cable type has been selected, the next decision involves wiring the classroom. Safe classroom wiring can be incorporated into the room design in a variety of ways. Some are very costly while others—such as raised floor, column, or conduit wiring—are cheaper. According to Beisse (1999), cabling and wiring should be installed so they cannot be damaged or stressed during use. When wiring an existing building, surface-mounted conduits carrying the cable can be installed along the walls. When no other solution exists, rubber conduits can be used to carry cable over or under any type of flooring. Plastic cable ties should be used to bundle cables to secure them to workstations, thus eliminating stress on the cable run and the possibility of accidents.

The following items also should be carefully considered when designing the room's wiring:

- Outlets. No two-pronged outlets should be used. "Cheater" plug adapters, which convert two-pronged plugs to three-pronged, should be avoided because they defeat the grounding feature. It is important to test outlets to ensure that they are properly wired and that the ground is working.
- Circuits. Separate circuits should be used for computer classrooms so they do not share circuits with other equipment that may draw heavily on the available amperage. Hard disk drives rely on electrical current for timing during read/write operations; inadequate power could cause loss of data.
- Power stability. It is a good idea to check with the electrical company to determine the stability of the area's power supply. A power conditioner, a device that regulates power and is placed between the computer and the power source, may be required. Power strips, devices that connect multiple plugs to the power supply, should not be used in place of power conditioners. Extension cords should never be used in connecting computer equipment to power sources. Each power strip should be plugged into an electrical outlet, not another power strip. When purchasing power strips, it is important to select those that include both a protective circuit to prevent damage due to surges and spikes, and a filter to protect against radio frequency interference.

Organizing and Controlling Facilities

Security is an important aspect of computer classroom management. While some phases are not difficult to manage, others are complex and emotional because they involve ethical and legal considerations. Security in a computer classroom means protection of users, systems, and information. Such protection involves user identification and passwords, antivirus software, as well as prevention of unauthorized log-ons, tampering, and illegal access. Information stored on computers must be considered confidential and must be protected against access unless the owner intentionally makes the information public.

The first step in managing a computer classroom is developing an acceptable-use policy (AUP). (See www.pde.psu.edu/bbpages_reference/41201/41201898.html and www.iusb.edu/agreement.html for sample policies.) Such a policy covers general computer use (access, ethics, and due process), Internet use, Internet etiquette, and security. The document should outline policies on access to computing resources, including peripherals, software, and hardware. It should also describe what are considered violations of computer security, unauthorized use of computer accounts, academic dishonesty, violation of software license agreements, harassment, and/or violation of other people's privacy. The document must include procedures for dealing with violators and the penalties for violations.

As part of their AUPs, schools can adopt certain rules to govern student behavior in computer classrooms. Developers of such rules can use the following as guidelines.

- Do not bring food or drink into the classroom.
- Be quiet and courteous to fellow students.
- Do not play games during class time.
- Use the recycling bins.
- Clean up your workstation at the end of class before leaving the room.
- Inform the teacher of equipment malfunctions.
- Do not use class time for e-mail or Web surfing.

The Internet provides access to a wide variety of resources, including e-mail, information and news services, public domain software and shareware, discussion groups, and chat rooms. It also makes available to students and teachers materials that may not be considered of educational value in the context of the school setting. The AUP should clearly outline what types of Internet access conform to the school's academic standards.

"Netiquette" refers to network etiquette or the generally accepted rules of conduct for using the Internet. These rules embrace, but are not limited to, the following:

- Be polite.
- Use appropriate language.
- Do not reveal personal addresses or telephone numbers.
- Be aware that e-mail may not be private.
- Use the network only in ways that will not disrupt other users.

It is critical that every user, whether student or teacher, take responsibility for security. A user should understand the level of protection each computer system automatically applies to files. A user should also be aware of computer viruses and should take steps to avoid contamination of the system and information stored on the system. He or she should remember that computer accounts are individual, not meant to be shared, and are to be protected by an obscure and frequently changed password.

Summary

In configuring new or upgraded classrooms, a team approach to design is strongly recommended. The team must conduct a needs assessment to determine projected use of the facility, appropriate hardware, and suitable layout. Results of this analysis will drive decisions about which computers to buy or which classrooms to upgrade or convert and will ensure that these decisions are made with careful regard to user needs and instructional objectives. School personnel must be creative in securing funding to meet these needs and objectives. Partnerships and alliances formed with technology-oriented companies can provide equipment, training, and curriculum to schools interested in expanding classroom facilities.

In planning for new or upgraded facilities, several components including acoustics, accessibility, safety, instructional media, and telecommunications must be addressed. Designers choosing configurations for computer classrooms or general-purpose classrooms that incorporate technology in instructional delivery must consider elements such as sight lines, desk space, lack of distraction, and group work space. Traditional classroom layouts can be reconfigured to integrate these elements within budgetary allowances.

In configuring the physical environment, important considerations include ergonomic concerns, safety, student and teacher comfort, and making the area task-specific. The choice of cabling is a cost factor, and designers must consider the high cost of reversing these decisions. They should also consider the safety issues involved with the location of outlets and wiring used to support the technology.

In controlling and organizing the technology classroom, security is a paramount concern. Security involves the user, the environment, and the files. Educational institutions must adopt AUPs that govern student conduct in the technology classroom.

The classroom environment is evolving. Thus, those responsible for the design of classrooms must ensure that the learning environment keeps up with learning. Planners of facilities must be aware of the latest design issues in order to provide the best facilities for learning.

References

Architectural graphic standards. (1994). Somerset, NJ: John Wiley & Sons, Inc.

Beisse, F. (1999). *A guide to computer user support.* Cambridge, England: Course Technologies.

Campbell, P. T. (1996). *Networking small office.* Alameda, CA: Sybex, Inc.

Cisco Systems Networking Academy. (1998). *Cisco academy of south west Ohio.* Retrieved July 13, 2000 from the World Wide Web: http://www.scoca-k12.org/cisco/about.htm

Designing the electronic classroom. (2000, November). Workspace Resources. Retrieved November 16, 2000 from the World Wide Web: http://www.workspace-resources.com/work/education/educ00.htm

Leamy, T. (1997). *Campus computer access.* Retrieved January 25, 2000 from the World Wide Web: http://lm.ucdavis.edu/pubs/access/

Merriam-Webster's collegiate® dictionary. (2000). Springfield, MA: Merriam-Webster Inc. Retrieved from the World Wide Web: http://www.m-w.com/dictionary.htm

Michael, K. (1995). Ergonomics for the CAD lab. *Tech Directions, 55*(4), 16.

Shelly, G. B., Cashman, T. J., & Serwatka, J. A. (1998). *Business data communications: Introductory concepts and techniques* (2nd ed.). Cambridge, England: Course Technologies.

Stenzel, J. (1996, June). *Some notes on computer-classroom design and configuration.* Retrieved November 16, 2000 from the World Wide Web: http://cai.ucdavis.edu/instruction/report.htm

Stenzel, J. (1997, December). *Computer classroom instructor's guide.* Retrieved November 16, 2000 from the World Wide Web: http://cai.ucdavis.edu/instruction/stenzel.htm

Sullivan, G. R. (1994, February 18). *Chapter 1-classroom XXI.* Retrieved July 13, 2000 from the World Wide Web: http://www-dcst.monroe.army.mil/crxxi/chap1.htm

Eye on the Future: Research Directions for Business Educators

James E. Bartlett II
Ball State University
Muncie, Indiana

Jim B. Mansfield
Central Missouri State University
Warrensburg, Missouri

The dramatic evolution of the work environment and the roles of business professionals are just a few of the factors driving change in business education. At the same time, societal trends—such as increasing diversity, the integration of Net Generation workers into the Generation X and Baby Boomer workforce, and less confidence in the ability of Social Security to provide a comfortable retirement—underscore the importance of shaping business education programs that prepare students for productive roles in the nation's economy.

For those with their eyes on the future, these changes in business and society raise fundamental questions about how business education curricula should evolve. Research offers one way of addressing such questions. And just as strong business education programs both prepare students for business and teach them about business, so must research address both these aspects of the field. This chapter argues that teachers be actively involved in reviewing and conducting research about their curricula. It also presents ideas about the substance and direction of such research with respect to the topics addressed in this *Yearbook*.

Research in Business Education: Who? Why? How?

Ary, Jacobs, and Razavieh (1996) have stated that teachers are professionals who must plan and make decisions. Research findings are a valuable contribution to these processes. Whether research is formal or informal, its results can provide business educators with reliable and valid data for making decisions about the business education curriculum and about how to deliver that curriculum. In fact, Borg, Gall, and Gall (1993) have stated that "action research" is a far better basis for decision making than personal experience.

Informal versus formal research methods. The idea of an informal action research model already exists in the literature of business education. For example, Bronner (1999) has said that action research for business educators is "research conducted in a classroom or in a clinical environment that usually addresses the 'itch' that business educators want to scratch when considering answers to problems that address personal teaching issues as contrasted with theoretical or more global problems" (p. 191).

In this model, teachers could start with a question about some aspect of their students' learning. For example, teachers may want to explore how the teaching/learning experience can be structured to address the diverse student population in their school. They might start by reviewing reports of published research to establish a strong theoretical knowledge base about the issue. Based on the literature review and on their own teaching experience, teacher-researchers can create a study to gather data.

Those who would conduct formal studies (qualitative or quantitative) should be familiar with specific research methodologies and statistical analysis procedures. It is often appropriate to use both action research and more formal research to investigate problems in managing business education, especially when considering broad issues such as effectively managing the curriculum and the classroom.

Solving problems of time and quality. Because the goal of collecting empirical evidence is to make decisions that will ultimately shape the business education classroom of the future, it is essential for teacher-researchers to conduct high-quality, representative, valid, and reliable studies. Yet the pressure on teachers at all levels to meet standards and also to be available to students may make teachers—no matter how well intentioned they are—shy away from any additional work-related burdens.

Business education teachers may want to consider adopting some of the shortcuts used by professionals in other fields who face similar time constraints. For example, professionals in medicine and science often collaborate on research projects so that no one individual has to assume the responsibility of conducting a study alone and so that the research team can draw on the strengths of its various members. For example, one researcher may be an expert in statistics, while another might be gifted in asking precisely the questions needed to yield meaningful results. Building research teams across grade levels offers collegial benefits as well as the opportunity for long-term and correlational studies.

Managing the Curriculum

Basic business and economic education. Educators today are challenged to produce students who are financially literate and able to function well in society. The Internet provides a wealth of materials and resources for developing and implementing programs in this area.

Basic business and economic education raises not only practical but also exciting research questions. The first step, of course, is to assess students' financial literacy. For example, how do students make decisions about money? How do personality and learning style influence the problem-solving process? Are there relationships between these factors that might yield valuable information about how best to educate students about handling personal and business finances? To launch this kind of research, teachers can use instruments such as the Myers-Briggs Type Indicator or Keirsey Temperament Sorter to measure personality type, the Motivated Strategies for Learning Questionnaire to measure learning strategies, and the Learning Style Inventory to measure learning styles.

Technology-related curriculum. Technology has been and will continue to be integrated throughout the curriculum. Because many business education programs are dissimilar and organized according to the needs of the local community and the perceptions of local school boards, teachers, and administrators, a combination of formal and action research is probably best when making decisions about the content of those programs. Teacher-researchers can present information about the types of technology that are being integrated into the business education curriculum at the national level (which is especially important because after they graduate students may move out of the local area to seek permanent employment) and how technology is being used to teach for and about business at all educational levels—elementary through collegiate.

Teacher-researchers can also investigate the impact of technology integration at different levels (elementary, middle, and high school). For example, does integrating technology into teaching and learning increase students' knowledge of a basic business unit, improve retention, change the students' perception of the unit, and affect the time students spend on the unit? Are there differences between students who learn the material interactively but "virtually" (such as by doing computer-based simulations) and those who participate interactively and "authentically" (such as by running a classroom business)? To find out, researchers can compare continuous variables (e.g., scores on tests, times to complete tests, and attitudes). This type of research can be applied not only to economic education but also to any of the basic business content areas contained in the *National Standards for Business Education* curriculum model (National Business Education Association, 1995).

Findings from this type of study can provide information about when and how much technology integration is most beneficial. As in all formal research, the studies should control for internal validity by measuring other factors that previous research has shown to be related to the topic. If research findings identify best practices, those practices can be incorporated into programs.

Integration with other content areas. Integrating business education with other disciplines reinforces the notion that business education is important for all students, regardless of their career or postsecondary education plans. Such integration can occur at all levels even though as Williams, Herrin, and Taylor's chapter commented, it has not yet reached the postsecondary/collegiate level. An important question, therefore, is how can business education courses best be integrated with other content areas, and what can be learned from best practices. A qualitative case study could provide a picture of the process and suggest benchmarks for implementing an integration program.

In states where such integration already prevails, researchers can explore how teachers and students perceive the integration process, i.e., what are the benefits and drawbacks? After reviewing related literature and interviewing students and teachers to examine factors that determine their perceptions, research-ers can develop a conceptual base that can be used by districts that have been slower to incorporate these learning models. To ensure that theoretical concepts drawn from the literature and interviews are measured validly and reliably, researchers can adopt the systematic process for developing survey instrumentation as described by Bartlett and Kotrlik (2000). The systematic process requires the researchers to (a) develop a conceptual definition of the construct of interest from a thorough review of the literature; (b) develop operational definitions and state-ments; (c) select an appropriate scaling technique; (d) conduct a review of the validity of the content of the statements and scaling technique; (e) develop directions for the instrumentation in respect to responding; (f) prepare a draft of the instrument and collect preliminary pilot data; (g) if needed, make corrections according to the pilot test and prepare the instrument for field testing; (h) conduct a field test of the instrument; (i) analyze the field test using item analysis, factor analysis, and estimates of reliability; (j) revise the instrument as needed (if major changes are made, repeat the field test, reanalyze the field test, and revise the instrument); and (k) conduct the study with the developed instrument.

Further, researchers can examine the characteristics of model programs in other integrated content areas, using regression analysis to explore significant variances in a summated scale of perceptions of a successful integration pro-gram. Business educators can use this model as a guide as they work to integrate their courses with other content areas.

School-to-Career: envisioning tomorrow's workplace. In a broad sense, there is a need for research that examines whether employers view School-to-Career programs as valuable preparation for the workplace. For example, are there significant differences in employers' perceptions of employees who have participated in School-to-Career programs and those who have not? Teacher-researchers can measure employer-employee ratings of such things as work satisfaction, general work ethic, technical skills, and the "softer" skills.

Because School-to-Career initiatives must reflect employer needs, research should continue to monitor workplace change. Further, this research must include a visionary component that examines which skills will best equip students to function successfully in the workplace. Educators must commit to continually aligning national standards for business education and the School-to-Career curriculum with the needs and objectives of community stakeholders and the best information available about future workplace needs.

Accountability—or program effectiveness—can be researched by tracking placement and retention rates of School-to-Career students in postsecondary programs and the workplace. A spin-off of this idea is to explore the characteristics of students in School-to-Career programs who go on to complete postsecondary/collegiate degrees and are successful in the workplace.

Diversity issues—such as the lack of women and members of minority groups in the information technology workforce—also lend themselves to research in the areas of career awareness, exploration, and preparation. New career paths are emerging every day, making vision an important component of research initiatives and curriculum management.

Program management in changing times. When challenged by rapid change such as increasing diversity, program innovations such as block scheduling, and evolving course content, schools and districts might consider using O'Neil's seven elements of program design to determine whether and how the business education curriculum should change. These seven elements—mission, goals, and objectives; needs assessment, occupational analyses, and advisory groups; management principles; instructional design model; organizational structure, controls, and political climate; resources and facilities; and program marketing—are a starting point for analyzing the district's adherence to the model and resulting enrollment in their programs. Data gathered from such an analysis could provide support for preservice and in-service training about program management.

Teacher-researchers can also explore whether and what kind of a relationship exists between the leadership styles of business educators and the extent to which they use the seven elements of program design. By computing correlations between leadership style and the use of design elements in combination with Davis's (1971) descriptors, researchers can determine both statistical and practical significance. Davis' descriptors are used to interpret correlations and are as follows: .01–.09 (negligible), .10–.29 (low), .30–.49 (moderate), .50–.69 (substantial), .70–.99 (very high), and 1.0 (perfect). For example, a correlation could be statistically significant at the .05 level and still only be a negligible correlation and not have practical significance.

Change, of course, is the only constant within this or any other discipline. Ongoing assessment of the skills, knowledge, attitudes, and abilities that employers seek and that are necessary for success in a given occupation must become part of what business educators do as they construct curriculum. Tools for these assessments are available: focus groups, interviews, surveys, and the Developing A Curriculum analysis recommended in McGrew's chapter on curriculum.

Business educators must then continually assess student mastery of business education content, including that delivered through distance learning programs. Using pretests and posttests, teacher-researchers can determine progress in knowledge and skill development. These data can be further analyzed to determine whether and where gaps between the curriculum and the needs of business and industry exist. Procedures outlined by Campbell and Stanley (1963) can be used to determine the internal validity of experimental and quasi-experimental research.

There is much to do, and little time in which to do it. Educators must, therefore, determine their research priorities in terms of their importance to community stakeholders and to the larger, global workplace. (This process should also be undertaken at the district and state levels.) Once priorities and goals are identified, they can be "dovetailed" using a chart technique similar to the one Davidson (1991) described in his book, *Breathing Space: Living and Working at a Comfortable Pace in a Sped-Up Society.*

Managing the Classroom and the Learning Process

Awareness of diversity is essential for students who will be working in an increasingly global environment and for the teachers who will prepare those students for the workplace. The questions are wide-ranging: How do gender, race, and socioeconomic class affect motivation and learning preferences? How can students learn to adapt to and work with others from different backgrounds and with different abilities? What adaptations must teachers make to create successful learning experiences for students, and how will teachers get this kind of training? How can we assist teachers experiencing the effects of the Americans with Disabilities Act, such as mainstreaming, and what kinds of instructional support can we give them and their students? How can we encourage everyone to view adaptation issues and strategies as necessary and beneficial rather than as inconvenient? How can we create conditions that allow all students to achieve and to succeed in their courses and in their experiences in business and industry?

The classroom setting. Effective classroom management determines whether or not curriculum takes hold, whether and what students learn, and how successfully students master the required learning standards. Expertise in managing course content, instructional methods, learning activities, and student behavior is probably one of the most difficult skills for new teachers to develop and for veteran teachers to change.

The Cochrane chapter's discussion of "boss" teacher and "lead" teacher approaches suggests an interesting method of self-assessment for business education departments. Teachers can describe which of the two styles they lean toward. They can also solicit feedback from students regarding how each style affects their interest in the subject matter, motivation to learn, perceptions of teacher effectiveness, and achievement in the course. The department can then use the data collected to determine which approach yields the sought-after results and then, based on this data, decide if changes or enhancements to the learning atmosphere are warranted.

Another area that deserves attention and is closely related to teaching style ("boss" versus "lead") is instructional methods. Research can be undertaken to compare mini-lectures (O'Connor, Bronner, and Delaney, 1996) followed by reinforcement activities with traditional methods of instruction (such as lecturing), small group methods, and cooperative learning techniques. For example, in a technology course on software applications, are there significant differences in student scores on hands-on and objective tests when the units are completed in cooperative learning groups versus individually?

The style of classroom management one uses not only affects learning but also classroom ambience. To develop their higher-level thinking skills, students can be asked to evaluate business environments and practices using the question, what if the classroom operated in that style? For example, how does it feel to work in a team as opposed to individually? Do student and teacher perceptions of work change based on the physical or emotional climate of the classroom? Does the classroom climate change based on the way work is organized?

Guided by the discussion Lytle presented in her chapter, a researcher could develop an instrument to measure how classroom management techniques relate to teacher satisfaction, student satisfaction, and student achievement. For example, how does the environment shape how happy, productive, or effective the classroom is, and how does this correlate with achievement levels? Are there best practices that can be adopted?

Planning for learning. Business education should be articulated in elementary, middle/junior, and high school curricula. A national needs assessment could examine students' knowledge of business subjects and their computer literacy. A professional organization or a consortium of organizations could provide resources to help achieve this objective.

As more sophisticated technology filters through a greater proportion of the population, curriculum will, of necessity, incorporate more sophisticated content at earlier levels. Correspondingly, teachers will need to become more sophisticated in what they know and in the breadth and depth of what they teach. For example, if students are learning PowerPoint in elementary school, then college business educators need to learn and to teach more than what the students have already mastered.

Based on the suggestions in Andelora's chapter, researchers can conduct in-service sessions to assist teachers with incorporating business education content into their curricula. Researchers can then examine the impact of the training by reviewing teacher evaluations of sessions, studying the information learned and retained, and observing how these ideas are being transferred to the classroom. Students can provide feedback about what they are learning from teachers who have completed the sessions (versus those who have not). This feedback can be used to determine whether the in-service training was effective.

At the postsecondary level, becoming more customer- and student-oriented are among the challenges business educators are facing. Initiatives include using distance learning, creating innovative schedules, and providing resources to assist nontraditional students (for example, offering alternative certification programs targeted toward students who have made career changes).

Each of the innovations above is worth exploring, especially when considering which teaching and learning methods are most appropriate for different student groups. Even with the rise of computer-based training and distance learning, many accrediting agencies, employers, and teachers question the quality of degree programs completed online. Research is needed to explore whether students who complete an online program test significantly better on standard content examinations than students in traditional programs. A quasi-experimental research design using pretest and posttest measures could provide empirical evidence about such achievement. Similarly, this design could be used to compare student achievement in and perceptions of effectiveness of Web-based, Web-enhanced, and Web-centric courses.

Preparing for and dealing with change. Change in business education affects both teachers and students. Teachers must rethink instructional delivery methods for the Net Generation, and become facilitators of learning rather than masters of teaching. Such an approach includes problem solving in a real-world context, the promotion of "discovery and doing" rather than lectures and listening, and an openness to shared knowledge. Students, too, must be prepared to adapt to a world of constant change. According to Bartlett (1999), a study of the resources that business professionals use to teach themselves on the job could yield information that is relevant and meaningful in this area.

Facilities management. The business education learning environment includes both traditional classrooms and computer-enhanced classrooms. In many cases existing facilities limit the amount of change that can take place.

Integrating technology into the classroom is time-consuming and challenging. At the most basic level, decisions about computer hardware purchases, computer software updates, and the integration of appropriate computer resources require a great deal of background knowledge. An action research project that tracks time allocations and skills related to teaching technology- and Web-based courses, including the duration of teachers' learning curves, could provide useful information for developing preservice and in-service training tools and for assisting teachers in configuring their classrooms to take advantage of advanced technology.

A study of who maintains, supports, and trains business teachers and others in schools to use technology is also needed. For example, research could investigate what the business teacher's role is in the maintenance, support, and training of colleagues who want to include technology in their classrooms, and what training business teachers have received for this role.

Summary

Because the business environment is changing at such a rapid pace, ongoing assessment of the workplace and of student competencies is a prerequisite for making informed decisions about curriculum. Similarly, a visioning component must be part of the decision-making process in order to create a curriculum that is meaningful and effective in preparing students for and educating them about business.

Research, whether formal or informal, can offer useful information for educators who must make decisions about the business education curriculum. Formal research methods begin with a review of the literature and a hypothesis about how an outcome will be affected by a given variable. Results may be generalizable to an entire field. Informal or action research methods are usually initiated to solve local (classroom- or school-based) problems and may or may not include a literature review. In both formal and informal research it is essential for teacher-researchers to conduct high-quality, representative, valid, and reliable research. Such research contributes the empirical evidence necessary to make sound decisions about curriculum and classroom management.

If the prospect of conducting research studies seems overwhelming in light of other teaching responsibilities, teachers can consider working in research teams whereby different team members take only part of rather than the entire responsibility for the study.

One of the most important areas of curriculum and classroom management is adapting to and preparing students for a workplace characterized by constant change. As teacher-researchers and as liaisons between students and the business world, business educators have the responsibility and the opportunity to model lifelong learning and constructive change as they, too, enhance their knowledge and skills to reflect business and industry demands. Studies that investigate how teachers accomplish these goals are useful for determining preservice and in-service training program content and for unearthing resources for on-the-job training for both students and teachers.

Business educators who have their eyes on the future will manage their classrooms and curricula with wisdom born of practical experience and knowledge generated by formal and informal research studies. Such educators will be instrumental in shaping the content and experiences that will enable students to assume their rightful and productive roles in tomorrow's economy.

References

Ary, D., Jacobs, L., & Razavieh, A. (1996). *Introduction to research methods* (3rd ed.). New York: Harcourt Brace College Publishing.

Bartlett II, J. E. (1999). *Analysis of self-directed learning in secondary business educators.* Unpublished doctoral dissertation, Louisiana State University.

Bartlett II, J. E., & Kotrlik, J. (2000, December). Instrument development: The survey design process. *Grand carousel mini-tips.* 2000 ACTE Convention, San Diego, CA.

Borg, W., Gall, J., & Gall, M. (1993). *Applying education research: A practical guide.* New York: Longman.

Bronner, M. (1999). Let's get serious about conducting action research. *Delta Pi Epsilon Proceedings*, pp. 191–198.

Campbell, D., & Stanley, J. (1963). *Handbook of research on teaching.* Houghton Mifflin Company.

Davidson, J. (1991). *Breathing space: Living and working at a comfortable pace in a sped-up society.* New York: MasterMedia Ltd.

Davis, J. A. (1971). *Elementary survey analysis.* Englewood Cliffs, NJ: Prentice-Hall.

National Business Education Association. (1995). *National standards for business education: What America's students should know and be able to do in business.* Reston, VA: Author.

O'Connor, B., Bronner, M., & Delaney, C. (1996). *Training for organizations.* New York: South-Western Publishing.